The ONE YEAR®

REAL LIFE ENCOUNTERS with GOD

365 Q&A Devotions

TYNDALE KIDS

Tyndale House Publishers, Inc.
Carol Stream, Illinois

Visit Tyndale's exciting website for kids at www.tyndale.com/kids.

The One Year is a registered trademark of Tyndale House Publishers, Inc.

Tyndale Kids logo is a trademark of Tyndale House Publishers, Inc.

The One Year Real Life Encounters with God

First printing by Tyndale House Publishers, Inc., in 2003.

Text edited by Cynthia Channell

Designed by Jacqueline Nuñez

General Editor and Project Coordinator: Lynda E. Pongracz

Development Team: Lisa J. Deam, Jerry Hanson, Deborah Koenig, Lynda E. Pongracz, Terrie Taylor, Elaine Weller

Writers: Dr. Martha J. Wright *(God the Father)*, Sharron R. Oyer *(God the Son)*, Lisa J. Deam *(God the Holy Spirit)*, Beverly Blades *(Victory)*, Brenda J. Hanson *(God's Word and Me)*, Emily C. Ramsdell *(Witnessing)*, Lora Oates *(Worshiping God)*, Sally A. Middleton *(Obeying God)*, Timothy J. Fisler *(Living for God)*, Lynda E. Pongracz *(Trusting God)*, Jean C. Torjussen *(Taking a Stand)*, Annette Haines *(What I Believe)*

Theological Consultants: Rev. Arthur Cobb, M. Joe Cox, Rev. Dair Hileman, Dr. Timothy D. Martin, Jim Neigh, Rev. John Romano, Rev. D. Bruce Seymour, Rev. Brian Thom, Dr. Mark Yelderman

Editorial Committee: Patricia R. Johann, Cheryl L. Oetting, Lynda E. Pongracz, Dr. Martha J. Wright

Special thanks to Child Evangelism Fellowship President Reese Kauffman, Marshall J. Pennell, Stephen Bates, Dr. A. A. Baker and the CEF worldwide family for their input, prayers, and support.

ISBN 978-0-8423-7206-0

Printed in the United States of America

16 15 14 13 12 11
9 8 7 6 5 4

ARE YOU READY FOR AN ADVENTURE?

Getting to know God is a great adventure! Did you know that God wants you to spend time with him each day? He does! Some people call that special time with God a "quiet time" or "devotions." It's a time to quietly sit and read and think about God and to talk to him in prayer.

The One Year Real Life Encounters with God has been written to help you in your quiet time. Each devotional will help you to learn more about God, about yourself, and about the world around you. The best part is that there's a new devotional adventure every day of the year!

Choose a special time each day for your quiet time—maybe when you first wake up in the morning or just before you go to bed at night. Be sure you have this book, a pen or pencil, and your Bible if you have one.

Are you ready to start on your adventure? Here's a road map to help you!

YOUR FIRST STOP—DEVOTIONAL STATION!

Here's what to do each day . . . starting with January 1!

- Talk to God. Ask him to help you to understand the things you will be reading during your quiet time.
- Read the Bible memory verse. It's at the side of the page. If you have a Bible, try to find the verse for yourself. See how quickly you can memorize this verse!
- Read the devotional. Each devotional will answer an important question such as: *Who is God? Does God always answer prayer? Why should I obey God when others don't?* Take your time reading the devotional and think about what it says.
- Write your answer. Read the question following the devotional and write or draw your answer. This helps you remember what you've learned!
- Talk to God again. There's a prayer starter at the end of each devotional that

can help you, but you can also make up your own prayer. You can pray about other things too. Thank God for all he does for you. Talk to God about problems or ask him to help you or someone you love. God is looking forward to hearing from you!

But that's not all! There are more exciting places to visit on your adventure!

MEMORY ZONE

Special pages scattered throughout *The One Year Real Life Encounters with God* list some great Bible verses for you to read. See how many of these verses you can memorize. Let a friend or family member test you to see if you can say all the verses on a page.

ACTIVITY CENTER

At the end of each month of devotionals in *The One Year Real Life Encounters with God*, you'll find a fun activity page. Fill in the missing words or solve the puzzle, and then write about what you've learned.

Wow! You have a whole year's worth of exciting places to visit in *The One Year Real Life Encounters with God!* Don't wait another day. Turn to today's date and get started on your daily adventures with God!

THE MAILBOX CLUB

Wouldn't it be cool to know that someone you'd never met was praying for you? That's exactly what can happen when you fill out the information below and send it to The Mailbox Club!

The people at The Mailbox Club will match you up with your own Mailbox Club friend. Your Mailbox Club friend will pray for you and will send you a note.

So go ahead and fill out the information on the next page. There's even a special place to write something you'd like your Mailbox Club friend to pray about for you.

When you finish, carefully tear the page out of your book. Put it in an envelope, add the address shown below, and stick on a postage stamp. Be sure to talk to your mom or dad or another adult before mailing in your information. Then send it to:

The Mailbox Club
P.O. Box 190
Warrenton, MO 63383-0190

If someone has already used the mail-in page in your book, write a note to the Mailbox Club people and tell them. Be sure to give them your name, birthday, grade, age, parent or guardian name, and complete mailing address. You can also write down your prayer requests.

Name

Birthday Age Grade

Parent/Guardian

Mailing address Apt. #

City State Zip

PRAYER REQUEST

Dear Mailbox Club friend,

Please pray for . . .

TABLE OF CONTENTS

JANUARY

God the Father

WHO IS GOD?

The heavens tell of the glory of God. The skies display his marvelous craftsmanship.
Psalm 19:1

YOU CAN PRAY:
Dear God, thank you for being a great God! Thank you for creating me. Help me to learn more about you so that I will love you. In Jesus' name. Amen.

Have you ever wondered who God is? Some people think that God is an old man who lives in the clouds. Others think that he is someone who causes bad things to happen when we do something wrong. Some people think that the sun and stars are gods because they give us light. Other people say, "There is no God."

The Bible, God's Word, tells us that the one true God is a Spirit. He doesn't have a body like you and me. That's why we can't see him, but he sees and hears and loves. God is everywhere. God is the Creator. He made the world and everything in it—the mountains, oceans, and animals. God also made you and me. We are his most special creation, and he loves us very much.

Grown-ups and children all need God. All people have something inside telling them there is a God. This book will help you learn about God. You will learn how great and wonderful God is. You will learn how to love him and live closer to him even though you cannot see him. Are you ready for the exciting adventure of getting to know God?

WRITE DOWN WHO YOU THINK GOD IS.

ARE THERE MANY GODS?

Some people worship many gods, but the Bible tells us that there is only one true living God. The Bible says that God is three Persons, but he is one God. That is something we cannot understand, but we know it is true. The Bible teaches us about God the Father, God the Son, and God the Holy Spirit. They are the three Persons.

God the Father lives in heaven, but he is everywhere. He is holy and without sin. God rules over his Creation. He is in control of all things. He loves everyone.

Jesus is God the Son. He died for our sins and rose again. All people can have their sins forgiven if they trust in Jesus as their personal Savior. After Jesus rose from the dead, he went up into heaven. Now Jesus is with his Father, God.

God the Holy Spirit came to earth after Jesus returned to heaven. He helps people to know that they are sinners. Then he comes to live in the hearts of those who trust in Jesus. The Holy Spirit also helps us understand God's Word, the Bible.

God the Father, God the Son, and God the Holy Spirit—they are the Trinity. They are three in one. All agree completely.

CAN YOU NAME THE THREE PERSONS OF THE TRINITY?

The heavens tell of the glory of God. The skies display his marvelous craftsmanship.
Psalm 19:1

YOU CAN PRAY:
Dear God, thank you for sending Jesus to be our Savior. Thank you for the Holy Spirit who lives in the hearts of those who believe in Jesus. In Jesus' name. Amen.

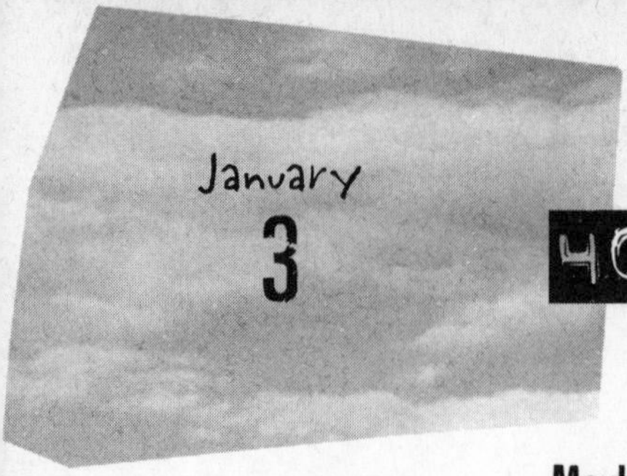

January

3

HOW OLD IS GOD?

Maybe you think that because God created the world, he must be at least two million years old! Wrong! God is eternal. There never has been a time that he has not existed. There will never be a time when he will stop existing.

Think of a circle. You cannot tell where the circle begins and ends. It is one continuous circle. A circle can remind you that God is eternal. The Father, the Son, and the Holy Spirit always have existed and always will. We have a hard time imagining that.

The Bible says, "You are God, without beginning or end" (Psalm 90:2). How long is that? It is forever. If you have believed in Jesus as your Savior, God has given you eternal life. Will it ever end? No! You are God's child forever! God wants to guide your life. Because he is eternal—he always has been and always will be—he can see what has happened, what is happening, and what will happen. What a guide to have! How great God is!

Will you trust your heavenly Father who is eternal? You cannot see what will happen in the future, but God sees and wants to direct your life.

The heavens tell of the glory of God. The skies display his marvelous craftsmanship.
Psalm 19:1

YOU CAN PRAY:

Dear God, thank you that you will never leave me because you are eternal. Thank you that I can trust you because you will always be there for me. In Jesus' name. Amen.

HOW WOULD YOU EXPLAIN TO A FRIEND THAT GOD IS ETERNAL?

HOW POWERFUL IS GOD?

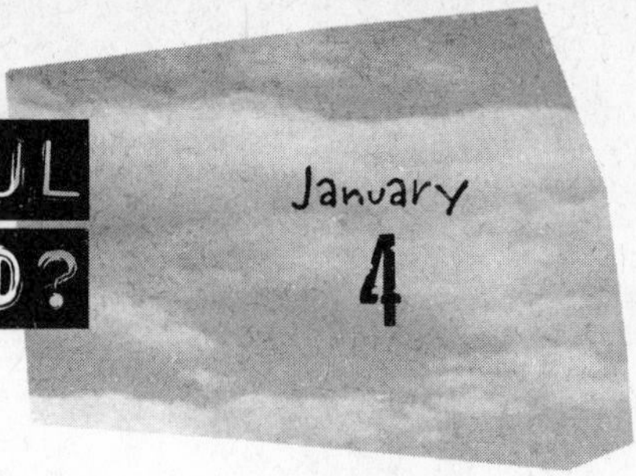

January
4

The 4.5 million–pound spaceship Columbia blasted off with a long fiery tail. Two minutes later, it had reached an altitude of 23 miles. It circled the globe at 17,000 miles per hour. Imagine the power that it took to push that huge rocket through space at that speed!

Did you know God is more powerful than that? The Bible says "his power is great" (Nahum 1:3). He made the heavens and earth. God spoke and it was there! He is almighty. He rules over all nations. God's power has no limits. He can make anything happen.

The Bible tells about Abraham and Sarah. God promised them that they would have many children, but no children were born. One day, God sent an angel to Abraham when he and Sarah were almost 100 years old. The angel told him that the following year Sarah would have a son. That was impossible! When Sarah laughed, the angel said, "Is anything too hard for the Lord?" (Genesis 18:14). Sure enough, Sarah had a son! Because God is all-powerful, he could make this impossible thing happen. The next time you have a problem, remember that God is very powerful and wants to help you.

The heavens tell of the glory of God. The skies display his marvelous craftsmanship.
Psalm 19:1

YOU CAN PRAY:
Dear God, you are the mighty God! Help me to trust you when I have a problem that seems impossible. Help me to remember that you are Ruler over all. In Jesus' name. Amen.

CAN YOU NAME SOME WAYS THAT GOD IS POWERFUL?

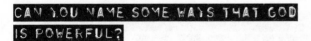

January

5

WHY DID GOD CREATE PEOPLE?

When Adam sinned, sin entered the entire human race. Adam's sin brought death, so death spread to everyone, for everyone sinned.
Romans 5:12

YOU CAN PRAY:

Dear God, thank you for creating me. I love you and praise you because you are so great. In Jesus' name. Amen.

Have you ever wondered where all the people on earth came from? God made them all! After God made the beautiful earth, he made one man. He made that man out of the dust of the earth and breathed life into him. God called that man Adam. Later, God caused Adam to sleep and took a rib from his side to make the first woman. God gave Adam this woman, Eve, to be his wife. Adam and Eve lived in the beautiful garden that God made.

Soon Adam and Eve had many children. When the children grew up, they had children. Soon there were many people on the earth. Today there are so many people it is hard to count them all!

God did not create people because he was lonely. He made us so that we could love him and praise him. The Bible says, "How great is the Lord, and how much we should praise him" (Psalm 48:1). God wants people to praise him because he is great and good.

When you see all that God has made, you can say, "How great God is!" You can praise him when you pray. Tell him that you love him and that you need him. You can never praise God enough.

WRITE DOWN THREE THINGS YOU CAN PRAISE GOD FOR TODAY.

HOW DID SIN ENTER THE WORLD?

God made everything in the world beautiful and good. But many things in our world are not beautiful and good anymore. There is sickness, sadness, fighting, and killing. Why did things go so wrong?

God placed the very first people, Adam and Eve, in the Garden. He told them they were not to eat the fruit from one certain tree or they would die. God's enemy, Satan, tricked Eve into eating the fruit. Adam ate it too. In choosing to disobey God, they sinned.

God told Adam that they would have to leave the Garden. They would have pain and sickness and their bodies would die. Sin separated Adam and Eve from God, who is holy and perfect.

Ever since Adam and Eve sinned, everyone is born sinful and separated from God. The Bible says "all have sinned" (Romans 3:23). Sin is thinking, saying, or doing things that break God's laws. It is sin in your heart that causes you to do bad things. You cannot get rid of your sin by yourself. You deserve to be punished for your sin. Only God can forgive you so that you will not be separated from him forever.

When Adam sinned, sin entered the entire human race. Adam's sin brought death, so death spread to everyone, for everyone sinned.
Romans 5:12

YOU CAN PRAY:

Dear God, thank you that you love me even though I have sinned. Thank you that you forgive me. In Jesus' name. Amen.

WHAT SAD THINGS HAPPENED WHEN ADAM AND EVE SINNED?

January 7

WHAT DID GOD DO ABOUT SIN?

The most wonderful story in all the world is the story of what God did so that we could have our sins forgiven.

After Adam and Eve sinned, God promised to send a Savior. You and I know today that the Savior is the Lord Jesus Christ, God's only Son. He was born into this world as a baby. When he became a man, he gave himself to die on the cross for our sins.

As Jesus died, God placed upon him the sins of the whole world. The Bible says, "God made Christ, who never sinned, to be the offering for our sin" (2 Corinthians 5:21). Jesus did not deserve to die. He had no sin of his own. He was perfect, but he took your place on the cross. If Jesus had not given his precious blood to take your punishment, you could never be forgiven of your sins. Jesus died and was buried. Three days later God brought him back to life. Jesus later returned to heaven where he is alive today. God kept his promise to pay for sin. He sent his own beloved Son to be the Savior of the world.

When Adam sinned, sin entered the entire human race. Adam's sin brought death, so death spread to everyone, for everyone sinned.
Romans 5:12

YOU CAN PRAY:
Dear God, thank you for sending your only Son, Jesus, to die on the cross for me. Thank you for your great love. In Jesus' name. Amen.

WRITE DOWN WHY YOU THINK JESUS HAD TO DIE.

HOW CAN I BE FORGIVEN?

January
8

Now you know Jesus died for your sins. Are you wondering how you can be forgiven? The Bible says that Jesus is the only way to God. Jesus said, "I am the way, the truth, and the life. No one can come to the Father except through me" (John 14:6).

Jesus wants to be your Savior. You cannot save yourself from sin. You're not saved from sin's punishment by doing good things. You can't be forgiven by saying prayers, giving money, or trying to please God. God says there is only one way, and that is through his Son, Jesus.

The Bible says, "Believe on the Lord Jesus and you will be saved" (Acts 16:31). To believe means to trust completely in the Lord Jesus. His death on the cross is the only payment for your sins that God will accept. When you choose to trust in the Lord Jesus as your Savior, God says you are forgiven. You are rescued from the punishment of your sins. You will not be separated from God in a place of punishment when you die. You'll live with God forever in heaven someday.

WHAT DO YOU NEED TO BELIEVE TO BE FORGIVEN OF YOUR SINS?

When Adam sinned, sin entered the entire human race. Adam's sin brought death, so death spread to everyone, for everyone sinned.
Romans 5:12

YOU CAN PRAY:

Dear God, I know that I'm a sinner. I believe in your Son, Jesus, who died to take the punishment for my sins and rose again. I want Jesus to be my Savior. In Jesus' name. Amen.

January

9

IS GOD REALLY PERFECT?

But now you must be holy in everything you do, just as God—who chose you to be his children—is holy.
1 Peter 1:15

YOU CAN PRAY:

Dear God, you are holy and perfect. You alone are good. Thank you that I can come to you through the Lord Jesus, who is my Savior. In Jesus' name. Amen.

Do you know someone who never does anything wrong or never makes a mistake? Certain people have searched for many years for someone who is perfect. They never found such a person.

The Bible says, "God is light and there is no darkness in him at all" (1 John 1:5). This verse means that God is holy and pure. There is no sin at all in him. There is not even one little bit of badness in God. He is set apart from sin—set apart from all that is evil or bad. God and sin are opposites like light and darkness. God is holy. The Father is holy; the Son, the Lord Jesus Christ, is holy; and the Holy Spirit is holy.

There is someone who is perfect—that is God! Only God is perfect. We have all sinned and sin separates us from God. Because God is holy, he has to punish sin. But he gave his Son to die for sin so that we could be forgiven and made holy. When you believed in Jesus as your Savior, you were forgiven of your sins and made holy before God. Aren't you glad?

HOW ARE WE DIFFERENT FROM GOD?

WHAT DOES IT MEAN THAT GOD IS HOLY?

January
10

Isaiah was one of God's great prophets. Prophets were men who told others what God said. God also spoke to Isaiah. God told Isaiah to tell people that one day the Savior of the world would come.

One day God spoke to Isaiah in a vision. A vision is like a dream. Isaiah said that he saw God seated on a throne, high and exalted. Above God were angels. The angels called out to each other, "Holy, holy, holy is the Lord Almighty! The whole earth is filled with his glory!" (Isaiah 6:3). When Isaiah saw the vision, he was afraid. He saw how sinful he was compared to God. The vision helped him to see that God is holy.

What does it mean that God is holy? He is 100 percent pure. He never sins—he is perfect. God always does what is right. He is completely good. God hates sin.

If we are sinners, how can we pray to God? God wants us to talk to him. He told Isaiah not to be afraid. He also tells us not to be afraid. When we believe in the Lord Jesus as our Savior, he takes our sin away and makes us clean so that we can talk to God who is holy.

WHAT DO YOU THINK IT MEANS THAT GOD IS HOLY?

But now you must be holy in everything you do, just as God—who chose you to be his children—is holy.
1 Peter 1:15

YOU CAN PRAY:

Dear God, you are a holy God. Thank you that the Lord Jesus has taken away my sin so that I can pray to you. In Jesus' name. Amen.

January

11

DOES GOD EXPECT ME TO BE HOLY?

But now you must be holy in everything you do, just as God—who chose you to be his children—is holy.
1 Peter 1:15

YOU CAN PRAY:

Dear God, thank you that you are a holy God. Please give me the power to live a holy life. In Jesus' name. Amen.

When the prophet Isaiah saw the vision of God surrounded by the angels covering their faces in reverence, he saw how holy God is. If you were Isaiah, what would you be thinking? Maybe you would think about how sinful you really are.

If you have trusted in Jesus as your Savior, God expects you to live a clean life. He expects you to be holy. You have a choice. You can give in to sin or you can choose God's way. God will help you to say "no" to sin. He expects you to obey his Word, the Bible, and do what is right. God expects you to tell the truth and always be kind, loving, and patient with others. He wants you to be honest and to behave in a way that pleases him.

Remember that God lives in you to give you the power to live a clean, holy life and to not sin. When you do sin, however, think about how holy God is. Confess your sin to him right away. God says if you will confess your sins—that is tell him about the wrong you have done—he will forgive you (1 John 1:9). Will you choose to be holy?

IN WHAT WAYS DOES GOD WANT YOU TO BE HOLY?

January
12

WHO'S IN CHARGE?

Has your mother ever said to you, "You're in charge"? When you're put in charge of something, you are like a king reigning over it. You have control and are responsible for seeing that the assignment is carried out.

Have you ever wondered who's in charge of the world? The Bible tells us that God is sovereign. That means he is in charge or in control of all things. He is the highest ruler. No one is over God. God reigns over everything and everybody all the time. Nothing can happen unless God allows it to happen. He is in control of everything day and night—24 hours a day, 7 days a week, 52 weeks a year. He never sleeps or goes away on vacation.

How long will God reign? The Bible says, "The Lord will reign forever and ever!" (Exodus 15:18). God was always in control and he always will be in control. What does that mean for you? No matter what happens in your life, you don't have to be afraid or upset because God is in control. He loves you, and he wants you to trust him completely. God is the greatest. He is sovereign. He is the King of kings.

But now you must be holy in everything you do, just as God—who chose you to be his children—is holy.
1 Peter 1:15

YOU CAN PRAY:

Dear God, I praise you because you are in control of all things. Help me to trust you each day. In Jesus' name. Amen.

WHAT DOES IT MEAN THAT GOD IS OVEREIGN?

January
13

WHAT ARE GOD'S RULES FOR US?

Long ago God gave his people 10 special laws to show them how holy he is and how sinful people are. The laws also tell us how God wants his people to live. We call these laws the Ten Commandments:

Do not worship any other gods besides me. (Worship God alone.)

Do not make idols of any kind. (Don't let anything take God's place in your life.)

Do not misuse the name of the Lord your God. (Only use God's name with respect.)

Remember to observe the Sabbath day by keeping it holy. (Rest and worship God one day a week.)

Honor your father and mother. (Respect your parents.)

Do not murder. (Protect life; never take life away.)

Do not commit adultery. (Married people are to be true to each other.)

Do not steal. (Don't take something that's not yours.)

Do not testify falsely against your neighbor. (Don't lie.)

Do not covet. (Don't want what belongs to others.)

When God spoke these commandments the people were afraid. But Moses, their leader, explained that God was showing them how great he is in order to keep them from sinning. The Israelites said they would obey God. Will you?

WHY DID GOD GIVE THE TEN COMMANDMENTS?

But now you must be holy in everything you do, just as God—who chose you to be his children—is holy.
1 Peter 1:15

YOU CAN PRAY:

Dear God, I want to live for you by keeping your laws. Help me to do what is right every day. In Jesus' name. Amen.

IS GOD SOVEREIGN OVER ME?

God is sovereign—he is always in control. God does whatever pleases him. He decides whether we can do what we have planned. He has total control over all people. Nothing that happens in our lives is ever out of God's control.

Have you ever thought that things in your life are out of control? Maybe someone you love has been injured in an accident or died of a terrible disease. Perhaps your family is having a hard time because one or both of your parents have lost their jobs. Maybe someone is being mean to you or treating you unfairly. When you are sick, or when troubles come, remember that God loves you and that everything is under his control. He will do what is best for you even though you may not think the situation is good.

The Bible says, "And we know that God causes everything to work together for the good of those who love God" (Romans 8:28). Nothing that happens to you is too small for God to know about. Nothing is too big for him to control it. When you can't understand why things happen, just remember that God is in control. You can trust your loving heavenly Father.

WHAT SHOULD YOU REMEMBER WHEN YOU ARE GOING THROUGH DIFFICULT SITUATIONS?

But now you must be holy in everything you do, just as God—who chose you to be his children—is holy.
1 Peter 1:15

YOU CAN PRAY:
Dear God, thank you that you are in control of my life. Help me to remember that you love me and will do what is best for me. In Jesus' name. Amen.

January

15

DOES MY LIFE SHOW THAT GOD IS IN CHARGE?

But now you must be holy in everything you do, just as God—who chose you to be his children—is holy.
1 Peter 1:15

YOU CAN PRAY:
Dear God, help me to trust you in the good times and the difficult ones. Thank you for your peace. In Jesus' name. Amen.

God never promised that his children would have a life free from problems and pain. God allows difficult things to happen in our lives as he carries out his plan for us.

It is just as important to trust God as it is to obey him. When you do not trust God, you are doubting that he is in control and that he is good. God wants you to learn to trust him every day, all day. He wants you to trust him in the good times and the difficult ones. Trusting God means believing with all your heart that he is in control and that he is doing what is best for you.

How does your life show that God is in charge? When you are facing a problem, your first response should be to trust God (rely on him). You can trust him because you know that God has allowed the problem for a certain reason. Talk to God in prayer and tell him your problems. As you trust God, he will give you peace, a calmness on the inside. Thank him for working in your life to make you more like Jesus.

WHY IS IT IMPORTANT FOR YOU TO TRUST GOD?

WHY DOES GOD PUNISH SINNERS?

January
16

Have you ever said, "That's not fair"? No one can ever say that of God. God is always fair (or just) in everything he does. The Bible says that God "does no wrong; how just and upright he is!" (Deuteronomy 32:4). God is our judge, and he judges fairly.

Since Adam and Eve, everyone is born into this world wanting to sin. God is holy; he hates sin. He cannot let people do wrong without punishing them, because he is just and fair. The Bible says, "For the wages of sin is death" (Romans 6:23). Wages are what we earn for what we do. What do we earn for sin? Yes, death. God said that because of sin we deserve to be separated from him forever. That's the punishment our just God placed on sin. It is called eternal death.

But God sent his only Son, the Lord Jesus Christ, to die on the cross and take the punishment we deserve for sin. People who reject the Lord Jesus will be lost forever in a terrible place called hell. All who believe in Jesus as their Savior are saved from the punishment they deserve (Acts 16:31).

HOW DOES GOD PUNISH SINNERS?

Give thanks to the Lord, for he is good! His faithful love endures forever.
Psalm 118:1

YOU CAN PRAY:

Dear God, you are always fair in everything you do. Thank you that Jesus took the punishment that I deserve for sin so that I can be saved. In Jesus' name. Amen.

January
17

HOW MUCH DOES GOD LOVE ME?

You know what love is, don't you? When you love someone, you want to be near him. You want to take care of him and do nice things for him. You're quick to forgive him if he does something wrong.

God's love is so much greater and more wonderful than the love we have for other people. God says, "I have loved you, my people, with an everlasting love" (Jeremiah 31:3). God's love is so great that it lasts forever! His love for you will never end.

There was never a time that God didn't love you. He loved you even before you were born. He knew exactly when you would be born, what color hair and eyes you would have, and who your parents would be. He loves you so much that he wants the best for you.

God has so much love that he sent his perfect, only Son, the Lord Jesus, to die in your place on the cross. Jesus' death on the cross is the greatest picture of God's love. He has promised that if you believe in Jesus as your Savior, he will someday take you to heaven to live with him forever. Can you see how much God loves you?

Give thanks to the Lord, for he is good! His faithful love endures forever.
Psalm 118:1

YOU CAN PRAY:
Dear God, thank you for your great love for me. Help me to love you and give you my best. In Jesus' name. Amen.

IN WHAT WAYS DOES GOD SHOW HE LOVES YOU?

WHAT IS GOD'S GRACE?

January
18

Have you ever received a gift you didn't deserve? The gift was given to you out of love. God is so great that he gives us his grace because of his love for us.

Grace is God showing his love to you even though you don't deserve it. You can't earn God's grace. You do not deserve to be saved from sin and to have eternal life. But God showed his grace by saving you from sin's punishment when you trusted in Jesus as your Savior. God also shows his grace by giving you strength and guidance, and by taking care of you each day. God, by his grace, gives you strength to handle difficult problems in your life. Isn't God's grace wonderful?

If you know Jesus as your Savior, you can be thankful that God saved you by his grace. The Bible says, "God saved you by his special favor when you believed" (Ephesians 2:8). You can also depend on God each day for the grace you need to live for him. Because God shows his grace to you, you should show his grace to others. Have you ever thanked God for his grace in your life?

Give thanks to the Lord, for he is good! His faithful love endures forever.
Psalm 118:1

YOU CAN PRAY:

Dear God, thank you for saving me by your grace. Thank you, too, for the blessings I do not deserve that you give me each day. In Jesus' name. Amen.

HOW DOES GOD SHOW HIS GRACE TO YOU?

January

19

WHAT IS GOD'S MERCY?

Have you ever thought about how merciful God is? The Bible says, "The Lord is merciful and gracious; . . . he has not punished us for all our sins" (Psalm 103:8-10).

Mercy is willingly forgiving someone who has done wrong rather than punishing him. It is showing kindness, especially when it is not deserved. That's what God has done for you. Instead of giving you the punishment you deserve for your sin, God in his mercy forgave you when you believed in Jesus as your Savior.

God shows mercy—kindness and love—to you every day in many ways, even though you don't deserve it. He provides for your needs. He hears and answers your prayers.

Now God expects you to be merciful to others. You can be kind and help those in need. You shouldn't look down on others or judge them. Being merciful may mean being a friend to someone others reject. It means being patient with younger brothers or sisters, even when they bother you.

God promises a special blessing to those who are kind and merciful. They will receive mercy. So if you show mercy, don't be surprised when others are merciful to you.

Give thanks to the Lord, for he is good! His faithful love endures forever.
Psalm 118:1

YOU CAN PRAY:

Dear God, thank you for showing me your mercy and grace that I don't deserve. Help me to be merciful to others. In Jesus' name. Amen.

WHY SHOULD YOU SHOW MERCY TO OTHERS?

WHY DO GOOD THINGS HAPPEN TO BAD PEOPLE?

January
20

Why do people who don't love God sometimes have so many good things happen to them? Maybe they have a lot of money or fame. Yet, some people who love God have so many struggles. It just doesn't seem fair.

God is sovereign, remember? He is in control of all things, including the lives of those who reject him. God directs their lives according to his purpose and plan. The Bible says, "We can make our plans, but the Lord determines our steps" (Proverbs 16:9). God allows people to make their own choices, yet they eventually do what God planned that they would do.

Sometimes it seems so unfair when we see good things happen to bad people. God allows these things to happen because of his mercy and grace. But God is just. One day, each person will stand before him. Those who have not believed in God's Son, the Lord Jesus, will be punished for their unbelief. Those who have trusted in Jesus as their Savior will be rewarded. Many who have not had very much in this world will be rich in heaven!

Don't be jealous of others who have more than you do. Thank God for what you have and for what he allows in your life—both good and bad. He loves you and is in control of everything that happens.

Give thanks to the Lord, for he is good! His faithful love endures forever.
Psalm 118:1

YOU CAN PRAY:

Dear God, thank you for being so good. Help me to trust what you are doing in my life and in the lives of other people. In Jesus' name. Amen.

WHY DO GOOD THINGS HAPPEN TO BAD PEOPLE?

January
21

WILL GOD EVER LET ME DOWN?

Has someone ever broken a promise to you? You were really counting on someone and he let you down. Maybe you have wondered whom you can really depend on.

The Bible says that there is someone who will never let you down, who will never break his promises to you—that is God! God will always be faithful to his Word and to every promise he has made in it. Since God is perfect, he cannot fail you even one time! The Bible says, "Understand, therefore, that the Lord your God is indeed God. He is the faithful God" (Deuteronomy 7:9). That truth should give you peace and confidence as you live each day.

What if you are unfaithful to God? What if you let him down? Will he still be faithful to you? Will he let you down? The amazing thing about God is that even though we are unfaithful to him, he will be continually faithful to us. When things are not going as you would like and you have problems that seem out of control, you can be confident that God will never let you down. Thank him for standing with you and being faithful each day.

Give thanks to the Lord, for he is good! His faithful love endures forever.
Psalm 118:1

YOU CAN PRAY:

Dear God, thank you that you will always be with me and will never let me down. Thank you for being faithful each day. In Jesus' name. Amen.

HOW DO YOU KNOW GOD WILL NEVER LET YOU DOWN?

CAN I REALLY BELIEVE GOD?

Has anybody ever lied to you? It is hard to believe people when it seems as if everyone lies from time to time. In many different situations people often ask, "What is the truth?"

God is all truth—he never lies. God sees and knows all things as they really are. The Bible says that "God is not a man, that he should lie" (Numbers 23:19). Because God is holy (without sin), he could not be anything else but true.

Not only God himself is truth, but his Word, the Bible, is the truth. His Word is totally trustworthy. The Bible says that all the commands of the Lord are true (Psalm 119:151). If you know Jesus as your Savior, you can trust God completely as you obey everything he says in his Word. God's promises are true. He has always kept his promises from the beginning of time. Many years ago God made a promise to a man named Noah never again to destroy the world with a flood (Genesis 9:11-13). When you see a rainbow, you can remember that God is truth. He kept his promise to Noah and he will keep his promise to you. You can believe with all your heart in the God of truth.

WHY CAN YOU BELIEVE WHAT GOD SAYS?

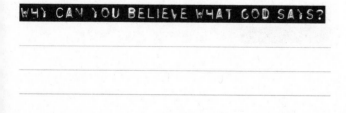

Give thanks to the Lord, for he is good! His faithful love endures forever.
Psalm 118:1

YOU CAN PRAY:

Dear God, thank you that you are Truth and that I can believe what you say. In Jesus' name. Amen.

January
23

DOES GOD KNOW EVERYTHING?

Have you ever met someone who thinks he knows it all? Maybe he can answer all your questions or get an *A* on tests at school. You think he's the smartest person in the world. But, no matter how much your friend knows, he doesn't know anything compared to God. God knows everything.

God has all knowledge—he knows everything in the whole world. Because God is all-wise, he uses all of that information in the best way possible. Since God made and understands all things, he has perfect plans. He knows what is best for you. In his wisdom, he carries out his plans for you. God knows exactly what he is allowing in your life even though some things may be hard. He is working through those situations for your good and his glory. Each thing that your loving heavenly Father allows to happen in your life is wise and good.

The Bible says, "O Lord, what a variety of things you have made! In wisdom you have made them all" (Psalm 104:24). God made everything and he knows everything. He loves you and wants you to trust him completely. Will you trust him today?

Give thanks to the Lord, for he is good! His faithful love endures forever.
Psalm 118:1

YOU CAN PRAY:
Dear God, you made everything and know everything. I will trust you today, knowing that everything that happens in my life is from you. In Jesus' name. Amen.

HOW DOES GOD USE HIS WISDOM IN YOUR LIFE?

WHAT IS THE FEAR OF THE LORD?

January
24

Moses, the great leader of the Israelite people, was old and would soon die. One day he told the priests they should read the law aloud to the people every seven years. He said, "Call them all together—men, women, children, and the foreigners living in your towns—so they may listen and learn to fear the Lord your God and carefully obey all the terms of this law" (Deuteronomy 31:12). When the law was read, a person would learn more about God and his Word. The children would also hear the law and learn to fear and obey the Lord.

What does it mean to fear the Lord? It means that you become so aware of how holy and powerful God is that you are really afraid of disobeying him. You do not want to displease God. When you fear God, you understand his greatness and you reverence him—show him respect and love. You think about him with awe and wonder because of his great power. Fearing God also means that you worship him, serve him, and trust him.

Do you realize how really great and awesome God is? If you do, you will want to please and obey him more than anything else.

Let us be thankful and please God by worshiping him with holy fear and awe.
Hebrews 12:28

YOU CAN PRAY:
Dear God, thank you for being my heavenly Father and for loving me so much. Help me to please you in all things by obeying you. In Jesus' name. Amen.

HOW DOES GOD WANT YOU TO FEAR HIM?

January
25

HOW DO I REVERENCE GOD?

How would you act if you were invited to visit a king? Would you run into his throne room laughing and talking? Would you ignore the king or call him by his first name? You would probably be quiet and respectful. What if you were invited to meet with the King of all kings, God himself? How would you act? No doubt you would show him great reverence.

To reverence God means to show loving respect for him and his Word. You do not show reverence for God when you speak about him in a careless way or use his name as a swear word. Because God is perfect and pure, it is a serious thing to him when his children fail to reverence him. You should not approach God lightly, as if he were not important. He is the most important one in all of the universe.

God is holy and he deserves your reverence. Be careful how you speak about God. Think about how holy God is before you use his name in a wrong way. Your reverence for God shows others that you have a special relationship with him. Will you show honor and reverence for God today with your life?

Let us be thankful and please God by worshiping him with holy fear and awe.
Hebrews 12:28

YOU CAN PRAY:
Dear God, thank you that you are a great and holy God. Help me to reverence you today and every day. In Jesus' name. Amen.

NAME THREE WAYS YOU CAN SHOW REVERENCE FOR GOD.

WHAT DOES GOD DO FOR ME?

January
26

All of us have needs—things we must have like food, clothing, and shelter. Probably your parents take care of these things for you. But did you know that it is God who has provided so that your needs will be met?

God knows about your basic needs. He also knows you have the need to be loved and accepted, and to feel safe and protected. Perhaps those who are supposed to take care of you have not been able to meet your needs. Your family might have to depend on others for help. At times, you may try to meet your own needs. But God wants you to look to him first to provide for you. He is your heavenly Father who cares for you more than anyone else could.

There is no need too great or too hard for God to supply. The Bible says, "God . . . will supply all your needs" (Philippians 4:19). God has all of the riches in the world. He never lacks anything, so he is well able to supply any need.

God does not promise to supply everything you want, but your needs will never go unmet. Depend on God. Tell him about your needs and trust him to provide for you.

HOW DOES GOD TAKE CARE OF YOU?

Let us be thankful and please God by worshiping him with holy fear and awe.
Hebrews 12:28

YOU CAN PRAY:

Dear God, thank you that you have the power to meet all my needs. Help me to trust you. In Jesus' name. Amen.

WHAT DOES GOD DO IN THE WORLD?

Let us be thankful and please God by worshiping him with holy fear and awe.
Hebrews 12:28

YOU CAN PRAY:
Dear God, thank you that you are in control of the world and everything in it. Help me to trust you and to not worry. In Jesus' name. Amen.

Have you ever wondered what God does all day? What in the world does God do? First, you know that God created the world and everything in it. The Bible says, "You made the skies and the heavens and all the stars. You made the earth and the seas and everything in them. You preserve and give life to everything" (Nehemiah 9:6). God is the owner of all.

Another thing that God does in the world is to rule over his Creation. God has complete control over all things. He has control over the universe, the animals, the nations of the earth, and over people. He has control over nature—the sunshine, thunder, lightning, rain, and snow. All nature obeys his will. God keeps everything in the world going according to his plan. He always has the good of his creation at heart.

Does it sometimes seem that God is not in control? Maybe it's because there are so many bad things happening in the world. God is taking care of all things. You don't need to worry because God is taking care of this big world and he's taking care of you!

NAME TWO THINGS THAT GOD DOES IN THE WORLD.

DO I APPRECIATE GOD?

January
28

When someone does something nice for you, you normally say "thank you." You tell that person how much you appreciate what he or she did. Sometimes you may even buy the person a gift.

God has done so many wonderful things for you. He loves and cares for you. How do you tell him that you appreciate all that he has done? One way is to give God honor. To give honor to God means to give him a high place in your thinking. You also show honor when you tell others how great God is. The Bible says, "Sing about the glory of his name! Tell the world how glorious he is" (Psalm 66:2). Instead of bragging when someone gives you a compliment, you honor God by saying, "Thank you. It was God who helped me." You are giving the honor to him for what he does in your life.

God is the one who is worthy of our praise and honor. Will you honor him today and every day? When God helps you, tell him how much you appreciate his help. Let others know how great your heavenly Father is. They will want to know him too.

Let us be thankful and please God by worshiping him with holy fear and awe.
Hebrews 12:28

YOU CAN PRAY:
Dear God, I love you and appreciate you. Thank you for all you have done for me. In Jesus' name. Amen.

HOW CAN YOU SHOW GOD THAT YOU APPRECIATE HIM?

January

29

DOES GOD KNOW ABOUT THINGS IN MY LIFE?

Let us be thankful and please God by worshiping him with holy fear and awe.
Hebrews 12:28

YOU CAN PRAY:
Dear God, thank you that you know all about me and you love me. Help me to trust you to do what is best for me. In Jesus' name. Amen.

Have you ever tried to explain something to a friend and he just stared at you? Maybe you think, "Doesn't anybody understand what I think or feel?"

God knows everything in the whole world, and God knows everything about you. The Bible says, "You [Lord] know when I sit down or stand up. You know my every thought. . . . Every moment you know where I am" (Psalm 139:2-3). God knows your thoughts and how you feel at any time of the day. He knows when you get up in the morning and when you go to bed. He sees your tears and hears your laughter. God knows when you're frustrated and when you're sad. He knows the tiniest movement that you make. He also knows every secret sin. Although God knows all about you, he still loves you!

Not one thing in your life goes unnoticed by God. Maybe no one else understands you and your situation, but God understands completely. He knows about your past, your present, and your future. Because God knows the future, he can prepare you for it. Isn't it great to know that God knows all about you? Trust him to do what is best in your life.

NAME FOUR THINGS THAT GOD KNOWS ABOUT YOU.

DOES GOD CARE ABOUT ME?

Do you ever feel like no one cares about you? When hard things happen, you might feel like you're all alone. But there is someone who always cares. That someone is God.

If you know the Lord Jesus Christ as your Savior, you can trust God to take care of you. Perhaps when you get home from school you have to be alone while your parents are at work. Maybe you live where there is violence and you worry about being safe. It's natural to feel afraid sometimes—our world can be a very scary place! Do you think God knows about the dangers in your life? Yes, and he cares. What should you do when you feel alone or scared? The Bible says, "Give all your worries and cares to God, for he cares about what happens to you" (1 Peter 5:7). No matter what the problem is, God can take care of you.

Because you're his child, God has a plan for your life. He can work out any situation no matter how difficult it may be. When you're in a difficult situation, tell God about it. Think about how powerful he is—he can do anything! Thank him that he loves and cares for you.

HOW DO YOU KNOW GOD CARES FOR YOU?

Let us be thankful and please God by worshiping him with holy fear and awe.
Hebrews 12:28

YOU CAN PRAY:

Dear God, thank you that you love and care for me. Help me to trust you in everything that happens. In Jesus' name. Amen.

January
31

HOW CAN I BE AWARE OF GOD EACH DAY?

Let us be thankful and please God by worshiping him with holy fear and awe.
Hebrews 12:28

YOU CAN PRAY:
Dear God, thank you that you are with me. Help me to think about you all the time and remember how great you are. In Jesus' name. Amen.

David was a shepherd boy. He took care of his sheep far from home. He led his sheep to eat green grass and to drink fresh water. At times David played his harp. He loved God and made up songs about him. David was always thinking about God.

Do you think about God during the day? Do you know that he is with you even though you can't see him? You can think about him many times every day. When you see the flowers or hear the birds sing, you can think about how wonderful God is. When you think about God while you're at school or when you're playing, you will want to please him.

If you are thinking about God while you play, you will not become angry or selfish. If you think about God while you do your schoolwork, you will do a good job. If you think about God a lot, how can you do sinful things? How can you worry or be sad? The Bible says, "You will keep in perfect peace all who trust in you, whose thoughts are fixed on you!" (Isaiah 26:3). God wants you to think of him very often.

NAME SOME SPECIFIC TIMES WHEN YOU CAN THINK ABOUT GOD.

Activity 1: God the Father

THE TRINITY

The Lord is God in three persons.
See if you can fill in the blanks below.

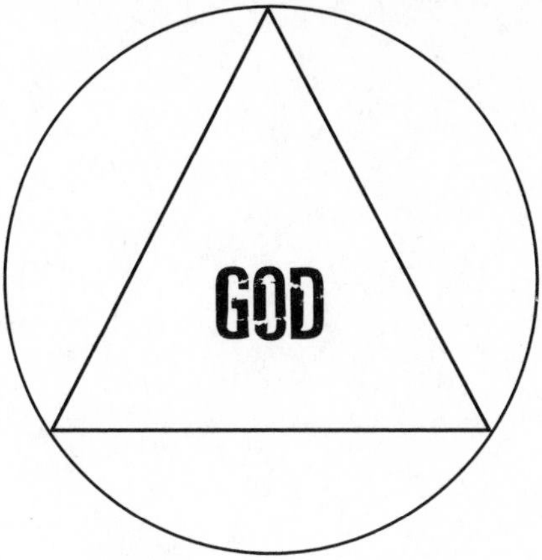

God the F______________

God the S______________

God the H__________ S__________

I show my reverence for God by . . .

____

THINKING IT OVER!

God the Father

Write the answers to these questions from your devotionals in the blanks.

1. What does it mean that God is eternal?

____

2. What is sin?

____

3. How can you be forgiven?

____

4. What does "God is holy" mean?

____

5. List two of God's rules for us:

____

6. How can you know God will keep his promises?

____

If you need help, you can look back in this month's devotionals. The number in ( ) tells you which devotional to check for each question. 1. (3) 2. (6) 3. (8) 4. (10) 5. (13) 6. (21)

FEBRUARY

God the Son

WHAT IS PROPHECY?

Can you imagine what it would be like to have God talk to you from heaven? What would he sound like? What would he say?

Hundreds of years ago God talked to special men called prophets. These men told others what God said. Sometimes they wrote it down for people to read. The prophets reminded people of God's great love for them. God also used the prophets to warn people to stop doing wrong or they would be punished.

God often told the prophets what was going to happen in the future. Since God knows everything, this was not hard for him to do. The people knew it was a message from God. Only he could know these things.

Because God spoke through a prophet, the message was called a "prophecy." Many of these special messages can be found in the Bible. These messages were not just for the people then. They're for you and me today! God's most exciting messages were about his Son, Jesus. You'll learn what these were as you keep reading in the next few days.

But when the right time came, God sent his Son.
Galatians 4:4

YOU CAN PRAY:

Dear God, thank you that you know all things, even before they happen. Help me to read your Word every day. In Jesus' name. Amen.

NAME SOMETHING YOU ARE GLAD GOD ALREADY KNOWS ABOUT.

WHO WERE GOD'S PROPHETS?

february
2

Who is the smartest person in the world? God, of course! He even knows what will happen in the future! The Bible says, "Lord, you know everything" (John 21:17). Nothing surprises God! Have you ever wished you knew what was going to happen like God does?

Before the Lord Jesus came to earth, God gave his chosen prophets special ability to know and write about the future. They told others what was going to happen. Many might have thought these men were very smart, but God's Holy Spirit told these prophets what to say. "It was the Holy Spirit who moved the prophets to speak from God" (2 Peter 1:21). Whatever they said came true!

The first prophet to write a book in the Bible was Isaiah. His book is near the end of the Old Testament.

The prophets spoke to groups of people. They loved God and the people very much. Some people treated them badly when they shared God's messages. Others did not believe them. Many didn't like what they said. But these bold prophets did not quit sharing God's messages with others.

HOW DID THE PROPHETS HAVE THE BOLDNESS TO SHARE GOD'S MESSAGES?

But when the right time came, God sent his Son.
Galatians 4:4

YOU CAN PRAY:

Dear God, help me to be bold like your prophets when I tell others about you. Thank you for giving me the courage not to quit. In Jesus' name. Amen.

February
3

WHAT DID GOD'S PROPHETS SAY ABOUT JESUS?

But when the right time came, God sent his Son.
Galatians 4:4

YOU CAN PRAY:
Dear God, I know Jesus is the one you promised to send. Thank you that he took the punishment for my sins. I believe in Jesus, your Son! In Jesus' name. Amen.

Do you like to read mysteries? A mystery is a secret that you figure out by using clues.

After God made the first man and woman, he promised to send a Savior to earth. This special person would take the punishment for the wrong things people had done. The Savior also would be punished for your sins. No one knew who it would be. It was a mystery. But God gave clues to the prophets, his messengers. We find them written in the Old Testament of the Bible.

Here are just a few of many clues the prophets wrote: God's promised Savior would be born in the city of Bethlehem. He would be born in a stable—like a barn. He would be from the family of King David. He would be rejected by the people and killed. The prophets told how he would die and why. They even said he would come back to life. Who is the promised Savior? You are right, the Lord Jesus Christ!

Some of these clues were written 700 years before Jesus ever came! There was no way the prophets could have known these things before they happened unless God had told them.

LIST THREE CLUES YOU LEARNED ABOUT THE PROMISED SAVIOR.

DID GOD'S PROPHECIES ABOUT JESUS COME TRUE?

february
4

"Could this be the Promised One from God?" many people wondered as they met the Lord Jesus. They had read the clues the prophets had written. They waited and watched. Then, at just the right time in history, Jesus came! "But when the right time came, God sent his Son" (Galatians 4:4).

One by one each clue the prophets had given about Jesus came true. Of all the cities in the world, he was born in Bethlehem. He was born in a stable. He was from the family of King David. Nazareth would become his hometown. All the prophecies about the Savior's birth had come true.

When he was grown, he did many amazing things that only God could do. But he was rejected by the people and treated very badly. He was nailed to a cross between two thieves. There he took the punishment for the sins of the whole world—including yours. All the prophecies about the Savior's death had come true. On the third day after Jesus died and was buried, he came back to life! Then, he returned to heaven to be with his Father. The prophets had written all this and more. Jesus is the Promised One!

WHY DON'T SOME PEOPLE BELIEVE JESUS IS GOD'S PROMISED SAVIOR?

But when the right time came, God sent his Son.
Galatians 4:4

YOU CAN PRAY:
Dear God, thank you for sending the Lord Jesus to earth at just the right time, as you promised. You are a great God! In Jesus' name. Amen.

February 5

IS JESUS REALLY THE SAVIOR GOD PROMISED?

But when the right time came, God sent his Son. Galatians 4:4

YOU CAN PRAY:
Dear God, I am glad I know the truth about your Son, Jesus. Keep me from being tricked by others. In Jesus' name. Amen.

"Follow me. I will help you get to heaven. Be good like me and someday you will be with God! I will show you the way." Many people have said this, but they were not telling the truth. Today, millions think men like Buddha or Muhammad will show them God's way. Others think they can find their own way to heaven.

When Jesus lived on earth, he said, "I am the way, the truth, and the life. No one can come to the Father except through me" (John 14:6). He was not only telling the truth, he *was* the truth! Only by believing (trusting) in Jesus, who died for your sins, can you be forgiven and come to God. Then, you can know you have life in heaven with God forever.

Who did the Father send to earth to be the promised Savior? The Bible says, "The Father sent his Son to be the Savior of the world" (1 John 4:14). *Savior* means the one who saves us from our sins. Only Jesus was God's perfect Son. Only Jesus was punished for your sins. Only Jesus came back to life. Only Jesus is the Savior God promised.

COPY 1 JOHN 4:14 BELOW AND SAY IT TO A FRIEND.

WHAT WILL JESUS DO IN THE FUTURE?

February

6

When Jesus entered the city of Jerusalem, the people shouted, "Bless the one who comes in the name of the Lord! Hail to the King of Israel!" (John 12:13). The prophets had said the promised Savior would someday rule the world. They thought that time had come, but Jesus hadn't come to earth for that reason. He came to die for our sins. The people didn't understand this. They were sad and confused when Jesus did not become king right away. Instead, he was put to death on a cross.

However, Jesus came back to life again and lives in heaven. God's Word says that someday Jesus will come back to rule the world as King. "When the Son of Man [Jesus] comes in his glory, . . . he will sit upon his glorious throne. All the nations will be gathered in his presence" (Matthew 25:31-32). Can you imagine what it will be like when Jesus is King? He is going to make a new earth. There will be no death, no tears, and no pain. What a wonderful place it will be!

All of those who have trusted the Lord Jesus as Savior will be with him forever! Those who haven't will be separated from God in a terrible place of punishment. If you haven't yet trusted in Jesus as your Savior, you can pray the prayer on this page.

WRITE THE DATE AND PLACE WHEN YOU TRUSTED JESUS AS YOUR SAVIOR.

But when the right time came, God sent his Son.
Galatians 4:4

YOU CAN PRAY:

Dear God, I know I am a sinner. I believe in Jesus, who died to take the punishment for my sin and rose again. Please forgive my sins. In Jesus' name. Amen.

February
7

WHY DOES GOD KEEP HIS PROMISES?

Have you ever made a promise you did not keep? "I promise I will be good from now on!" "I promise I will never speak to you again as long as I live!" "I promise I will never ask for another thing if you just get me what I want now!"

Has God ever made a promise he did not keep? No! God always keeps his promises because God is truth. You can believe what he says. Some things he told the prophets have not happened yet, but we know they will someday. The Bible says, "For the word of the Lord holds true, and everything he does is worthy of our trust" (Psalm 33:4). We have already seen hundreds of prophecies come true, just as God promised!

The greatest promise God has made was to send Jesus to earth. Why did God make that promise? God knew you needed a Savior. You have sinned and need to be forgiven. Why has God kept his promise? Because God is truth—he does not lie (Titus 1:2). Another reason he has kept his promise is because he loves you. You don't deserve his love or kindness, but because of Jesus, you can now be a child of God.

But when the right time came, God sent his Son. Galatians 4:4

YOU CAN PRAY:
Dear God, thank you for your love. I don't deserve your love or kindness. You love me even when I sin. You are wonderful! I love you, too. In Jesus' name. Amen.

WRITE A POEM TO GOD, THANKING HIM FOR HIS LOVE.

WHERE DID JESUS COME FROM?

February

8

Before time began on earth, the Bible says Jesus lived. He did not begin as a baby in Bethlehem. He was in heaven before coming to earth. He did not have a beginning, and he will live forever. How could this be? Because Jesus was, and is, God!

Jesus was not an angel who became God. He was not a man who later became like God. He has always been God. In fact, Jesus made the universe. "Christ is the one through whom God created everything in heaven and earth" (Colossians 1:16).

At just the right time in history, God sent his Son, Jesus, to be born as a baby so he could live on earth like you and me. "The Word [Jesus] became human" (John 1:14). While living on earth, Jesus proved he was God by his words and actions. He healed the sick, brought dead people back to life, and calmed storms! He forgave sins and never once sinned!

During Jesus' life on earth, God the Father spoke about him from heaven. God said, "This is my beloved Son, and I am fully pleased with him" (Matthew 3:17). God the Father wanted us to know for certain that Jesus truly is God the Son.

In the beginning the Word already existed. He was with God, and he was God. John 1:1

YOU CAN PRAY:

Dear God, I know Jesus is your Son. Thank you for helping me know and believe the truth. In Jesus' name. Amen.

WRITE DOWN A VERSE FROM TODAY'S LESSON THAT COULD HELP YOU EXPLAIN WHO JESUS REALLY IS.

February 9

HOW COULD JESUS BE BOTH GOD AND MAN?

The King of the universe born as a baby? How could this be? That is exactly what happened. Jesus, God the Son, left his wonderful home in heaven to come to earth and be born as a baby. The Bible says, "The Word [Jesus] became human and lived here on earth among us" (John 1:14). It was a miracle!

In heaven, Jesus had all power and authority as God. When he became a human, Jesus willingly gave up his right to those things. He became like you and me. He got hungry, thirsty, and tired. He felt pain and sadness. But because Jesus was still God the Son, he never sinned. He was completely God and man—perfect in every way.

Why did Jesus come to earth as a human? He came to take your punishment for sin. "He obediently humbled himself . . . by dying a criminal's death on a cross" (Philippians 2:8). He came to earth to make a way for you to go to heaven. Even when he was dying, there was never a moment that he was not God.

You don't have to understand how Jesus could be both God and man. You just need to believe that he was. God can do anything!

In the beginning the Word already existed. He was with God, and he was God.
John 1:1

YOU CAN PRAY:

Dear God, even though I can't understand all about you and your Son, Jesus, I believe what the Bible says. You are the mighty God! In Jesus' name. Amen.

WHAT ARE TWO THINGS JESUS GAVE UP WHEN HE CAME TO EARTH AS A HUMAN?

HOW WAS JESUS BORN?

February
10

Mary was amazed at what she heard! An angel told her, "You will become pregnant and have a son, and you are to name him Jesus. He will be very great and will be called the Son of the Most High" (Luke 1:31-32). Mary didn't know how this could happen. She was a virgin. Without touching her in any physical way, God would place the baby within her. It was a miracle!

God gave Mary a husband named Joseph. He would help Mary take care of the baby Jesus. Joseph knew that God himself was Jesus' real Father. An angel had visited Joseph, too, with the news. Perhaps he had read what the prophets had said about the coming Savior.

There was no room to stay in Bethlehem. Jesus was born in a stable. The Bible says Mary "wrapped him snugly in strips of cloth and laid him in a manger [a feeding place for animals]" (Luke 2:7). This was all part of God's plan. Everything about his birth had come true, just as the prophets had said. This tiny baby lying in the manger was the Savior of the world!

WRITE DOWN THE WORDS TO YOUR FAVORITE CHRISTMAS SONG ABOUT BABY JESUS.

In the beginning the Word already existed. He was with God, and he was God. John 1:1

YOU CAN PRAY:
Dear God, thank you for sending Jesus to earth in such a special way. It may not be Christmas now, but Happy Birthday, Jesus! In Jesus' name. Amen.

February

11

WAS JESUS LIKE ME?

What was Jesus like as a boy? As the perfect Son of God, Jesus was different from you in many ways. But there are some ways in which he was like you. He had a human body that got hungry and tired. He could be happy or sad.

Because he had a human body, he "grew both in height and in wisdom, and he was loved by God and by all who knew him" (Luke 2:52). These are ways that you should be growing too!

Jesus grew in height. His body became bigger and his muscles grew stronger.

Jesus grew in wisdom. When Jesus was 12 years old, he went to the temple (place of worship) where he talked with the religious leaders. They were impressed with his understanding and his answers. This story is in Luke 2:41-52.

Jesus was "loved by God." Everything he did pleased his Father, God. Jesus knew his Father was watching and helping him all the time!

Jesus was loved "by all who knew him." Others admired and respected him.

Are you growing in these important ways? Are you making wise choices? Are you getting bigger and stronger? Are you pleasing God in all that you do? Do you treat others with respect and kindness?

In the beginning the Word already existed. He was with God, and he was God. John 1:1

YOU CAN PRAY:

Dear God, help me to grow up to be like your Son, Jesus. Thank you. In Jesus' name. Amen.

HOW CAN YOU GROW TO BE MORE LIKE JESUS?

WHAT DID JESUS DO ON THE EARTH?

february
12

"It's a miracle!" Jairus must have joyfully shouted. "My little girl was dead, but Jesus brought her back to life!" News spread quickly throughout the countryside (Matthew 9:18-26). Blind people could suddenly see (Luke 18:35-43). Crippled people could walk (Luke 5:17-26). Many sick people were being healed (Mark 6:53-56). And that's not all! Jesus walked on water (Mark 6:45-51). He made giant storms go away by simply speaking (Mark 4:35-41). Demons obeyed his commands (Matthew 17:14-18). Twice he fed thousands of people with just a little bit of food (John 6:3-13; Mark 8:1-10).

It seemed there was no limit to Jesus' mighty power! Whatever the problem, he could take care of it. These miracles showed God's power and love. Jesus was proving that he truly was the Son of God, just as the prophets had said!

The Bible says, "I suppose that if all the other things Jesus did were written down, the whole world could not contain the books" (John 21:25). What problem do you have in your life today? Whether it's big or small, Jesus can help! Tell him about it and trust him to do what's best for you.

WRITE DOWN A BIG PROBLEM THAT JESUS CAN HELP YOU WITH.

In the beginning the Word already existed. He was with God, and he was God. John 1:1

YOU CAN PRAY:

Dear God, your power proves you can take care of my problems. Please help me to trust you with my problem today. In Jesus' name. Amen.

february

13

WHY IS JESUS CALLED THE WORD?

Words can be important! They tell others what you think, feel, or know to be true. Imagine a world without words!

The Bible says that Jesus "was the Word." This means that Jesus was God's message to you. Everything Jesus spoke told us how God thinks and feels. Everything Jesus did showed us what God would do.

Jesus was "the Word" as he taught how God wants you to think and behave. Not only did he say it, he showed you perfectly how to do it!

Jesus also taught about God's plan for you to have eternal life by believing in him as your Savior. He is called "the Word of life." The Bible says, "The one who existed from the beginning is the one we have heard and seen. We saw him with our own eyes and touched him with our own hands. He is Jesus Christ, the Word of life" (1 John 1:1).

When people listened to and looked at Jesus, they were listening to and looking at God!

Since Jesus is God's message to you, it is very important that you know him! What Jesus said and did is found in the books of Matthew, Mark, Luke, and John in the Bible. Other books may help you too, like this devotional book.

In the beginning the Word already existed. He was with God, and he was God.
John 1:1

YOU CAN PRAY:
Dear God, help me get to know you better every day. In Jesus' name. Amen.

WHAT HAVE YOU LEARNED ABOUT JESUS THAT YOU DIDN'T KNOW BEFORE?

WAS JESUS EVER TEMPTED TO SIN?

February
14

Have you ever wanted to be perfect? Maybe you have even tried. If someone told you he or she was perfect, I am sure you would watch very carefully for proof!

When Jesus lived on earth, he proved he was perfect! Satan tempted him many times to do wrong, but he never did! One day Satan visited Jesus in a wilderness in Judea. "If you are the Son of God," he taunted, "change these stones into loaves of bread" (Matthew 4:3). He was tempting Jesus not to follow God's plan.

Two other times Satan tempted Jesus to become proud and show his power. Satan even tried to get Jesus to worship him! Jesus knew God's plan for his coming to earth, and this was not it! He was determined to do only what his Father wanted.

Did Jesus ever give in? No! He could not sin, for he was God's perfect Son. He was exactly who he claimed to be, and he proved it! Jesus spoke the truth to Satan from God's Word. Satan eventually left him.

Jesus proved many times his power over Satan. That is why the Lord Jesus can help you when you are tempted to do wrong.

In the beginning the Word already existed. He was with God, and he was God.
John 1:1

YOU CAN PRAY:
Dear God, please help me when I am tempted to disobey you. I will depend on your power to help me say "no." In Jesus' name. Amen.

WHAT CAN YOU DO WHEN YOU ARE TEMPTED TO SIN?

February

15

WHAT HAPPENED IN THE ROOM UPSTAIRS?

It was the night before Jesus was to be killed. His 33 years on earth were almost over. The special Jewish holiday called the Passover had come. The prophets had said this would be the time of his death. Jesus met with his 12 close followers in an upstairs room for their last meal together (Luke 22:7-23).

The bread and wine Jesus passed to his disciples that night had special meaning. The next day he would die on a cross. The bread and wine were to be reminders of his wounded body and his blood that would flow on the cross as payment for our sins.

Judas Iscariot was there eating with Jesus. Before the meal was over, Judas left the room to go and betray Jesus by leading his enemies to him (John 13:21-30).

Jesus made some wonderful promises to his followers. Then they sang one last song together and left. It was a night they would never forget.

Jesus told his followers to continue to remember his death in the same way he had demonstrated in the upstairs room. Today we call this Communion, or the Lord's Supper. We are to remember his death in this way until he comes again.

For God so loved the world that he gave his only Son, so that everyone who believes in him will not perish but have eternal life. John 3:16

YOU CAN PRAY:

Dear God, thank you for giving this special way to remember what Jesus did for me. In Jesus' name. Amen.

HOW WAS THE NIGHT IN THE UPSTAIRS ROOM IMPORTANT FOR US TODAY?

WHY WAS JESUS ON TRIAL?

february
16

The night in the upstairs room had been special to Jesus and his disciples. But the religious leaders who hated Jesus wanted to have him killed! Why? Because Jesus had said he was the Son of God. He claimed to be the Messiah—the one God promised to send into the world to save everyone from sin. The leaders refused to believe him. They arrested Jesus and put him on trial.

Since Jesus had done nothing wrong, the religious leaders had to get men to tell lies about him. For hours, Jesus listened to their lies and he was painfully beaten. The religious leaders wanted Jesus put to death, so they took him to Pilate, the governor. "By our laws he ought to die because he called himself the Son of God," the leaders declared. Jesus did not say a word (John 19:7-9).

Pilate asked Jesus, "Don't you realize that I have the power to release you or to crucify you?" Jesus answered, "You would have no power over me at all unless it were given to you from above" (John 19:10-11). Jesus knew that being on trial was part of God's plan. The time had come for him to suffer and die for the sins of the world.

IF YOU HAD BEEN AT JESUS' TRIAL, WHAT WOULD YOU HAVE TOLD ABOUT JESUS?

For God so loved the world that he gave his only Son, so that everyone who believes in him will not perish but have eternal life. John 3:16

YOU CAN PRAY:
Dear God, I believe Jesus is your Son, just as he said. Thank you that he was willing to suffer and die for my sin. In Jesus' name. Amen.

February
17

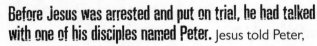

WHERE WERE JESUS' FRIENDS?

Before Jesus was arrested and put on trial, he had talked with one of his disciples named Peter. Jesus told Peter, " 'This very night, before the rooster crows, you will deny me three times.' 'No!' Peter insisted. 'Not even if I have to die with you! I will never deny you!' And all the other disciples vowed the same" (Matthew 26:34-35). But that night, when Jesus was arrested, his disciples ran away. They were afraid.

Peter followed at a distance. It was a horrible sight! Jesus was accused of things he didn't do. He was whipped, beaten, slapped, punched, mocked, and spit upon. One could hardly recognize him because of the bruises and blood.

Peter sat outside, warming himself by the fire. A servant girl pointed to him and said, "You were one of those with Jesus" (Matthew 26:69).

"I don't know what you are talking about," Peter replied (Matthew 26:70). Two other servants said they recognized Peter as one of Jesus' followers, but two more times Peter denied that he knew Jesus. Then the rooster crowed. As Jesus was led out of the trial, he looked at Peter, and Peter remembered Jesus' words. How could he have denied Jesus? Peter went away, crying bitterly.

For God so loved the world that he gave his only Son, so that everyone who believes in him will not perish but have eternal life. John 3:16

YOU CAN PRAY:

Dear God, I am sorry for the times I have pretended not to know you. Help me to be brave to speak up for you. In Jesus' name. Amen.

WRITE ABOUT A TIME WHEN YOU SPOKE UP FOR JESUS, EVEN THOUGH IT WAS HARD.

WHY DID JESUS HAVE TO DIE?

February
18

Jesus' arms were stretched out as soldiers nailed him to a wooden cross. The pain was horrible. The Lord Jesus was being crucified.

The mocking crowd said, "So he is the king of Israel, is he? Let him come down from the cross, and we will believe in him!" (Matthew 27:42). Because Jesus was the Son of God, he would not come down. God the Father placed on his perfect Son the sin of the whole world. "God made Christ, who never sinned, to be the offering for our sin" (2 Corinthians 5:21). Jesus willingly bled and died on the cross to take the punishment that God required for sin.

Hours later, darkness came over the whole countryside. Jesus cried out, "My God, my God, why have you forsaken me?" (Matthew 27:46). The perfect, holy God could not look at his Son, who had taken upon himself the sin of the world.

Later Jesus said, "Father, I entrust my spirit into your hands!" (Luke 23:46), and Jesus died. Some of the soldiers who had seen all that had happened said, "Truly, this was the Son of God!" (Matthew 27:54). When Jesus took the punishment for sin on the cross, he did all that was necessary to be called the Savior.

FINISH THIS SENTENCE: JESUS HAD TO DIE BECAUSE . . .

For God so loved the world that he gave his only Son, so that everyone who believes in him will not perish but have eternal life.
John 3:16

YOU CAN PRAY:
Dear God, thank you for being willing to send your Son to die in my place. In Jesus' name. Amen.

February

19

WHO MOVED THE STONE?

A friend named Joseph asked for permission to take Jesus' dead body down from the cross and bury him. After his body was wrapped in special cloths, they placed him in a tomb, or cave. A huge stone, requiring several men to move it, was rolled in front of the entrance. The religious leaders asked Pilate to assign armed soldiers to guard the tomb day and night (Matthew 27:57-66).

Suddenly, on the third day, there was an earthquake! An angel came down from heaven and rolled the stone from the door! The guards shook with fear and fell down as if they were dead. A few women, who were Jesus' friends, came to visit the tomb. They brought spices to put on Jesus' body, but when they arrived, the women were surprised to see a shining angel sitting on top of the stone (Matthew 28:1-4).

The tomb was empty! Jesus was gone! The angel said, "Don't be afraid! . . . I know you are looking for Jesus, who was crucified. He isn't here! He has been raised from the dead, just as he said would happen. . . . Go quickly and tell his disciples he has been raised from the dead" (Matthew 28:5-7). The women ran to tell the disciples.

WHAT WOULD YOU HAVE SAID TO JESUS THE DAY HE CAME BACK TO LIFE?

For God so loved the world that he gave his only Son, so that everyone who believes in him will not perish but have eternal life.
John 3:16

YOU CAN PRAY:

Dear God, because your Son came back to life, I can live forever with you in heaven! You are an awesome God! In Jesus' name. Amen.

CAN I KNOW FOR SURE THAT I AM FORGIVEN?

February
20

Have you ever wondered if you are really forgiven? One of the last things Jesus said as he hung on the cross was, "It is finished!" He meant that he had done all that is necessary to pay for your sin. God loved you when you didn't deserve it. Jesus died for you so you could be forgiven. If you have trusted Jesus as your Savior, God kept his promise. He has forgiven you and you have eternal life. One Bible writer says, "I write this to you who believe in the Son of God, so that you may know you have eternal life" (1 John 5:13). Also, the Bible says that when God forgives you, he won't remember your sins anymore (Hebrews 8:12).

Maybe you're thinking, "But I don't feel like I'm forgiven!" Your forgiveness does not depend on how you feel. It is based on your faith in Jesus and what he has done for you. Put your name in his promise: "For God so loved [your name] that he gave his only Son, so that everyone who believes in him will not perish but have eternal life" (John 3:16).

For God so loved the world that he gave his only Son, so that everyone who believes in him will not perish but have eternal life.
John 3:16

YOU CAN PRAY:
Dear God, thank you for keeping your promise to me. Thank you for forgiving me and for the gift of eternal life. In Jesus' name. Amen.

HOW DO YOU KNOW YOU ARE FORGIVEN?

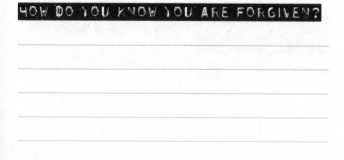

February

21

WHAT CAN I GIVE TO GOD?

For God so loved the world that he gave his only Son, so that everyone who believes in him will not perish but have eternal life. John 3:16

YOU CAN PRAY:

Dear God, I give myself to you. I will go where you want me to go, do what you want me to do, and be what you want me to be. In Jesus' name. Amen.

If you've received the Lord Jesus Christ as your Savior, you're probably just beginning to realize the wonderful gift he is! Jesus is your friend and helper. He is God's free gift to you!

When someone gives you a wonderful gift, you usually want to give that person something in return. Perhaps you are so grateful for God's gift of the Lord Jesus that you would like to give him something special. But what do you give to God, who owns everything? The gift he wants most is you! One of the Bible writers said, "I plead with you to give your bodies to God. Let them be a living and holy sacrifice—the kind he will accept" (Romans 12:1).

A sacrifice is an offering or gift. You can tell God you want to give yourself to him. Give him your eyes and ears, your feet and your hands. Give him your mind and your heart. Give him every part of you to do what pleases him. Why should you present your body to God? Because you love him. He wants you to be holy, set apart, for him to use in whatever way he chooses. Will you give yourself to God now?

WRITE A THANK-YOU NOTE TO GOD FOR HIS GIFT TO YOU.

DID JESUS REALLY COME BACK TO LIFE?

february 22

"Jesus, alive from the dead? I'll prove it's not true!" Many people have said this from the first day Jesus came back to life. Some are still saying it today. Maybe you've also wondered if Jesus truly came alive again. He did! And there is much evidence to prove it is true.

Some have tried to prove Jesus didn't really die. They say he just fainted and that his disciples pretended that he died and came alive again. But Jesus' enemies made sure he was dead before his body was taken down from the cross. They also made sure no one could steal his body and pretend he had risen.

After Jesus came back to life, over five hundred people saw him on at least 15 different occasions! They touched him, talked to him, and ate with him. Many of these witnesses were later tortured and killed by Jesus' enemies. If it were not true, they certainly would have said so to save their own lives.

For hundreds of years, millions of people all over the world have testified that Jesus is alive! Even though we can no longer see him with our eyes, we can see Jesus changing lives and answering our prayers.

Christ died for our sins, just as the Scriptures said. He was buried, and he was raised from the dead on the third day, as the Scriptures said.
1 Corinthians 15:3-4

YOU CAN PRAY:

Dear God, thank you that Jesus is alive and that he is working in my life today. In Jesus' name. Amen.

HOW DO YOU KNOW THAT JESUS IS ALIVE?

February

23

WHAT WERE JESUS' LAST WORDS?

If you were not going to see your family and friends for a very long time, what would you say to them? I am sure you would choose your words very carefully. It would be important for them to remember your last instructions.

After Jesus came back to life, he stayed on earth for 40 more days (Acts 1:3). Then it was time for him to return to heaven. His family and friends would not see him for a very long time. What were Jesus' last words to those he loved? "Go into all the world and preach the Good News to everyone, everywhere" (Mark 16:15).

Jesus' instructions are for you and me as well. Tell others everywhere the Good News about the Lord Jesus Christ. He died, taking the punishment for your sin. He came back to life three days later. Now anyone can believe in him and receive his gift of everlasting life.

Do you know someone who needs to hear about Jesus? Plan a time to tell him or her. Do you know others who are sharing the good news about Jesus? Perhaps you could pray or give money to help them.

Christ died for our sins, just as the Scriptures said. He was buried, and he was raised from the dead on the third day, as the Scriptures said.
1 Corinthians 15:3-4

YOU CAN PRAY:

Dear God, help me to tell others about you. Also, use me to help others share your good news. In Jesus' name. Amen.

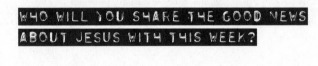

WHO WILL YOU SHARE THE GOOD NEWS ABOUT JESUS WITH THIS WEEK?

HOW DID JESUS RETURN TO HEAVEN?

February
24

One day, Jesus had taken his disciples up on a mountain. He had finished giving his last instructions to them. Now it was time for him to return to heaven. Suddenly, as the disciples watched in silent amazement, Jesus began rising into the air. As he rose higher and higher, the disciples had to strain their eyes to see him. Finally, a cloud hid him from their sight. It was amazing! Jesus' mighty power had taken him back to his home in heaven (Acts 1:9).

As the disciples continued to stare into the sky, two angels appeared and spoke to them. "Jesus has been taken away from you into heaven. And someday, just as you saw him go, he will return!" (Acts 1:11). One day Jesus will return from heaven in the clouds!

What did the disciples do next? First they worshiped the Lord Jesus. Then they returned to the city with great joy (Luke 24:52). Can you imagine how the disciples felt telling others what they had just seen? What an exciting day it had been. And how exciting to know that, one day, Jesus will return!

Christ died for our sins, just as the Scriptures said. He was buried, and he was raised from the dead on the third day, as the Scriptures said.
1 Corinthians 15:3-4

YOU CAN PRAY:
Dear God, I'm glad you are alive in heaven! Help me to tell the Good News about you to others. In Jesus' name. Amen.

WHAT WOULD YOU HAVE DONE IF YOU HAD SEEN JESUS GO UP INTO HEAVEN?

february

25

WHAT IS JESUS DOING IN HEAVEN?

About 2,000 years have passed since the Lord Jesus Christ left the earth to return to heaven. What has he been doing all this time? One thing he's been doing is preparing a beautiful place for each of his children! Jesus promised, "There are many rooms in my Father's home, and I am going to prepare a place for you" (John 14:2).

Will this home look like a fine house in Asia, Africa, or America? Will it look like a grand castle in Europe or a beautiful island dwelling? We can't begin to imagine! Nothing on earth will come close to its beauty! A perfect God who loves you very much is making this perfect place.

Not only is the Lord Jesus preparing a place for you, he is preparing you for that place. He wants you to be ready to enjoy all that he is making for you. For this reason, he is also praying for you. Jesus "is sitting at the place of highest honor next to God, pleading for us" (Romans 8:34). Isn't it wonderful to know that Jesus is thinking about you right now? He loves you, he prays for you, and he looks forward to being with you forever!

Christ died for our sins, just as the Scriptures said. He was buried, and he was raised from the dead on the third day, as the Scriptures said.
1 Corinthians 15:3-4

YOU CAN PRAY:

Dear God, thank you for preparing a special place just for me. Thank you that Jesus prays for me so I will be ready for that special place. In Jesus' name. Amen.

WHAT DO YOU THINK YOUR PLACE IN HEAVEN MIGHT LOOK LIKE?

IS JESUS REALLY PRAYING FOR ME?

february
26

Yes, Jesus is praying for you. One thing he is praying is that you will stand strong against the temptation to sin. Jesus remembers what it was like when Satan tempted him on earth. He knows that you still have that desire to sin. He prays that you will say "no" to temptation.

The Bible says that Satan stands before God's throne, day and night, accusing us of our sins (Revelation 12:10). Every time we give in to sin, Satan points out our guilt to God. That's when the Lord Jesus speaks to God the Father for us. The Bible says, "There is someone to plead for you before the Father. He is Jesus Christ, the one who pleases God completely" (1 John 2:1). Jesus, the perfect One, is like your lawyer. He tells the judge, God the Father, that you are not guilty because he already paid for your sin by dying on the cross. No accusation from Satan can stand up to Jesus' defense!

When God declares you "not guilty" and forgives you, it's not because you deserve it. God is being merciful to you because of his Son, Jesus, who has prayed for you. Aren't you glad that the Lord Jesus prays for you every day?

WHY DO YOU NEED JESUS TO PRAY FOR YOU?

Christ died for our sins, just as the Scriptures said. He was buried, and he was raised from the dead on the third day, as the Scriptures said.
1 Corinthians 15:3-4

YOU CAN PRAY:
Dear God, thank you for Jesus, who prays for me. Thank you for your forgiveness. In Jesus' name. Amen.

February
27

WHEN WILL JESUS RETURN TO EARTH?

Christ died for our sins, just as the Scriptures said. He was buried, and he was raised from the dead on the third day, as the Scriptures said.
1 Corinthians 15:3-4

YOU CAN PRAY:
Dear God, thank you that Jesus is coming back again. Help me to be ready for his return. In Jesus' name. Amen.

Suddenly, when we least expect it, Jesus will come back to earth! The prophets foretold that Jesus would come the first time, and he did. The prophets have also told us to look for his coming again. The Bible says, "For the Lord himself will come down from heaven with a commanding shout, with the call of the archangel, and with the trumpet call of God" (1 Thessalonians 4:16). Jesus himself also promised his return to earth someday. "When everything is ready, I will come and get you, so that you will always be with me where I am" (John 14:3). He is coming to take his children home to heaven.

When will it happen? He didn't say. It could happen any day at any time. The Bible does tell us certain events to look for that would be clues to Jesus' return. His coming could take place in your lifetime! If you have not trusted the Lord Jesus as your Savior, this could be frightening news! You will be left to endure much suffering. But you can trust in him today! If you have already trusted the Lord Jesus Christ as your Savior, you should be excited about seeing him face-to-face!

IF YOU KNEW JESUS WAS COMING TODAY, HOW WOULD YOU SPEND YOUR TIME?

HOW CAN I BE READY FOR JESUS' RETURN?

february
28

If you have ever taken a trip, you know it is important to prepare. Right now you need to prepare for your trip to heaven. If you've never trusted Jesus Christ as your Savior, now is the time to do that. The Bible says, "Indeed, God is ready to help you right now. Today is the day of salvation" (2 Corinthians 6:2). Tell God you are sorry for your sin. Thank the Lord Jesus for taking your punishment for sin on the cross. Ask him to make you his child. Don't wait; you may not get another chance.

If you have already trusted the Lord Jesus as your Savior, now is the time to get to know God better. Now is the time to obey his Word. The Bible says, "And now, dear children, continue to live in fellowship with Christ so that when he returns, you will be full of courage and not shrink back from him in shame" (1 John 2:28). If you are living close to Jesus Christ, you will not be ashamed to see him when he appears. As you continue reading the devotionals in this book, you'll learn many more things you can do to prepare for your trip to heaven.

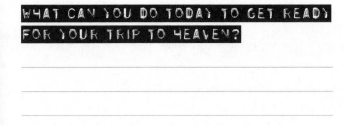

WHAT CAN YOU DO TODAY TO GET READY FOR YOUR TRIP TO HEAVEN?

Christ died for our sins, just as the Scriptures said. He was buried, and he was raised from the dead on the third day, as the Scriptures said.
1 Corinthians 15:3-4

YOU CAN PRAY:

Dear God, thank you that I can be with you in heaven someday. Help me to prepare now for the day I will see you. In Jesus' name. Amen.

Activity 2:
God the Son

WHO IS JESUS?

Color in each space that does NOT describe the Lord Jesus.

False	Savior	Angel
Alive	God	Holy
Unloving	Lord	Dead
Sinner	King	Criminal

Others can see that I love Jesus because . . .

____

THINKING IT OVER!

God the Son

Write the answers to these questions from your devotionals in the blanks.

1. How did the prophets know what was going to happen in the future?

____

2. What will happen to those who trust Jesus as Savior?

____

3. Why did Jesus come to earth as a human?

____

4. Name one miracle Jesus did while he was on earth.

____

5. What happened three days after Jesus took the punishment for our sin?

____

6. What is Jesus doing in heaven?

____

If you need help, you can look back in this month's devotionals. The number in ( ) tells you which devotional to check for each question. 1. (2) 2. (6) 3. (9) 4. (12) 5. (19) 6. (25)

MARCH

God the Holy Spirit

March

1

WHO IS THE HOLY SPIRIT?

Don't you realize that all of you together are the temple of God and that the Spirit of God lives in you?
1 Corinthians 3:16

YOU CAN PRAY:
Dear God, thank you for giving me your Holy Spirit as a guarantee so I can know I have eternal life. In Jesus' name. Amen.

Have you ever received something that came with a guarantee like a CD player or a Walkman? A guarantee is a promise that the item will work. When you receive Jesus as your Savior, God gives you a guarantee of eternal life with him in heaven someday. This guarantee is the Holy Spirit.

The Holy Spirit is a person, not a force. He has feelings just like a person. He can choose and decide things because he has a will. He has a mind and is able to teach. He is a person and he is God. Our God is a three-in-one Person. He is God the Father, God the Son, and God the Holy Spirit.

When you receive Jesus as your Savior, the Holy Spirit comes to live inside you. Since he is God, your body becomes the house where God lives. The Bible says, "Don't you realize that . . . the Spirit of God lives in you?" (1 Corinthians 3:16). Even though you cannot see him, he is very real. The Holy Spirit is your reminder that God is always with you. He is your guarantee of eternal life!

WRITE DOWN THREE THINGS YOU HAVE JUST LEARNED ABOUT THE HOLY SPIRIT.

WHAT DOES THE HOLY SPIRIT DO?

March
2

The Holy Spirit lives in people who have trusted Jesus as their Savior. But what does the Holy Spirit do for people who have not trusted Jesus? The Bible says, "[The Holy Spirit] will convince the world of its sin, and of God's righteousness, and of the coming judgment" (John 16:8). The Holy Spirit uses God's Word to show people that they are sinners. He helps them see that they need Jesus to forgive their sins.

Maybe you've never trusted Jesus as your Savior. Has the Holy Spirit spoken to you? Admit to God that you are a sinner. Tell him that you trust in Jesus, who died on the cross for your sins. He will forgive you today.

If you do know Jesus as your Savior, the Holy Spirit can help you tell others about Jesus. You can share Bible verses about Jesus with them. The Holy Spirit will use those verses to help them understand that they are sinners and need to be forgiven. Can you think of someone who does not know Jesus as his Savior? Will you let the Holy Spirit use you to show that person how to trust in Jesus? Share the truth about Jesus and then let the Holy Spirit do his work.

Don't you realize that all of you together are the temple of God and that the Spirit of God lives in you?
1 Corinthians 3:16

YOU CAN PRAY:
Dear God, thank you for the Holy Spirit. Help me to share about Jesus' forgiveness with someone who does not know you. In Jesus' name. Amen.

WHAT DOES THE HOLY SPIRIT DO FOR THOSE WHO DO NOT KNOW JESUS AS THEIR SAVIOR?

March

3

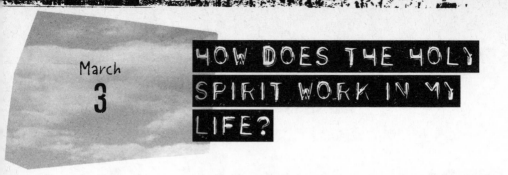

HOW DOES THE HOLY SPIRIT WORK IN MY LIFE?

Don't you realize that all of you together are the temple of God and that the Spirit of God lives in you?
1 Corinthians 3:16

YOU CAN PRAY:
Dear God, thank you for your Holy Spirit, who is my Helper. I will listen to him as I learn more about you. In Jesus' name. Amen.

Maps are used to give directions. Often maps are hard to understand. You need someone to show you how to read them. The Bible is like a map. It gives you directions for how to get to heaven. It shows you how to live for Jesus. The Holy Spirit is the person who helps you read this map.

If you have trusted Jesus as your Savior, the Holy Spirit lives inside you. The Holy Spirit helps you to understand the Bible. He also helps you to know God. He gives you strength to do right and to say "no" to sin. When you sin, the Holy Spirit lets you know you have done wrong. He helps you understand that you need to tell God what you have done wrong.

The Bible calls the Holy Spirit your Counselor, which means helper. Before Jesus left this earth to return to heaven, he told his followers, "And I will ask the Father, and he will give you another Counselor, who will never leave you" (John 14:16). Jesus called this Counselor, or Helper, the Spirit of truth who will live in God's children forever (John 14:17). Isn't it wonderful to know that God's Holy Spirit will live in you forever? He is your helper!

CAN YOU THINK OF THREE WAYS THE HOLY SPIRIT HELPS YOU? WRITE THEM HERE:

WHAT DOES IT MEAN TO BE FILLED WITH THE SPIRIT?

March
4

When you receive Jesus as your Savior, the Holy Spirit comes to live in you forever. This is called his indwelling. God also wants you to be filled with the Holy Spirit. Let him control your life. The Bible says, "Let the Holy Spirit fill and control you" (Ephesians 5:18). When the Holy Spirit fills you, he controls your thoughts, words, and actions. The Holy Spirit will indwell you forever, but you need to ask God to fill you with his Spirit each day. Then you can live to please him.

How do you know if you're filled with the Holy Spirit? When the Holy Spirit fills you, he gives you power to win over sin. He controls your thoughts, words, and actions so they are pleasing to God. Do your thoughts, words, and actions show that you are filled with the Holy Spirit? If not, you need to ask God to fill you again.

God wants to fill you with his Spirit each day. But did you know you can ask God to fill you with his Spirit for special jobs that he wants you to do? God's Spirit dwells in you always. But don't forget that he wants to fill you each day so you can serve him better.

HOW CAN YOU TELL IF YOU'RE FILLED WITH THE HOLY SPIRIT?

Don't you realize that all of you together are the temple of God and that the Spirit of God lives in you?
1 Corinthians 3:16

YOU CAN PRAY:
Dear God, please fill me with your Holy Spirit today. I want your Spirit to control every area of my life. Thank you. In Jesus' name. Amen.

March
5

CAN THE HOLY SPIRIT HELP ME NOT TO SIN?

Amanda stood looking at the computer. Mom had told her, "No computer games until after your homework is done." *Mom will be gone for another hour*, Amanda thought. She was tempted (had a strong desire) to play just one game but knew that would be sinning.

Before you trusted Jesus as your Savior, you were under the power and control of sin. But now the Holy Spirit dwells in you. The Bible says you are his living temple. The Holy Spirit wants to help you to keep that temple clean from sin. He dwells in you to set you free from sin's power and control. The Bible says, "Sin is no longer your master" (Romans 6:14).

However, that doesn't mean you'll never be tempted to sin. When you are tempted to sin, the Holy Spirit convicts you. He helps you to know that your behavior is wrong. But it's up to you to choose to obey God. Pay attention to what he is showing you. The Holy Spirit is working in you. He will give you the ability to choose to obey God and not to sin. Will you choose to listen to the Holy Spirit and do what is right?

Don't you realize that all of you together are the temple of God and that the Spirit of God lives in you?
1 Corinthians 3:16

YOU CAN PRAY:
Thank you, God, that the Holy Spirit convicts me before I sin. Help me to listen to him and not to sin. In Jesus' name. Amen.

WHAT DOES THE HOLY SPIRIT DO WHEN YOU ARE TEMPTED TO SIN?

WHAT HAPPENS IF I SIN?

March
6

Have you ever done something wrong to a friend and wanted to hide it from him? Were you sad and afraid he would find out? Did you stay away from him? Because you did something wrong to your friend, you have broken your fellowship (friendship) with him. However, when you tell your friend what you did, it makes everything right. You want to spend time with him again.

If you sin against God, it is the same. You do not want to talk to him in prayer. You do not want to read your Bible. Sin spoils your fellowship (friendship) with God. He will never leave you, but sin makes him sad. Sin will also make you sad. It will take away your peace and joy. Sin also blocks your prayers so that God will not answer. The Bible says, "If I had not confessed the sin in my heart, my Lord would not have listened" (Psalm 66:18).

If you sin, you are no longer allowing the Holy Spirit to control your life. It is then that he begins to convict you (points out your sin). He causes you to want to make things right with God. You need to confess your sins to God (agree with him that you've sinned) to make things right again.

HOW DOES SIN AFFECT YOUR FRIENDSHIP WITH GOD?

Don't you realize that all of you together are the temple of God and that the Spirit of God lives in you?
1 Corinthians 3:16

YOU CAN PRAY:

Dear God, thank you for the Holy Spirit, who convicts me when I sin. Help me to listen to him and do what is right. In Jesus' name. Amen.

March

7

HOW DO I CONFESS MY SINS TO GOD?

Tamika sat in the principal's office. She was in big trouble. Her teacher caught her writing on the bathroom wall. The principal came into his office and closed the door. "Tamika," he said, "I am disappointed in you."

"I'm sorry," Tamika said.

"Are you really?" he asked. "Are you sorry because you did something wrong, or are you sorry because you got caught?"

When you sin, the Holy Spirit living inside you convicts you. He lets you know that things are no longer right between you and God. You should feel sorry because you sinned against God, not because you were caught. Confessing your sins to God makes things right again.

To confess means to name your sins—to agree with God that you did wrong. God already knows, but he wants you to tell him. The Bible says, "If we confess our sins to him, he is faithful and just to forgive us" (1 John 1:9). Tell God, "I admit I was wrong when I [name the sin]." God promises to forgive you. Thank him for his forgiveness and ask him to help you not to sin that way again. You may also need to say "I'm sorry" to someone else who has been hurt by your sin.

Don't you realize that all of you together are the temple of God and that the Spirit of God lives in you?
1 Corinthians 3:16

YOU CAN PRAY:
Dear God, thank you for your forgiveness. Help me to do right and not to give in to sin. In Jesus' name. Amen.

WHAT DOES GOD PROMISE TO DO WHEN YOU CONFESS YOUR SINS TO HIM?

WHAT HAPPENS WHEN I CONFESS MY SINS?

March
8

When you come in from playing outside and are dirty, what do you do? You take a bath. The "real you" inside gets dirty when you sin. It needs to be cleaned. Confessing your sins to God is like taking a spiritual bath for the "real you."

Do you remember what you have been learning about the Holy Spirit? When you receive Jesus as your Savior, the Holy Spirit comes to live inside you. Your body is the temple where he lives. He is your helper. And when you give in to sin, he convicts you.

God promises to forgive you if you confess your sins to him. "If we confess our sins to him, he is faithful and just to forgive us and to cleanse us from every wrong" (1 John 1:9). Confessing your sins to God is like taking a spiritual bath.

When you confess your sins, your relationship with God is made right again. Your peace and joy return. God hears and answers your prayers. You are once again filled by him. He is in control.

Taking a bath and being clean feels great, but taking a spiritual bath and being forgiven feels even better!

WRITE DOWN THREE THINGS THE HOLY SPIRIT DOES AFTER YOU CONFESS YOUR SINS TO GOD.

Don't you realize that all of you together are the temple of God and that the Spirit of God lives in you?
1 Corinthians 3:16

YOU CAN PRAY:

Dear God, help me to listen to the Holy Spirit and not to give in to sin when I am first tempted. Thank you for your promise to forgive me when I confess my sin. In Jesus' name. Amen.

March
9

HOW DOES THE HOLY SPIRIT TEACH ME?

Do you have a favorite teacher? Why do you like this teacher the best? Is it because he or she helps you learn new things? Is it because he or she helps you understand what is being taught? Good teachers make you think. They make learning fun and interesting.

The Holy Spirit is your teacher also. The Bible says, "The Holy Spirit . . . will teach you everything and will remind you of everything I myself have told you" (John 14:26). The Bible is the textbook the Holy Spirit uses to teach you. When you read God's Word, the Holy Spirit helps you understand what is being said. He helps you to learn about God. He helps you to grow in your Christian life and to please God.

Before you read God's Word, it is important to stop and pray. Ask the Holy Spirit to help you understand what you are about to read. When you are finished reading, ask God to help you obey what you have just read. Don't be upset if you do not understand everything that is written in the Bible. Even adults do not understand everything. But the Holy Spirit will teach you just what he wants you to know right now.

When the Spirit of truth comes, he will guide you into all truth.
John 16:13

YOU CAN PRAY:
Dear God, thank you for the Holy Spirit who is my teacher. Help me to obey what he teaches me. In Jesus' name. Amen.

WRITE DOWN TWO THINGS THE HOLY SPIRIT HELPS YOU TO LEARN OR UNDERSTAND.

HOW DOES THE HOLY SPIRIT GUIDE ME?

March
10

The Holy Spirit is not just a teacher; he is also your guide. The Holy Spirit will direct you in little things. He will help you to speak to a friend about Jesus. He will show you how to help someone who is hurting. He will also guide you in big things like what you should do when you grow up and whom you should marry (if he wants you to get married).

If you know Jesus as your Savior, you need to ask God for guidance. Then listen quietly for his plan. One way the Holy Spirit may guide you is through God's Word. Reading the Bible will help you to know God's thoughts. A second way he guides you is through things that happen. Look for ways God is working things out. God will cause things to happen that will show you his plan step by step. A third way the Holy Spirit guides you is through other Christians. He may use your parents or others who love God to give you good advice.

God promises, "I will guide you along the best pathway for your life" (Psalm 32:8). You don't know what will happen in the future, but God does. He knows what's best for you. You can trust the Holy Spirit to guide you.

When the Spirit of truth comes, he will guide you into all truth.
John 16:13

YOU CAN PRAY:
Dear God, help me to trust in you and allow the Holy Spirit to guide me each day. In Jesus' name. Amen.

HAVE YOU BEEN ALLOWING THE HOLY SPIRIT TO GUIDE YOU? IF YOU HAVE, WRITE DOWN ONE WAY HE HAS GUIDED YOU THIS PAST WEEK.

March

11

WHAT DOES IT MEAN TO "QUENCH" THE SPIRIT?

When the Spirit of truth comes, he will guide you into all truth.
John 16:13

YOU CAN PRAY:

Dear God, help me not to quench the Holy Spirit but to let him do his work in my life. In Jesus' name. Amen.

The Bible uses symbols to help you understand how the Holy Spirit works in your life. One symbol of the Holy Spirit is fire. Fire makes things pure. The Holy Spirit cleans away things in your life God does not like. He convicts you when you do wrong. He helps you and guides you.

Have you ever watched a campfire or leaves burning? The fire grows stronger when it is fanned with air. It is quenched, or put out, with water. The Holy Spirit's fire grows stronger in your life when you pray, witness, read the Bible, and obey God. When you disobey, you quench the Spirit. You also quench him when you refuse to allow him to guide you and lead you in serving God. Without the Spirit's leading, you have no joy or inner peace.

The Bible says, "Do not stifle the Holy Spirit" (1 Thessalonians 5:19). This does not mean the Holy Spirit will leave you. He is your guarantee of eternal life! It means you are not controlled and filled by him. Confess your sins. Start obeying God and allow the Holy Spirit to do his work in your life.

NAME TWO WAYS YOU MIGHT QUENCH THE HOLY SPIRIT.

WHAT DOES IT MEAN TO "GRIEVE" THE SPIRIT?

March
12

Have you ever heard the word grieve? It means to have deep feelings of pain or sadness. When someone you love—or maybe your pet—dies, or when you have to say good-bye to a good friend who moves away, you grieve over your loss. Did you know that your actions or attitudes might cause others to grieve over you? You grieve your parents when you disobey.

In your Christian life, there may be times you grieve the Holy Spirit—cause him pain and sadness. You grieve the Holy Spirit when you are mean or when you talk in a harsh or angry way. Fighting and arguing also grieve the Holy Spirit. You cause him sadness when you do not confess your sins to God. You grieve him when you doubt God's Word about your being saved from sin.

God says, "Do not bring sorrow to God's Holy Spirit by the way you live. Remember, he is the one who has identified you as his own, guaranteeing that you will be saved on the day of redemption" (Ephesians 4:30). You are still God's child. You still have God's promise of eternal life, but it hurts him when you grieve the Holy Spirit. If someone grieves over you, it means he loves you. God loves you and is sad when you grieve his Spirit. Confessing your sins to God allows the Holy Spirit to have control of your life once again.

WHAT ARE THREE WAYS YOU MIGHT GRIEVE THE HOLY SPIRIT?

When the Spirit of truth comes, he will guide you into all truth.
John 16:13

YOU CAN PRAY:

Dear God, thank you for forgiving me. Help me not to grieve the Holy Spirit. In Jesus' name. Amen.

March

13

HOW DOES THE HOLY SPIRIT CHANGE ME?

When you were born, you could not feed yourself. Someone had to take care of you. As time passed, you began to crawl and then walk. Soon you began to talk. You were growing and changing.

When you trust in Jesus as your Savior, you are born into God's family. You are changed into a new person on the inside. The Bible says, "Those who become Christians become new persons. They are not the same anymore, for the old life is gone. A new life has begun!" (2 Corinthians 5:17). You are a newborn baby in Christ with a new desire to please God. Now you need to grow up in your new life. Jesus is your example of how God wants his children to grow and live. It pleases God when you act like his Son.

The Holy Spirit living in you helps you grow and change so you can live to please God. He teaches you and guides you through the Bible. He helps you pray and gives you power to obey God. When you do sin, he convicts you so you will confess your sins to God. Little by little, the Holy Spirit is working in your life to change you.

When the Spirit of truth comes, he will guide you into all truth.
John 16:13

YOU CAN PRAY:

Dear God, I want the Holy Spirit to work in my life to change me and help me grow. In Jesus' name. Amen.

WRITE THREE WAYS THE HOLY SPIRIT IS CHANGING YOU.

WHAT IS THE FRUIT OF THE SPIRIT?

March
14

Have you ever seen bananas growing on an apple tree? It's impossible! Apple trees produce (grow) apples, and banana trees produce bananas. When you become God's child, he wants you to produce fruit. This is not fruit like apples or bananas. This is spiritual fruit. This fruit shows in your actions and words. It is what you *are* on the inside—your character. Obeying and serving God is what you *do,* but spiritual fruit is produced by what you *are.*

The Bible lists the fruit you should produce. "But when the Holy Spirit controls our lives, he will produce this kind of fruit in us: love, joy, peace, patience, kindness, goodness, faithfulness, gentleness, and self-control" (Galatians 5:22-23).

This fruit is produced in your life when you listen to the Holy Spirit and allow him to be in control. What is the result of controlling your own life? Bad fruit like jealousy, anger, and selfishness are produced. When you obey the Spirit and allow him to control you, good fruit is produced. The more you obey the Holy Spirit, the more the fruit of the Spirit grows and develops. What kind of fruit is seen in your life? Is it good fruit or bad fruit?

CAN YOU LIST THE FRUIT OF THE SPIRIT THAT GOD WANTS TO PRODUCE IN YOU?

But when the Holy Spirit controls our lives, he will produce this kind of fruit in us: love, joy, peace, patience, kindness, goodness, faithfulness, gentleness, and self-control. Galatians 5:22-23

YOU CAN PRAY:

Dear God, help me to give my life to the Spirit and allow him to produce good fruit in my life. In Jesus' name. Amen.

March

15

CAN THE HOLY SPIRIT HELP ME LOVE OTHERS?

Do you know what love means? You may think that love is just a feeling, but that is not true love. If you love someone only because that person loves you, you are not showing true love. True love comes from God.

The Bible says that "God is love" (1 John 4:8). God loves you even though you are a sinner. God showed his love by sending his Son to die on the cross for your sin. When you trust in Jesus as your Savior, God fills you with his love. The Bible says, "For we know how dearly God loves us, because he has given us the Holy Spirit to fill our hearts with his love" (Romans 5:5). When the Holy Spirit is in control, he will produce love for others in your life.

True love is loving others like Jesus does. This means to think of others more highly than yourself. True love is to want God's best for others. When the fruit of love is produced in your life, you will not expect to receive anything in return for the love you give. Is the Holy Spirit producing the fruit of love in your life?

But when the Holy Spirit controls our lives, he will produce this kind of fruit in us: love, joy, peace, patience, kindness, goodness, faithfulness, gentleness, and self-control. Galatians 5:22-23

YOU CAN PRAY:

Dear God, thank you for loving me with your true love. Please produce the fruit of love in my life. In Jesus' name. Amen.

LIST TWO WAYS YOU CAN SHOW THE SPIRITUAL FRUIT OF LOVE TO OTHERS.

HOW DOES THE HOLY SPIRIT GIVE ME JOY INSIDE?

March
16

It was midnight. All the prisoners were locked in their jail cells. Suddenly there was singing! Two prisoners, Paul and Silas, were singing praises to God. They had been beaten and thrown into jail because they were telling others about Jesus. How could Paul and Silas praise God at a time like this? They had joy inside (Acts 16:16-40).

Joy is a fruit the Holy Spirit produces in your life when you allow him to be in control. You can have joy even when things are not going well. This joy is not a happiness that comes and goes. It is a deep inner gladness and delight that you know God is faithful and keeps his promises.

Even when problems come, the Holy Spirit can produce joy in your life. Joy comes when you obey God and trust in his promises. God gives you joy and strength to handle problems. The Bible says, "Don't be dejected and sad, for the joy of the Lord is your strength!" (Nehemiah 8:10). When you remember that God is in control, you will have a song of joy in your heart. You will be able to praise God like Paul and Silas.

But when the Holy Spirit controls our lives, he will produce this kind of fruit in us: love, joy, peace, patience, kindness, goodness, faithfulness, gentleness, and self-control.
Galatians 5:22-23

YOU CAN PRAY:
Dear God, thank you for the strength and joy you give me to handle my problems. In Jesus' name. Amen.

HOW CAN YOU HAVE JOY IN YOUR LIFE EVEN WHEN THINGS ARE NOT GOING WELL?

March

17

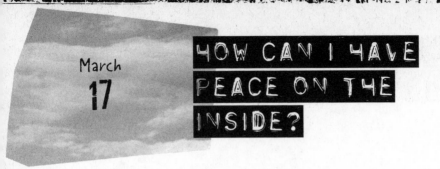

HOW CAN I HAVE PEACE ON THE INSIDE?

But when the Holy Spirit controls our lives, he will produce this kind of fruit in us: love, joy, peace, patience, kindness, goodness, faithfulness, gentleness, and self-control. Galatians 5:22-23

YOU CAN PRAY:

Dear God, help me to keep my thoughts on you so the fruit of peace is produced in my life. In Jesus' name. Amen.

Megan looked out the window. It was raining. "When will Mom get home?" she asked softly. Thoughts raced through her mind. *What if lightning strikes the house? What if Mom dies in a car accident?* Then Megan remembered her grandmother's words. "Trust in the Lord and give him your fears. Keep your thoughts on him and he will give you peace."

Have you ever been afraid or worried? Jesus said, "I am leaving you with a gift—peace of mind and heart" (John 14:27). When you trust in Jesus as your Savior, you have peace with God. Sin no longer makes you God's enemy. You have forgiveness because Christ paid for your sin when he died and came back to life. Jesus has become your peace.

Not only do you have peace with God, but you also have the peace of God. Peace is a fruit of the Spirit. It is an inner quietness in your heart and mind that comes as you trust God and keep your thoughts on him (Isaiah 26:3). When the Holy Spirit is in control, he produces peace in your life. When worries or fears come, you can pray to God and depend on him to give you peace.

WHAT SHOULD YOU DO WHEN WORRIES OR FEARS COME INTO YOUR LIFE?

HOW DOES THE HOLY SPIRIT GIVE ME PATIENCE?

March
18

Hurry up, I can't wait any longer. *Why is she taking so long? When will we get there?* Do you ever talk like this? Talking this way shows you do not have patience. Patience is the ability to go through hard or boring times calmly. It is the ability to wait without getting restless or upset. If you have trusted in Jesus as your Savior, the Holy Spirit can produce the fruit of patience in your life.

Patience is produced as you wait for the Lord to work and allow the Holy Spirit to be in control. As you go through hard things in life, the Holy Spirit will give you strength to have patience. He will help you accept trouble or pain, even for a long time. The Bible says, "Be glad for all God is planning for you. Be patient in trouble, and always be prayerful" (Romans 12:12). The Holy Spirit will also help you show patience to others who do wrong to you or are unkind.

The next time you find yourself thinking, I can't wait any longer, stop and pray. Thank God for the Holy Spirit who is living in you. Ask him for the strength to show patience.

WRITE DOWN A TIME WHEN YOU HAVE TROUBLE BEING PATIENT.

But when the Holy Spirit controls our lives, he will produce this kind of fruit in us: love, joy, peace, patience, kindness, goodness, faithfulness, gentleness, and self-control. Galatians 5:22-23

YOU CAN PRAY:

Dear God, I have trouble being patient when [name the situation]. Please produce the fruit of patience in me. In Jesus' name. Amen.

March
19

CAN THE HOLY SPIRIT HELP ME TO BE KIND?

But when the Holy Spirit controls our lives, he will produce this kind of fruit in us: love, joy, peace, patience, kindness, goodness, faithfulness, gentleness, and self-control. Galatians 5:22-23

YOU CAN PRAY:
Dear God, thank you for giving me strength to show kindness to someone today. In Jesus' name. Amen.

Jake sat all alone in the lunchroom. Ever since his father had gone to jail, the other boys made fun of him. They called him names. They said he would end up in jail too. Their words hurt Jake. He wanted to say unkind words in return but knew that it would not be right.

It surprised Jake as Jerome sat down beside him. Jerome had made fun of him earlier that day. "Jake, I've been watching you," Jerome said. "You never get mad when we laugh at you. In fact, you are nice to us. I saw you help Desmond pick up the books he dropped the other day. What's with you?"

"Well," Jake said, "I know it pleases God when I am nice to others even when they are unkind to me. I'm a Christian, and God's Spirit living in me helps me to be kind."

God was producing the fruit of kindness in Jake's life. Instead of getting mad, he showed kindness. The Bible says, "Be kind to each other, tenderhearted, forgiving one another, just as God through Christ has forgiven you" (Ephesians 4:32). Are you letting God produce the fruit of kindness in your life?

WRITE SOMETHING YOU CAN DO TO SHOW KINDNESS TO SOMEONE ELSE.

WHAT DOES IT MEAN TO BE GOOD?

March
20

"Wait up!" Jerome called as he ran towards Jake. "I didn't get my homework done. Can I copy yours?"

"Sorry," Jake answered. "That would be cheating."

Later as Jake was going out to recess, he saw Jerome sitting at his desk. Jake ran to talk with his teacher. Minutes later he walked up to Jerome's desk. "Mrs. Snow said I could help you learn your spelling words."

Yesterday Jake showed kindness to Jerome. Today he is showing the fruit of goodness. Goodness is doing what is right. Jake knew it was wrong to help Jerome cheat. He chose to do right. He was being good.

God is the only one who is perfectly good. God wants his children to be like him. You should do good. The Bible says, "A good person produces good deeds from a good heart" (Luke 6:45). When the Holy Spirit is in control, the fruit of goodness will show in your life.

Goodness is more than doing what is right. Goodness is shown in your words and actions. Jake decided to give up his recess and help Jerome. He spoke kind words. Goodness is love in action.

WRITE TWO WAYS YOU COULD SHOW THE FRUIT OF GOODNESS IN YOUR LIFE.

But when the Holy Spirit controls our lives, he will produce this kind of fruit in us: love, joy, peace, patience, kindness, goodness, faithfulness, gentleness, and self-control. Galatians 5:22-23

YOU CAN PRAY:

Dear God, thank you for being good to me. Help me to be good in all I think, say, and do. In Jesus' name. Amen.

March

21

HOW CAN THE HOLY SPIRIT HELP ME TO BE FAITHFUL?

But when the Holy Spirit controls our lives, he will produce this kind of fruit in us: love, joy, peace, patience, kindness, goodness, faithfulness, gentleness, and self-control.
Galatians 5:22-23

YOU CAN PRAY:
Dear God, thank you for your faithfulness to me. Help me be faithful to you and others in my life. In Jesus' name. Amen.

Do you keep your promises? A faithful person is someone you can depend on and who keeps his promises. God always keeps his promises. He is faithful. When you trust the Lord Jesus Christ as your Savior, his Holy Spirit wants to produce the fruit of faithfulness in your life. Faithfulness means to be true to God in your thoughts, words, and actions. The Bible says, "God, who calls you, is faithful; he will do this" (1 Thessalonians 5:24).

As God develops the fruit of faithfulness in your life, others will see it in what you do and say. They will notice that you keep your promises. They will know that you do things on time and to the best of your ability. They will notice that you put God first in everything you do. Most importantly, God will notice your faithfulness and he will be pleased. When God sees that you are faithful with a few things, he will put you in charge of many things (Matthew 25:21).

When you keep your promises, you are allowing the fruit of faithfulness to be seen in your life. Will you be someone others depend on and trust?

LIST THREE WAYS THE HOLY SPIRIT CAN HELP YOU BE FAITHFUL.

AM I A GENTLE PERSON?

March
22

Chris was a gentle person. He was kind and respectful of others. He did nice things for people whenever he could. He didn't allow anger to control his words and actions. Do you think Chris had many friends? Yes! People enjoy being around a gentle person.

Gentleness is treating others with love, kindness, and respect because you appreciate them and understand their needs. When you allow the Holy Spirit to be in control, he produces the fruit of gentleness in your life. You may think that gentleness is being weak, but it's not. It shows great inner strength.

Jesus showed gentleness many times when he lived on earth. He accepted and helped many people whom others rejected. He welcomed children, showed kindness to the poor, and healed the sick. Jesus' life is an example of how you should show gentleness to others.

When you say, "Excuse me," "Please," and "Thank you," you show gentleness. When you quietly do kind things for others, you show gentleness. When you respond to people with gentle words instead of being rude or shouting angrily, you show gentleness. God tells us in the Bible, "Let everyone see that you are considerate in all you do" (Philippians 4:5). Will you respond to others with gentleness?

WHAT ARE SOME WAYS YOU CAN SHOW GENTLENESS TO SOMEONE TODAY?

But when the Holy Spirit controls our lives, he will produce this kind of fruit in us: love, joy, peace, patience, kindness, goodness, faithfulness, gentleness, and self-control. Galatians 5:22-23

YOU CAN PRAY:

Dear God, thank you for Jesus Christ who shows me how to be gentle. Please help me to be gentle with others. In Jesus' name. Amen.

March
23

HOW CAN THE HOLY SPIRIT HELP ME TO CONTROL MYSELF?

But when the Holy Spirit controls our lives, he will produce this kind of fruit in us: love, joy, peace, patience, kindness, goodness, faithfulness, gentleness, and self-control. Galatians 5:22-23

YOU CAN PRAY:

Dear God, thank you for the Holy Spirit's power to give me self-control. Please produce this fruit in my life each day. In Jesus' name. Amen.

Have you ever watched a star athlete receive a medal or trophy? What did the athlete do to win? He trained hard. He disciplined himself. He spent many hours getting his body under control.

The Bible compares the Christian life to running a race (1 Corinthians 9:24-27). If you are God's child, your spiritual life needs a workout. Exercising self-control is like training to be a spiritual star athlete.

Self-control means staying in charge of your thoughts, feelings, and actions instead of letting them control you. It means being disciplined. The Bible says, "Stay alert and be sober" (1 Thessalonians 5:6).

The Holy Spirit living in you can produce the fruit of self-control in your life. Through the Holy Spirit's power, you can have self-control in what you eat. He can help you have self-control in what you say or do. Your thoughts and the things you look at can be under his control. When he is in control, instead of getting angry and losing your temper, you respond with gentleness. Will you be a spiritual star athlete by allowing the Holy Spirit to produce the fruit of self-control in your life?

WHEN ARE SOME TIMES THAT YOU NEED THE HOLY SPIRIT TO GIVE YOU SELF-CONTROL?

WHAT ARE SPIRITUAL GIFTS?

March
24

If you have trusted the Lord Jesus as your Savior, you are part of the body (family) of Christ. The Bible says, "Now all of you together are Christ's body, and each one of you is a separate and necessary part of it" (1 Corinthians 12:27). Each member of God's family is special. He has given each one at least one special gift. It is not a natural talent, like the ability to play an instrument or be a star athlete. It is a spiritual gift. This gift is given to you by God to help you serve him and others in the body of Christ.

We all have times when we need help. Sometimes we feel sad or discouraged or have physical problems. As members of the body of Christ, we all need to work together and look after each other. We can use our spiritual gifts in many ways to meet each others' needs.

Some of the spiritual gifts God gives are helping, giving, showing mercy, teaching, and leading. In the next few devotionals, you will learn more about these spiritual gifts. You'll also learn how to discover what your gifts are and how to use them for God.

Now all of you together are Christ's body, and each one of you is a separate and necessary part of it.
1 Corinthians 12:27

YOU CAN PRAY:
Dear God, thank you for giving your children spiritual gifts. Help me to learn what my gift is and to use it to help others. In Jesus' name. Amen.

WHY DOES THE HOLY SPIRIT GIVE EACH CHRISTIAN A SPIRITUAL GIFT?

March

25

DO I HAVE A SPIRITUAL GIFT?

When you choose a gift for someone, you think about what that person is like. The better you know the person, the better you know the right gift to give. God knows you best of all. He made you! His plan for you is to serve him and build up the body of Christ. To help you fulfill God's plan, the Holy Spirit gave you at least one spiritual gift. How do you know what your spiritual gift is?

Once you know what the spiritual gifts are, you need to pray and ask God to show you what gift (or gifts) he has given to you. Then, as you are serving God, notice what you are good at. What do you enjoy doing the most? These things are evidence that God has most likely given you spiritual gifts in these areas. Also, others may point out to you areas where God is using you in a special way.

Pay special attention to the next few devotionals. See if you can identify your spiritual gifts among those mentioned. Ask God to help you discover your spiritual gift and how you can best use it to serve him.

Now all of you together are Christ's body, and each one of you is a separate and necessary part of it.
1 Corinthians 12:27

YOU CAN PRAY:

Dear God, thank you for giving me a spiritual gift. Help me to learn what it is and to be willing to use it to serve you and others. In Jesus' name. Amen.

HOW CAN YOU KNOW WHAT YOUR SPIRITUAL GIFT IS?

WHAT IS THE GIFT OF SERVING?

March
26

Trisha likes to help. Without being asked, she runs to help her mother bring in the groceries from the car. At school, she helps the teacher put away books. At church, she picks up the papers left on the benches and throws them away. Trisha has trusted in the Lord Jesus Christ as her Savior. The Holy Spirit has given her the spiritual gift of serving.

Serving is one of the spiritual gifts the Holy Spirit gives God's children. Spiritual gifts are used to help others who are in the body of Christ. Serving is the ability to see jobs that need to be done and to do them. People with the gift of serving help in a way that frees others to use their own gift for the Lord.

Do you like to help others? When you see a need, do you often help without being asked? If you answered yes, you may have the gift of serving. The Bible says, "Work with enthusiasm, as though you were working for the Lord rather than for people" (Ephesians 6:7). If you have the gift of serving, will you use it to help others in God's family, the body of Christ?

HOW CAN YOU TELL IF SOMEONE HAS THE GIFT OF SERVING?

Now all of you together are Christ's body, and each one of you is a separate and necessary part of it.
1 Corinthians 12:27

YOU CAN PRAY:

Dear Lord, please show me my spiritual gift. If I have the gift of serving, help me use it to help others in the body of Christ. In Jesus' name. Amen.

March
27

WHAT IS THE GIFT OF GIVING?

Now all of you together are Christ's body, and each one of you is a separate and necessary part of it.
1 Corinthians 12:27

YOU CAN PRAY:

Dear God, please show me my spiritual gift. If I have the gift of giving, help me to give joyfully to meet the needs of others. In Jesus' name. Amen.

Austin knocked on the door of Mr. Young's house. Mr. Young opened the door and smiled at him. "What can I do for you today, Austin?" Mr. Young asked.

"I was wondering if you have any jobs I could do to earn some extra money," Austin replied. "There's a new kid at school named Todd. He only has one pair of shoes, and they are full of holes. I want to earn some money to buy him a new pair."

"That's so nice of you!" Mr. Young replied. "I think I can find something for you to do."

Austin saw that Todd had a need and wanted to give to meet this need. Austin has the spiritual gift of giving. You do not need lots of money to have the gift of giving. You can use your time and talents to give to others. Austin was willing to give his time and talents to earn money for Todd's new shoes.

The Bible says, "God has given each of us the ability to do certain things well. . . . If you have money, share it generously" (Romans 12:6, 8). If you have the gift of giving, will you give joyfully?

WRITE TWO THINGS, BESIDES MONEY, THAT YOU COULD GIVE.

WHAT IS THE GIFT OF MERCY?

March
28

Kim could tell that something was wrong with Ann. She walked over to where Ann was sitting and sat beside her. "Is there something wrong?" Kim asked.

"My grandma is very sick," Ann said.

"God can help," Kim encouraged her. "Let's talk to him right now." The two girls bowed their heads and Kim prayed.

If you are quick to sense the hurts of others, you may have the spiritual gift of mercy (showing kindness). This gift of the Spirit causes you to comfort a friend who gets a bad grade or loses a pet. If you have the gift of mercy, you quickly offer help and pray for others.

People with the gift of mercy comfort others in a way that gives them strength to go on. The Holy Spirit living in you gives you wisdom to use this gift. The Bible says, "But the wisdom that comes from heaven is . . . full of mercy" (James 3:17). Since people with this gift want to help, the Spirit can also give wisdom not to do things for others they should do for themselves. If you feel you have the gift of mercy, ask God to use you to help others who are hurting.

Now all of you together are Christ's body, and each one of you is a separate and necessary part of it.
1 Corinthians 12:27

YOU CAN PRAY:
Dear God, please show me my spiritual gift. If I have the gift of mercy, give me wisdom to use it to comfort others. In Jesus' name. Amen.

LIST TWO WAYS THAT SHOW THAT SOMEONE HAS THE GIFT OF MERCY.

March

29

WHAT IS THE GIFT OF TEACHING?

Now all of you together are Christ's body, and each one of you is a separate and necessary part of it.
1 Corinthians 12:27

YOU CAN PRAY:
Dear God, please show me my spiritual gift. If I have the gift of teaching, help me to use it so others can learn more about you. In Jesus' name. Amen.

After his teacher had given an assignment, Terrance asked to use the computer. He could hardly wait to search for the answers himself. Whenever Terrance learned something new, he was eager to share it with his friends. Terrance has the spiritual gift of teaching.

Teaching is another spiritual gift given by the Holy Spirit. If you find yourself asking questions like "Why?" or "Is this correct?" you may have the gift of teaching. People with this gift like to search for answers. When they find the answer, they enjoy sharing what they learned with others.

If you have the gift of teaching, you will want to know if something is true or not. You will want to learn more about God's Word and share what you learned with others. One day, you might become a teacher of God's Word! The Bible says, "God has given each of us the ability to do certain things well. . . . If you are a teacher, do a good job of teaching" (Romans 12:6, 7).

Each person who trusts in the Lord Jesus as his Savior receives at least one spiritual gift. These gifts are used to help others in the body of Christ. If your gift is teaching, will you use it to help others learn more about God?

HOW CAN YOU TELL IF SOMEONE HAS THE GIFT OF TEACHING?

WHAT IS THE GIFT OF LEADING?

March
30

"Mom!" Ryan called as he ran into the house. "My teacher made me the leader of our class project!"

Ryan's mother smiled. "That's great!" she said. "You'll make a good leader."

Do you like to be in charge of projects? Are you quick to come up with a plan to get a job done? Is it easy for you to get others involved so they can help too? If you answered "yes," you may have the spiritual gift of leading.

The Bible tells us that the Holy Spirit gives different gifts. It says, "If God has given you leadership ability, take the responsibility seriously" (Romans 12:8). To govern diligently means to lead carefully—to do your best and not quit.

The church needs people with the gift of leading to serve the Lord Jesus Christ. People with this gift are not afraid to stand alone for something they believe is right. Leaders are people who come up with a plan and get things done. A good leader does not stand back and give orders but gets involved and helps with the job. If you have the gift of leading, ask God to help you use it to serve the body of Christ.

Now all of you together are Christ's body, and each one of you is a separate and necessary part of it.
1 Corinthians 12:27

YOU CAN PRAY:
Dear God, please show me my spiritual gift. If I have the gift of leading, help me to use it to serve the body of Christ. In Jesus' name. Amen.

LIST THREE WAYS THAT SHOW YOU THAT SOMEONE HAS THE GIFT OF LEADING.

March

31

HOW CAN I USE MY SPIRITUAL GIFT?

As you have been reading about some of the spiritual gifts, have you discovered your gifts? The Bible says that spiritual gifts are given "to equip God's people to do his work and build up the church, the body of Christ" (Ephesians 4:12). Let's review the gifts you've been reading about:

Serving—Seeing jobs that need to be done and doing them

Giving—Finding joy in giving to others

Mercy—Noticing when others are hurting, and comforting them

Teaching—Enjoying the study of God's Word and helping others understand it

Leading—Organizing others and helping them get a job done

Are you like Trisha, who enjoys serving others? Maybe you're like Austin, who gave to help a friend in need. Perhaps you're like Kim, who was quick to comfort a friend who was hurting. Are you like Terrance? He has the gift of teaching and enjoyed sharing what he learned with others. Maybe you're like Ryan, who liked being in charge of a project and getting it done.

Will you use your spiritual gift to build up others in the body of Christ? God will bless you and give you joy as you use your gift for him.

LIST THE SPIRITUAL GIFTS YOU FEEL YOU HAVE.

Now all of you together are Christ's body, and each one of you is a separate and necessary part of it.
1 Corinthians 12:27

YOU CAN PRAY:

Dear God, thank you for giving me the spiritual gift of [list the gifts you feel you have]. Help me to use them to serve you and others. In Jesus' name. Amen.

THE MEMORY ZONE

Here are some great Bible verses about what you've learned so far. Put a check mark in the box as you memorize each one!

- ❑ **1 John 1:9** "But if we confess our sins to him, he is faithful and just to forgive us and to cleanse us from every wrong."
- ❑ **Psalm 32:8** "I will guide you along the best pathway for your life. I will advise you and watch over you."
- ❑ **Psalm 66:18** "If I had not confessed the sin in my heart, my Lord would not have listened."
- ❑ **John 14:26** "But when the Father sends the Counselor as my representative—and by the Counselor I mean the Holy Spirit—he will teach you everything and will remind you of everything I myself have told you."
- ❑ **2 Corinthians 5:17** "What this means is that those who become Christians become new persons. They are not the same anymore, for the old life is gone. A new life has begun!"
- ❑ **Ephesians 4:30** "And do not bring sorrow to God's Holy Spirit by the way you live. Remember, he is the one who has identified you as his own, guaranteeing that you will be saved on the day of redemption."
- ❑ **Luke 6:45** "A good person produces good deeds from a good heart, and an evil person produces evil deeds from an evil heart. Whatever is in your heart determines what you say."
- ❑ **Ephesians 4:3** "Always keep yourselves united in the Holy Spirit, and bind yourselves together with peace."

Activity 3: God the Holy Spirit

THE FRUIT OF THE SPIRIT

Complete the crossword puzzle with the nine words that describe the fruit of the spirit. (See Galatians 5:22-23.)

The Holy Spirit helps me by . . .

____

THINKING IT OVER!

God the Holy Spirit

Write the answers to these questions from your devotionals in the blanks.

1. What kind of people does the Holy Spirit live in?

____

2. What is one thing the Holy Spirit helps you do?

____

3. What should you do if you sin as a believer?

____

4. What are some fruits of the Holy Spirit?

____

5. Why does God give you spiritual gifts?

____

6. What do people with the gift of mercy do?

____

If you need help, you can look back in this month's devotionals. The number in ( ) tells you which devotional to check for each question. 1. (2) 2. (5) 3. (7) 4. (14) 5. (24) 6. (28)

APRIL

Victory

April 1

ARE ANGELS REAL?

Have you ever watched a movie or TV program about angels? Do you wonder if they are real? Most of what you see in the movies or on TV about angels is not true. However, it is true that God made angels, and they are very real.

Angels are special creations of God and each one is different. We don't know exactly what angels look like. We do know they are not people—people who die don't become angels. We do know that some angels have wings and some look like us. God made these wonderful, strong, heavenly creatures to worship, praise, obey, and serve him. Angels also watch over God's children. Angels are more powerful than people but not as powerful as God. Angels can appear and disappear very quickly. They do not die. Some people pray to angels, but that is wrong. Only God can answer prayers.

One angel, named Lucifer, was called an angel of light. At some time Lucifer turned against God. Now we call him Satan—the devil. Some of the angels followed Satan. They are called "fallen angels" or demons. Satan and his demons are God's enemies. They are also the enemies of God's people. In the next few days, you'll learn more about your enemy, Satan.

WHAT ARE TWO THINGS YOU LEARNED ABOUT ANGELS?

Be careful! Watch out for attacks from the Devil, your great enemy. He prowls around like a roaring lion, looking for some victim to devour.
1 Peter 5:8

YOU CAN PRAY:
Dear God, thank you for creating angels to serve and obey you. In Jesus' name. Amen.

April
2

WHO IS SATAN?

Some people think Satan wears a red suit and has horns and a tail. That is not what he looks like. The Bible tells us that when God first made him he was one of the most beautiful angels. He was called Lucifer. He probably watched as God made the first man and woman. One terrible day he chose to turn against God and become his enemy. He became Satan.

The Bible calls Satan "the god of this evil world" (2 Corinthians 4:4). He is completely bad and evil. His plan is to trick people. He wants them to turn against God like he did. He wants to ruin God's plan for you. It may seem that Satan can do whatever he wants. But he is still under the control of God, who is all-powerful. When Jesus returns to earth, Satan will be punished. When the judgment is over, Satan will be thrown into the lake of fire, where he will stay forever.

Satan wants you to think he is just a pretend character in a funny red suit. Remember, he is real and he is your enemy. But the Bible says, "The Spirit who lives in you is greater than the spirit who lives in the world" (1 John 4:4).

WHY IS SATAN GOD'S ENEMY?

Be careful! Watch out for attacks from the Devil, your great enemy. He prowls around like a roaring lion, looking for some victim to devour.
1 Peter 5:8

YOU CAN PRAY:

Dear God, thank you that you are more powerful than Satan. Help me to be careful not to be tricked by Satan but to obey you. In Jesus' name. Amen.

April
3

HOW DID SATAN BECOME GOD'S ENEMY?

"I will do what I want, not what you want me to do." Have you ever said or thought something like that? Do you know where that sort of thought comes from?

One day Lucifer, God's special angel, had that thought. He decided he wanted to be like God. His thoughts may have been, "I will ascend to heaven and set my throne above God's stars. I will preside on the mountain of the gods far away in the north. I will climb to the highest heavens and be like the Most High" (Isaiah 14:12-14). Do you hear the words "I will"? Only God could truly speak with that authority because only God is all-powerful.

What caused Lucifer to turn against his Creator? It was pride. Pride is thinking more highly of yourself than you should. Lucifer thought he was as good as God. His sinful pride separated him from God. When Lucifer rebelled, God had to separate himself from Lucifer. Lucifer and his angel followers had to leave heaven. Now Lucifer is known by a different name—Satan or the devil. He is God's enemy, and he is your enemy.

The Bible says, "God sets himself against the proud" (1 Peter 5:5). Don't let pride take control of you and turn you away from God. Remember that God is your Creator. Worship and obey him only.

Be careful! Watch out for attacks from the Devil, your great enemy. He prowls around like a roaring lion, looking for some victim to devour.
1 Peter 5:8

YOU CAN PRAY:
Dear God, thank you for being my great Creator. Help me to guard against pride that would turn me against you. In Jesus' name. Amen.

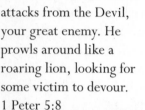

HOW CAN YOU GUARD AGAINST LETTING PRIDE TAKE CONTROL OF YOUR LIFE?

WHY IS SATAN MY ENEMY?

April 4

What does the word enemy mean? An enemy is someone who hates you and wants to hurt you. Satan hates God and wants to hurt him. Because you are God's child, Satan hates you and wants to hurt you too. He wants to destroy everything that belongs to God.

Satan shows that he is your enemy in many ways. He lies to you. The Bible says he is "the father of lies" (John 8:44). He tries to trick you into doing wrong things so you will disappoint God. He tries to get you to sin against God. What does the Bible verse at the side of this page tell you about Satan? He is your enemy; he prowls around like a lion looking for someone to devour (destroy).

Is Satan always successful in finding someone to destroy? Does Satan always win? No! You can escape the danger and guard against Satan's attacks. When you obey God, Satan loses. If you have trusted Jesus as your Savior, you have God's Holy Spirit living in you. God is greater than Satan. When you let the Holy Spirit control you, you will obey God and do what is right. You need to be alert, listening to God and watching out for Satan's attacks.

WHAT ARE TWO THINGS YOU CAN DO TO GUARD AGAINST SATAN'S ATTACKS?

Be careful! Watch out for attacks from the Devil, your great enemy. He prowls around like a roaring lion, looking for some victim to devour.
1 Peter 5:8

YOU CAN PRAY:
Dear God, thank you for loving me. Please help me to listen to you and to watch out for Satan's attacks. In Jesus' name. Amen.

April
5

WHAT ARE SOME OF SATAN'S TRICKS?

"Come on, Jeron! All you have to do is watch for the store clerk," Sam said. "You don't have to take anything. You won't be stealing. You are just watching. If you want to be my friend, you'll help me."

Sam didn't care about being Jeron's friend. He just wanted to trick Jeron into helping him do wrong.

Satan doesn't want you to love and obey God. He tries to trick you into doing wrong things. One of his tricks is to tell you the lie that you won't have any friends if you don't do drugs or drink. Another of his tricks is to get you to want new things so much that you would do something wrong to get them. Have you ever thought that God isn't real? Have you ever thought that God doesn't really love you? Those are other lies that Satan tells.

Satan would like to trick you into believing that Jesus did not die on the cross to pay for your sins. Satan doesn't want you to know how much God loves you. He wants you to believe you can take care of yourself and don't need Jesus. Watch out for Satan's tricks. Remember that he is a liar.

Be careful! Watch out for attacks from the Devil, your great enemy. He prowls around like a roaring lion, looking for some victim to devour.
1 Peter 5:8

YOU CAN PRAY:
Dear God, please help me to see when Satan is trying to trick me. Help me to believe your Word instead. In Jesus' name. Amen.

CAN YOU THINK OF ONE WAY SATAN HAS TRIED TO TRICK YOU?

IS SATAN AS POWERFUL AS GOD?

April
6

Satan is very powerful. He is more powerful than we are. Who do you think has more power, God or Satan? God made the world in six days. God made our bodies. God raised Jesus from the dead. Satan cannot do anything like that. God is much more powerful than Satan.

However, Satan has power. His attacks on God's people are powerful and hard to fight, but Satan is not as powerful as God. Satan tried with all of his might to stop Jesus from paying for your sins. He may have thought he had won when Jesus died on the cross. People took Jesus' body from the cross and buried him. But, on the third day, God raised Jesus back to life again! God is always the winner over Satan.

God is sovereign. He is the highest ruler, and he is always in control. Our God is above all and rules over all; he has all power. God has the power to hear and answer your prayers. Only he has the power to forgive your sins and make you his child. God even has control over Satan. One day God will punish Satan by putting him and his followers into the lake of fire forever.

Be careful! Watch out for attacks from the Devil, your great enemy. He prowls around like a roaring lion, looking for some victim to devour.
1 Peter 5:8

YOU CAN PRAY:

Dear God, thank you that you are more powerful than Satan. Thank you for loving me. In Jesus' name. Amen.

WHAT ARE THREE THINGS THAT SHOW YOU GOD'S POWER?

April 7

WHY DOES GOD ALLOW SATAN TO TEMPT ME?

Think of your very best friend. Do you love that person because you have to or because you want to? Love is something you choose to give.

God chose to love you, and he wants you to choose to love him. When God allows Satan to tempt you (try to get you to disobey), he is allowing you to choose whom you will love and serve. God wants you to obey him because you love him.

One of the ways you obey God is by saying "no" when Satan tempts you to do something wrong. You can't do that by yourself—you need God's help. That is another reason why God allows you to be tempted. He wants you to learn to depend on him to give you strength to say "no" to Satan. The Bible says, "The Lord is my helper" (Hebrews 13:6). You can ask God to help you be a winner over Satan's temptations.

When you ask God for help and you obey him, you get to know him better. The better you know someone, the more you love him. God wants you to choose to love him. Do you?

Be careful! Watch out for attacks from the Devil, your great enemy. He prowls around like a roaring lion, looking for some victim to devour. 1 Peter 5:8

YOU CAN PRAY:

Dear God, please help me to say "no" to Satan's temptations. Help me to show that I love you by obeying you. In Jesus' name. Amen.

WHAT ARE TWO REASONS WHY GOD ALLOWS SATAN TO TEMPT YOU?

CAN I REALLY WIN OVER SATAN?

April 8

If you were in a battle with a very strong enemy all by yourself, do you think you could win? No! However, if you were in a battle with that same enemy and had the biggest and the strongest helper, could you win? Yes!

The Bible tells us about a man who lived a long time ago. His name was Elijah. One day, God asked Elijah to do something very scary. God asked Elijah to go to the king and tell him God was going to punish all the people because they were doing very bad things. The people were serving Satan, not God. The king got very angry and tried to kill Elijah, but Elijah escaped. Elijah continued living and serving God. How did that happen? What made it possible for Elijah to win? He didn't have any super power. The Bible says he was just like you and me. He won because he had God on his side. If you know Jesus as your Savior, he is on your side too. The Bible says when you have Jesus, "the Spirit who lives in you is greater than the spirit who lives in the world" (I John 4:4). With Jesus you can win.

WHAT MADE IT POSSIBLE FOR ELIJAH TO WIN?

Be careful! Watch out for attacks from the Devil, your great enemy. He prowls around like a roaring lion, looking for some victim to devour. 1 Peter 5:8

YOU CAN PRAY:

Dear God, thank you that because of Jesus I can win over Satan. In Jesus' name. Amen.

April 9

WHAT IS GOD'S BATTLE PLAN FOR ME?

Be careful! Watch out for attacks from the Devil, your great enemy. He prowls around like a roaring lion, looking for some victim to devour.
1 Peter 5:8

YOU CAN PRAY:
Dear God, thank you that you are my helper. Please help me to remember how to win over Satan. In Jesus' name. Amen.

Soldiers need a battle plan to tell them the best way to fight. God has a battle plan for you. You are in a war every day because Satan hates you. It is a war you can win because you have the biggest and strongest helper—God. If you follow God's battle plan, you will win.

Here's the plan. It has four parts: (1) Believe Jesus died for your sins. (2) Remember you don't have to sin. God says if you will obey him and refuse to listen to the devil, Satan will run away from you (James 4:7). (3) Obey God. Sin makes God sad and it can keep God from hearing your prayers. If you do sin, you need to confess your sin to God. (4) Thank God for victory over Satan. The Bible says, "How we thank God, who gives us victory over sin and death through Jesus Christ our Lord!" (1 Corinthians 15:57).

God has given you special protection in your battle against Satan. It's called the armor of God. This armor can't be seen, but it defends you against Satan's attacks. If you use it correctly, God will help you to defeat Satan in every battle. You'll read more about this armor in the next few days.

CAN YOU NAME FOUR THINGS YOU CAN DO TO WIN OVER SATAN'S ATTACKS?

WHAT MUST I DO BEFORE I CAN HAVE VICTORY OVER SATAN?

April 10

Do you want to be a winner (have the victory)? Before you can have victory over Satan, you need to receive Jesus as your Savior.

The Bible says, "But to all who believed him and accepted him, he gave the right to become children of God" (John 1:12). You receive him (Jesus) by admitting you have sinned. You were born with a desire to sin. You sin when you lie, steal, hurt someone, or even think bad things. Everyone sins (Romans 3:23), and God must punish sin. The punishment for sin is to be away from God forever.

What does it mean to believe in his name? It means you believe that Jesus is God and never sinned. He died on the cross to be punished for your sins. He died willingly because he loves you. Jesus did not stay dead; on the third day he came alive again. He is in heaven now, praying for you. You receive him by telling God you have sinned. Tell him you believe Jesus was punished for your sins. Ask him to forgive you. Then, you become God's child. Once you are God's child, you can begin to have victory over Satan.

WHAT DOES IT MEAN TO RECEIVE JESUS AS YOUR SAVIOR?

Put on all of God's armor so that you will be able to stand firm against all strategies and tricks of the Devil.
Ephesians 6:11

YOU CAN PRAY:

Dear God, I have sinned. I believe Jesus died to take the punishment for my sins. Please forgive me and make me your child. In Jesus' name. Amen.

April
11

HOW CAN I BE PREPARED FOR THE BATTLE?

Put on all of God's armor so that you will be able to stand firm against all strategies and tricks of the Devil.
Ephesians 6:11

YOU CAN PRAY:
Dear God, help me to remember to confess my sins and to watch out for Satan's attacks so I will be ready for battle. In Jesus' name. Amen.

Every day you are in a battle against Satan. He hates God and wants you to sin against him. You need to be prepared for the battle, because you can't win over Satan in your own strength.

An important part of being prepared for the battle is to confess your sins to God. God is with you to help you say "no" to sin. However, sometimes you don't accept his help. Sometimes Satan tricks you into sinning. And sometimes you just choose to sin. Whenever you realize you have sinned, you should confess that sin to God. That means you should agree with God that what you did was sin. The Bible says, "If we confess our sins to him, he is faithful and just to forgive us" (1 John 1:9).

Another important part of being prepared for battle is to watch out for Satan's attacks. He always looks for ways to cause you to sin. Be careful to avoid places, people, or things that often tempt you to sin.

To be strong for the battle, you need to spend time with God each day. Reading his Word and praying will strengthen you against Satan's attacks.

HOW CAN YOU BE PREPARED FOR YOUR BATTLE AGAINST SATAN?

WHAT IS THE ARMOR OF GOD?

April
12

Do you know what armor is? Maybe you've seen suits of armor that soldiers used to wear into battle. Police officers today also wear armor to protect them—bulletproof vests and helmets. Firefighters wear helmets and heavy coats and boots as protective armor.

If you know Jesus as your Savior, God has given you armor to protect you in your battle against Satan. You can't see this armor—it's invisible. But it is described in the Bible in Ephesians 6:13-17. The helmet of salvation protects your mind. The "body armor of God's righteousness" protects your heart so that you will do what's right. The "belt of truth" helps you to learn God's Word and to tell the truth. The shoes of "the peace that comes from the Good News" help you to stand firm in your battle with Satan. The "shield of faith" protects you from Satan's attacks that would cause you to doubt God. The "sword of the Spirit" is the Word of God. It is your weapon against Satan.

The armor God has given you will never wear out or break. In the next few days, we will talk more about what each piece of the armor means and how it can help you.

WHY IS THE ARMOR OF GOD IMPORTANT TO YOU?

Put on all of God's armor so that you will be able to stand firm against all strategies and tricks of the Devil.
Ephesians 6:11

YOU CAN PRAY:

Dear God, thank you for giving me your armor so I can win when Satan attacks me. In Jesus' name. Amen.

April
13

WHY DO I NEED GOD'S ARMOR?

Why would someone need armor? Armor is designed to protect something. A soccer goalie wears armor—shin guards to protect his legs. A baseball catcher wears armor—a mask and chest guard so he won't be hurt if the ball hits him. Did you know that Christians need armor too?

Christians need armor to protect us from Satan's attacks. Satan is God's enemy. Because you are God's child by trusting in Jesus as your Savior, Satan is your enemy too. The Bible says that Satan is sneaking around looking for someone to destroy (1 Peter 5:8). There are many ways Satan tries to destroy you. He attacks your mind, tempting you to believe his lies and doubt God's love and care. He attacks your heart, tempting you to do things your own way instead of God's way.

You are not strong enough to fight against Satan yourself. God knows that, so besides giving you his armor, he has promised to be your helper. The Bible says, "The Lord is my helper, so I will not be afraid" (Hebrews 13:6). A good soldier knows that without his armor the enemy can destroy him. You need God's armor for your protection.

Put on all of God's armor so that you will be able to stand firm against all strategies and tricks of the Devil.
Ephesians 6:11

YOU CAN PRAY:
Dear God, help me to remember I have your armor and you as my helper. In Jesus' name. Amen.

WHAT ARE TWO THINGS GOD HAS GIVEN TO HELP YOU WIN AGAINST SATAN?

HOW DO I USE THE BELT OF TRUTH?

April
14

We have talked about your enemy, Satan, and his attacks. God has given you armor for protection, but armor won't help you unless you use it. For the next few days, we're going to talk about each piece of the armor and how it can help you.

One of the pieces of armor God has given you is the "belt of truth." This important piece helps you to know what is true and not to be fooled by Satan's lies. How do you use the belt of truth? There are two ways: First, you use the belt of truth by learning as much as you can from God's Word. You can do this by reading the Bible and memorizing Bible verses from this devotional book. Remembering truths from God's Word will help you when Satan tempts you to doubt God.

Another way to use the belt of truth is to be sure that you are always truthful in everything you do. One of Satan's names is the "father of lies." Satan is happy when you tell even a small lie. The belt of truth will protect you against Satan's temptations to lie. God can help you remember to use the belt of truth each day.

Put on all of God's armor so that you will be able to stand firm against all strategies and tricks of the Devil.
Ephesians 6:11

YOU CAN PRAY:
Dear God, please help me to use my belt of truth every day by reading your Word and telling the truth. In Jesus' name. Amen.

NAME TWO WAYS TO USE THE BELT OF TRUTH.

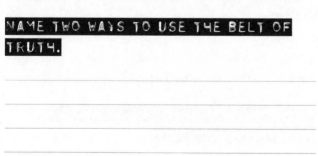

April 15

WHAT IS THE BODY ARMOR OF RIGHTEOUSNESS?

Put on all of God's armor so that you will be able to stand firm against all strategies and tricks of the Devil.
Ephesians 6:11

YOU CAN PRAY:
Dear God, thank you for the body armor of righteousness that helps me to have right attitudes and to do the right thing. In Jesus' name. Amen.

One of the most important parts of the body that a soldier must protect in battle is his heart. As a child of God, you need protection for your heart too—not the organ in your body that keeps you alive, but your feelings, attitudes, and emotions. For this reason, God has given you the body armor of righteousness.

Righteousness is a big word. It means being right before God and doing right. None of us is perfect or righteous all the time. But since you trusted Jesus as your Savior, God no longer sees you as a sinner. He sees you through his perfect Son, Jesus, who died for your sin.

Satan may try to attack you by reminding you of your sin. He wants you to think that God rejects you. When you have your body armor of righteousness on, you know Satan is lying. God says in the Bible, "I have loved you, my people, with an everlasting love" (Jeremiah 31:3).

Living the right way is a protection to you, just like a shield. Only God can help you have a right attitude and the strength to do right. Choosing God's way—being truthful, obedient, and kind—shows that you are using the body armor of righteousness.

HOW DO YOU USE THE BODY ARMOR OF RIGHTEOUSNESS?

WHY DO I NEED THE HELMET OF SALVATION?

April
16

What do motorcycle riders, skateboarders, and soldiers all wear to protect their heads? A helmet. As God's child, your head needs protection too—especially your mind.

Satan wants to attack your mind and lead you away from God. He may put wrong thoughts in your mind like "I hate you!" or "Nobody loves me." Satan can use things like TV, music, or the Internet to put wrong thoughts in your mind. That is why you need to use your helmet of salvation. It helps you to believe God's promise that you are saved from the punishment of your sin. It also gives you confidence that God can guard your mind from Satan's attacks.

How do you use the helmet of salvation? When you read your Bible and think about good things, you are using your helmet to guard your mind. Be careful what enters your mind—what you think about, read, watch, and listen to. The Bible tells you to "conquer . . . rebellious ideas" (2 Corinthians 10:5). You need the helmet of salvation to help you choose right things to look at and listen to. Remember that God is more powerful than Satan. Use your helmet and trust God to guard your thoughts.

HOW WILL YOU USE THE HELMET OF SALVATION TODAY?

Put on all of God's armor so that you will be able to stand firm against all strategies and tricks of the Devil.
Ephesians 6:11

YOU CAN PRAY:
Dear God, thank you for the helmet of salvation that guards my mind. Please help me to choose good things to look at and listen to. In Jesus' name. Amen.

April 17

WHAT ARE THE SHOES OF THE GOSPEL OF PEACE?

Put on all of God's armor so that you will be able to stand firm against all strategies and tricks of the Devil.
Ephesians 6:11

YOU CAN PRAY:
Dear God, thank you for the shoes of the gospel of peace. Help me to use them every day so that I can share your peace and love with others. In Jesus' name. Amen.

Firefighters wear special shoes to protect their feet. These shoes are made of rubber, and they have metal inside for extra protection. They also have sturdy soles to keep them from slipping on wet floors.

Special shoes are part of the armor God has given you. Satan wants you to slip and fall. He wants you to worry about whether you truly belong to God. He doesn't want you to tell others about Jesus or to let them see God's peace in your life. That's why you need to use the shoes of the gospel of peace every day!

Peace is a calm and quietness on the inside. It is a steady confidence that everything is okay. The Bible says that "Christ himself has made peace" (Ephesians 2:14). You have peace with God when you trust Jesus as your Savior. God also gives you peace with yourself because he helps you to see yourself as he sees you. You are loved by him, forgiven, and accepted into his family! In addition, God gives you peace with others. He helps you to show kindness, to forgive, and to share his love with others. Are you using your special shoes today?

WHAT WILL THE SHOES OF THE GOSPEL OF PEACE DO FOR YOU?

HOW DO I USE THE SHIELD OF FAITH?

April
18

Soldiers from years ago often went into battle carrying a shield. Usually the shields were large and heavy. They covered almost every part of the soldier's body to protect against the enemy's arrows. The sides of the shield were often made to hook together with the shields of other soldiers. The soldiers could join together to form a wall of protection against the enemy.

If you are God's child, he has given you a shield of protection against the attacks of Satan. It's called the shield of faith. Faith is believing that what God says, he will do. Faith is also acting on what you believe, even when you have doubts. Satan is constantly firing arrows of doubt at you. He wants you to doubt God's promises, doubt God's faithfulness, doubt God's goodness, and doubt God's power.

You need to hold your shield of faith up high by trusting God's Word. Trust the truths you know about God. Trust the words you have memorized from the Bible. Even when things seem to be going wrong, trust that God is with you and is in control of everything. Like soldiers, join together with your Christian friends. You can encourage each other to stand strong.

WHAT ARE TWO WAYS YOU CAN USE YOUR SHIELD OF FAITH?

Put on all of God's armor so that you will be able to stand firm against all strategies and tricks of the Devil.
Ephesians 6:11

YOU CAN PRAY:
Dear God, thank you for my shield of faith. Help me to trust you, no matter what. In Jesus' name. Amen.

April
19

WHAT IS THE SWORD OF THE SPIRIT?

Put on all of God's armor so that you will be able to stand firm against all strategies and tricks of the Devil.
Ephesians 6:11

YOU CAN PRAY:
Dear God, please help me to memorize at least one Bible verse each week so I will be able to use the sword of the Spirit to keep Satan away. In Jesus' name. Amen.

Do you know what a sword is? It's like a huge knife. It is a weapon with sharp edges that could cut and stab the enemy. All the rest of your armor is something you put on to protect yourself. Your sword is a weapon you use to attack your enemy. The sword of the Spirit is the Word of God—the Bible.

The Lord Jesus used the sword of the Spirit when Satan attacked him. Three times Satan came and tried to get Jesus to sin. Each time, Jesus quoted words from the Bible. Satan finally went away.

You can use your sword when Satan tries to get you to sin. You need to be learning verses from the Bible by memory. If you don't have a Bible, learn some of the verses in this devotional book. God's Holy Spirit will bring these verses to your mind when Satan tempts you to sin. These verses will help you remember what God wants you to do—or what he doesn't want you to do. Each time you remember and use a verse from God's Word, you are becoming skillful in using your powerful weapon, and you are keeping Satan far away.

HOW CAN YOU USE THE SWORD OF THE SPIRIT?

HOW DO I PUT ON GOD'S ARMOR?

April
20

If you were a soccer goalie, would you be ready to play if you did not have your shin guards on? As a Christian, you're not ready to fight your enemy without your armor.

In today's Bible verse, God says to put your armor on. You need to be constantly aware that you have God's armor of protection. When you have your quiet time with God, think about the armor and what it is for. It might help you to "put on" each piece by talking to God about it. Thank him for the helmet; ask him to protect your mind. Thank him for the belt; ask God to help you be truthful. Thank him for your body armor; ask God to guard your feelings and help you to do right. Thank him for your shoes; ask God to give you his peace on the inside. Thank him for your shield; trust that God will be with you and help you. Practice using your sword by saying a Bible verse aloud as you get dressed. Remember that your armor is invisible to you, but God sees it and so does Satan.

Put on all of God's armor so that you will be able to stand firm against all strategies and tricks of the Devil.
Ephesians 6:11

YOU CAN PRAY:
Dear God, thank you for giving me your armor to protect me today. In Jesus' name. Amen.

WHY DO YOU NEED GOD'S ARMOR EACH DAY?

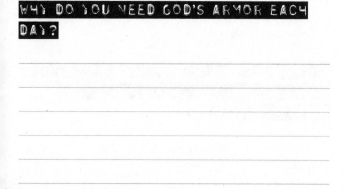

April
21

DID JESUS USE GOD'S ARMOR?

Throughout his earthly life, the Lord Jesus Christ gave us the example of how to use God's armor. If you read about him in the first four books of the New Testament—Matthew, Mark, Luke, and John—you will see how he perfectly used the armor of God.

Jesus used the body armor of righteousness by always doing what was right. He used the shield of faith, believing the promises of his Father, God. Jesus used the helmet of salvation by keeping his thoughts focused on doing his Father's will. He used the belt of truth by speaking only what was true. He used the shoes of peace by demonstrating how we could have peace with God. Jesus also used the sword of the Spirit as he resisted temptation by quoting verses from God's Word.

Did the Lord Jesus use God's armor? Yes—in fact, he is the armor! He is your righteousness (Philippians 3:9), your salvation (Psalm 27:1), and your peace (Ephesians 2:14). He is the truth (John 14:6), and he is the Word of God (John 1:1). As you put your faith in the Lord Jesus and use his Word, you can be a winner over sin and Satan.

Put on all of God's armor so that you will be able to stand firm against all strategies and tricks of the Devil.
Ephesians 6:11

YOU CAN PRAY:
Dear God, thank you for the Lord Jesus, who showed me how to use your armor. Help me to follow his example. In Jesus' name. Amen.

WRITE A NOTE TO JESUS THANKING HIM FOR SHOWING YOU HOW TO USE THE ARMOR OF GOD.

WHAT IF I FORGET TO USE THE ARMOR?

April
22

Imagine a firefighter carrying his protective equipment to the fire but then trying to fight the blaze without using it. That wouldn't be a very good idea. He would get seriously hurt—possibly even killed!

You have been learning all about the protective armor that God gives to his children. You have that armor in the Lord Jesus Christ. He is with you all the time. But what if you choose not to let the Lord Jesus give you the strength to resist the temptations to do wrong? Maybe you think you are strong enough to fight the battle against sin and Satan without God's help. But you cannot win without God.

If you don't use your armor, how will you say "no" when that bad thought comes to you? What will you do when something makes you afraid? You won't have the strength on the inside to be a winner over sin.

God never meant for you to fight your battles alone. He is with you every day and everywhere you go to help you and to make you a winner. When temptations to do wrong come, remember your armor. Thank God for each piece and use it. You will win the battle!

Put on all of God's armor so that you will be able to stand firm against all strategies and tricks of the Devil.
Ephesians 6:11

YOU CAN PRAY:
Dear God, please remind me each morning to use my armor throughout the day. In Jesus' name. Amen.

WHAT HAPPENS IF YOU DON'T USE YOUR ARMOR?

April
23

IS PRAYER PART OF MY PROTECTION?

How would you like to have a super weapon that no one could resist or defend against? Did you know you do have one? It is called prayer. The Lord Jesus used the weapon of prayer many times in his earthly life. He wanted always to do his Father's will. He also took time to thank his Father, God.

Jesus told his followers always to pray and not to give up. Prayer is an important part of your protection against the enemy. Each day your enemy, Satan, prowls around looking for someone to hurt (1 Peter 5:8). You could try to fight him, but you would not win by yourself. You need to pray and ask your heavenly Father for help.

Prayer is talking to God. Satan trembles when God's children pray. He knows that if you pray, God listens, and Satan will lose. Part of prayer is learning to listen and obey. It's not just a time for you to talk to God, it's also a time for him to talk to you. Prayer is a super weapon, but it won't help you if you don't use it. You can pray anytime, anyplace, about anything. Just do it!

Put on all of God's armor so that you will be able to stand firm against all strategies and tricks of the Devil.
Ephesians 6:11

YOU CAN PRAY:
Dear God, please help me to remember to talk to you every day. Help me to listen to you and obey. In Jesus' name. Amen.

WHY IS PRAYER AN IMPORTANT PART OF YOUR PROTECTION?

DID PEOPLE IN THE BIBLE FACE TEMPTATION?

April
24

Sometimes we think that the people in the Bible were super people. We think they had some kind of special power that we don't have. Maybe you've read the stories of Noah and the ark, David and Goliath, and Daniel in the lions' den. Perhaps you wonder how they had such courage. You wish you were as brave as they were. Maybe you are! The people we read about in the Bible were just like us. They had many problems, and they also had temptations to sin.

Everyone faces temptation to do wrong. Satan attacks everyone. He wants the whole world to serve him and turn against God. Satan attacked the people you read about in the Bible, too. God put their stories in his Word so you and I could learn from them. Some of the people in the Bible were true heroes. They trusted God for the strength to say "no" to the temptation to sin and "yes" to obeying God. The people you read about in the Bible had to make hard choices. Not all of them chose to trust and obey God. When you are tempted, what will you choose to do?

WHAT SHOULD YOU DO WHEN YOU ARE TEMPTED TO SIN?

So humble yourselves before God. Resist the Devil, and he will flee from you.
James 4:7

YOU CAN PRAY:

Dear God, please help me to be like heroes in the Bible who trusted and obeyed you when tempted to sin. In Jesus' name. Amen.

April

25

HOW DID JOSEPH HANDLE TEMPTATION?

The Bible tells about a young man named Joseph and what he did when he was faced with temptation (Genesis 37–47). He submitted to (trusted and obeyed) God. He resisted (said "no" to) the devil. God helped Joseph to be a winner over temptation.

Joseph had 10 brothers who hated him. They sold him as a slave. He was taken far away from his family. He was probably tempted to hate his brothers, but he didn't. Years later when Joseph saw his brothers again, he was a very important man in Egypt. His brothers came there to buy food for their families because there was a famine—no food was growing in their land. There was food in the land of Egypt because God had told Joseph to save it. The king put Joseph in charge of selling food to the people. When his brothers knew it was Joseph, they were afraid. Joseph could have given in to the temptation to get revenge, but he didn't. He told his brothers, "It was God who sent me here, not you!" (Genesis 45:8). Joseph submitted to God and resisted the devil. God helped Joseph to be a winner over temptation.

So humble yourselves before God. Resist the Devil, and he will flee from you.
James 4:7

YOU CAN PRAY:
Dear God, please help me to resist the temptation to be angry and want to get revenge. In Jesus' name. Amen.

HOW CAN YOU RESIST TEMPTATION?

HOW DID DANIEL AND HIS FRIENDS TAKE A STAND FOR GOD?

April
26

The Bible tells about a group of young men who were taken as captives to a foreign land. They were to be trained for service to a king who did not worship the true and living God. Unlike the other young men, Daniel and his three friends decided to take a stand for God and honor him by doing what was right. Their first test came at mealtime. They knew that the food in the king's court had probably not been prepared according to the laws God had given his people. Also, it had most likely been offered to false gods.

Daniel determined he would not dishonor God by eating this food. God gave Daniel courage and wisdom to ask the guard for permission to eat vegetables and drink water for 10 days. Afterward, Daniel and his friends were healthier than the other men were. From that time on, God helped them in their training, giving them special wisdom and knowledge. Daniel and his friends were determined to take a stand for God. God gave them strength to do what was right (Daniel 1:6-20).

The next time you are in a hard situation, remember that God can give you strength and courage to stand for him and do what's right.

HOW CAN YOU HAVE COURAGE TO STAND FOR GOD?

So humble yourselves before God. Resist the Devil, and he will flee from you.
James 4:7

YOU CAN PRAY:

Dear God, please give me strength and courage to take a stand for you and to do what's right, no matter what others may do. In Jesus' name. Amen.

April
27

WHAT HAPPENED WHEN DAVID FAILED TO RESIST TEMPTATION?

So humble yourselves before God. Resist the Devil, and he will flee from you.
James 4:7

YOU CAN PRAY:
Dear God, when temptations come, please help me submit to you. Please give me the strength to resist. In Jesus' name. Amen.

King David wanted something that was not his. He wanted another man's wife for his own. He knew that what he wanted was wrong and sinful, but the temptation was strong. Instead of submitting to God (obeying God), King David gave in to the temptation and took the other man's wife. He even purposely sent the other man into battle so he would be killed. Then, David was free to marry the woman. But the Bible says that God knew what David had done, and God was not pleased.

Several terrible things happened because David failed to resist temptation. First, an innocent man died. Then, the baby that was born to David and his new wife also died. But, even worse than these things, David knew that he had sinned against God. David finally confessed his sin to God, and his relationship was healed. However, David must have never forgotten the danger of failing to resist temptation (2 Samuel 11–12).

God will not let you get away with sin. Failing to resist temptation hurts your relationship with him. It may hurt others, too. When temptation comes, submit to God and he will help you to resist!

WHAT MIGHT HAPPEN IF YOU FAIL TO RESIST TEMPTATION?

HOW DID GIDEON HAVE COURAGE TO STAND FOR GOD?

April
28

Gideon was scared! His country, Israel, was being overrun by its enemy. Gideon was so afraid that he hid so the enemy couldn't find him. God sent an angel who told Gideon that God had chosen him to lead his country in battle against the enemy! Gideon was doubtful, but God said, "I will be with you" (Judges 6:16). God was reminding Gideon that he would not have to stand alone.

As Gideon prepared for the coming battle, God gave him some very strange instructions. Gideon and his small army did exactly what God had told them to do. The night of the battle, they circled the enemy camp, blew trumpets, and broke clay pitchers. Then, holding blazing torches high in the air, they cried out, "For the Lord and for Gideon!" (Judges 7:16-25). As they watched in amazement, the startled enemy ran away in fear and confusion. Gideon's army chased and defeated their enemy! How did Gideon have courage to stand for God? He remembered God's promise and obeyed what God said (Judges 6–7).

You can do the same! When you need courage to stand for God, submit to him. Remember his promise to be with you, and obey him. He will give you victory!

HOW DID GIDEON HAVE COURAGE TO STAND FOR GOD?

So humble yourselves before God. Resist the Devil, and he will flee from you.
James 4:7

YOU CAN PRAY:

Dear God, I need courage to stand for you. Help me to remember that you are with me, and help me to obey you. In Jesus' name. Amen.

April
29

HOW DID RAHAB USE THE SHIELD OF FAITH?

A woman named Rahab lived in Jericho. The people in her city didn't believe in the true and living God and had done many evil things. God had commanded his people, Israel, to conquer Jericho. The Israelite leader sent spies into the city, but the king of Jericho found out and was searching for them (Joshua 2).

Rahab helped the spies to hide. She told them that she believed in the God of Israel. Later, she helped them escape by lowering them down the high stone wall by a rope. Before they left, they made a promise to Rahab. Because of her faith, God would save her during the battle. They told her to tie a red rope in her window and gather her family inside. They promised that when the day of battle came, she and her family would be safe (Joshua 2:17-20).

It may have seemed strange to Rahab and her family, but she believed God's promise and did exactly as she was told. Because of her faith, Rahab and her family were saved. In another part of the Bible, God lists Rahab as a hero of faith (Hebrews 11:31). Trust and obey God—that's how you use your shield of faith!

So humble yourselves before God. Resist the Devil, and he will flee from you.
James 4:7

YOU CAN PRAY:
Dear God, I want to trust and obey you. Please help me to remember to use my shield of faith. In Jesus' name. Amen.

HOW DID RAHAB USE HER SHIELD OF FAITH?

WHAT HAPPENED WHEN PETER FAILED THE LORD JESUS?

April
30

Have you ever told someone you would do something? If you don't keep your word, how do you feel? How would you feel if your close friend pretended he didn't even know you?

When the Lord Jesus told his disciples that he was going to die, Peter promised Jesus he would always be there for him. Peter said, "Not even if I have to die with you! I will never deny you!" (Matthew 26:35). But Peter failed the Lord Jesus. For three years, they had been close friends. However, when Jesus needed Peter, Peter pretended he didn't know him.

I am sure Jesus felt just as bad as you would, but he didn't stop loving Peter. Jesus died before Peter had a chance to say he was sorry. Peter must have felt awful. But Jesus didn't stay dead. When he came back to life, he forgave Peter and gave him another chance. He even gave him a very special job. You can read about it in John 21:15-19. You can't make Jesus stop loving you, even if you fail him. If you know Jesus Christ as your Savior, he is always ready to forgive you and give you another chance.

So humble yourselves before God. Resist the Devil, and he will flee from you.
James 4:7

YOU CAN PRAY:
Dear God, thank you for always loving me. I am sorry when I fail you. Thank you for forgiving me. In Jesus' name. Amen.

WHAT SHOULD YOU DO IF YOU FAIL THE LORD JESUS?

Activity 4:
Victory

THE ARMOR OF GOD

Fill in the blanks to name each piece of armor we are given as Christians.

Helmet of ______________________

Body armor of ______________________

Shield of ______________________

Sword of the ______________________

Belt of ______________________

Shoes of the ______________________ of ______________________

I can have victory over sin by . . .

____

THINKING IT OVER!

Victory

Write the answers to these questions from your devotionals in the blanks.

1. How does Satan show that you are his enemy?

____

2. Satan is powerful, but who is more powerful?

____

3. What do you have to do before you can have victory over Satan?

____

4. Why do you need God's armor to fight against Satan?

____

5. How will knowing Bible verses help you when you are tempted?

____

6. Why doesn't Satan like for you to pray?

____

If you need help, you can look back in this month's devotionals. The number in ( ) tells you which devotional to check for each question. 1. (4) 2. (6) 3. (10) 4. (13) 5. (19) 6. (23)

MAY

God's Word and Me

WHAT IS THE BIBLE?

You may wonder what makes the Bible special. It is a book from God. It isn't like any other book you can read. Other books have the thoughts and ideas of people, but the Bible is God's own Word. Every single word in the Bible is true.

The Bible is one way God tells us what he wants us to know. The Bible says it "is useful to teach us what is true and to make us realize what is wrong in our lives. It straightens us out and teaches us to do what is right" (2 Timothy 3:16). The Bible tells what God is like. It shows you what you are doing wrong and how God can take care of those things. The Bible will train you to live in the way God says is right.

Do people ever call you by other names? Your name might be Robert, but you may be called Bob or Robbie. The Bible is sometimes called by different names too. It may be called "God's Word" or "Holy Bible." That is because it comes from our perfect, holy God. The Bible is also called the "Scripture," which means writing. Even though it is called by other names, it is still God's book, his message to us.

All Scripture is inspired by God and is useful to teach us what is true and to make us realize what is wrong in our lives. It straightens us out and teaches us to do what is right.
2 Timothy 3:16

YOU CAN PRAY:
Dear God, thank you for giving us the Bible. Help me to use it to learn more about how you want me to live. In Jesus' name. Amen.

WHAT ARE SOME WAYS THE BIBLE CAN HELP YOU?

WHERE DID THE BIBLE COME FROM?

You already know the Bible came from God. Our Bible verse says, "All Scripture is inspired by God." But how did God give us the Bible? Did it just fall from heaven? No, God's Spirit told 40 different men what to write. God used their own style and personality to write his words. The Holy Spirit inspired and guided them in such a way that there were absolutely no mistakes in any of the words as they were originally written.

This didn't happen all at once. It took 1,600 years for the whole Bible to be finished! Just think about taking that long to write a book! No one could ever live 1,600 years, but time isn't a problem for God. He has always lived and will live forever. He told men at different times in history what to write. Sometimes they wrote what was happening right then. Other times they wrote about what had already happened. God even had them write what would happen in the future.

The men wrote what God told them to write in their own languages. Later, the Bible was put into many other languages as well. That way people all over the world could read it and learn about God.

HOW DOES HAVING THE BIBLE IN YOUR OWN LANGUAGE HELP YOU?

All Scripture is inspired by God and is useful to teach us what is true and to make us realize what is wrong in our lives. It straightens us out and teaches us to do what is right.
2 Timothy 3:16

YOU CAN PRAY:

Dear God, thank you for the Bible. Thank you that it is in my language so I can read it and learn what you want me to do. In Jesus' name. Amen.

IS THE BIBLE TRUE?

How can you tell if something you read is true? One way is to compare it with other things you know are true. The Bible says God's Word is true (John 17:17). The facts prove that. Much of the Bible was written by eyewitnesses. They were people who actually saw the things they wrote about. Archaeological and historical writings from Bible times agree with what the Bible says. That helps you know it is true.

The Bible told about many things hundreds of years before they happened. These are called prophecies. Many of those things have already come true. God said something would happen and it did. You can be sure all the other prophecies will come true too. God knows what will happen in the future. He knew just what to tell the men to write.

God has protected the Bible for thousands of years. Many people in history have tried to destroy the Bible. God didn't let that happen. He kept his true Word safe so you can have it today. The Bible says, "The grass withers, and the flowers fade, but the word of our God stands forever" (Isaiah 40:8).

All Scripture is inspired by God and is useful to teach us what is true and to make us realize what is wrong in our lives. It straightens us out and teaches us to do what is right.
2 Timothy 3:16

YOU CAN PRAY:
Dear God, thank you for protecting the Bible so I can read it today. Help me to remember that everything in your Word is true. In Jesus' name. Amen.

WHAT HELPS YOU BELIEVE THE BIBLE IS GOD'S TRUE WORD?

WHY ARE THERE TWO PARTS TO THE BIBLE?

May
4

Did you know that our calendar tells something about Jesus? Each year tells about how long it's been since Jesus was born. The years before Jesus was born have "before Christ," or "BC," numbers. The years after he was born have "in the year of our Lord," or "AD," numbers. All the years are numbered starting with Jesus' birth!

The parts of the Bible are divided by Jesus' birth too. The Bible is made up of 66 books. Each book is part of either the Old Testament or the New Testament. The Old Testament is in the front of the Bible. It tells about Creation and other things that happened before Jesus became a man.

The New Testament is in the back part of the Bible. The books in it were written after Jesus was on earth. The New Testament tells about Jesus' life. If you read the New Testament, you can find out how to have your sin forgiven by believing in Jesus. The New Testament also tells what Jesus' followers did after he returned to heaven.

Knowing the Bible is divided by time will help you find things in it more easily.

WHAT ARE THREE THINGS YOU COULD FIND IN THE NEW TESTAMENT PART OF THE BIBLE?

All Scripture is inspired by God and is useful to teach us what is true and to make us realize what is wrong in our lives. It straightens us out and teaches us to do what is right.
2 Timothy 3:16

YOU CAN PRAY:

Dear God, thank you for giving us both parts of the Bible. Help me to find out more about you by reading it. In Jesus' name. Amen.

HOW DOES THE BIBLE FIT TOGETHER?

Have you ever tried to write a story or a report? Sometimes it's hard to get it just right. What if lots of people tried to write a book together? What if they lived in different times and places? Would it be likely to fit together right? Amazingly enough, that is the way the Bible was written.

It is wonderful that the Bible fits together the way it does. It was written by 40 men over hundreds of years. It is hard to believe all those authors could agree on everything! That's just what happened though. The later authors agree exactly with the earlier ones.

Another way the Bible fits together is in telling about Jesus. In the Old Testament, God promised he would send a Savior. This Savior would take the punishment for sin. People waited hundreds of years for God to keep his promise. In the New Testament, God sent Jesus as our Savior. That was his plan all along.

Why does the Bible fit together? "All Scripture is inspired by God" (2 Timothy 3:16). Only God could make all the parts of the Bible fit together perfectly! You can always trust God's Word. It will never change.

All Scripture is inspired by God and is useful to teach us what is true and to make us realize what is wrong in our lives. It straightens us out and teaches us to do what is right.
2 Timothy 3:16

YOU CAN PRAY:
Dear God, thank you for making the Bible all go together just right. Help me to trust you to take care of my life just right too. In Jesus' name. Amen.

WHY IS IT IMPORTANT THAT THE BIBLE ALL FITS TOGETHER?

HOW DID THE OLD TESTAMENT PEOPLE DEAL WITH SIN?

May
6

You already know that Jesus died for sin. You can have your sin forgiven by believing in him as your Savior. What happened to people before Jesus came? Could those people have their sins forgiven?

God's people often chose to disobey him. God is perfectly fair. He couldn't ignore the people's sin. The Bible says, "Without the shedding of blood, there is no forgiveness of sins" (Hebrews 9:22). God made a way for the people to have their sin covered (forgiven). God told them to bring animals to sacrifice for their sin. The people deserved to be punished, but the animals were killed instead. The people knew they had done wrong. The animals died in their place. The blood of the animals covered the people's sin. Someday a Savior would come to take away that sin forever. The people needed to believe that promise.

Jesus was that Savior. He took the punishment for sin forever. Now animals don't have to be sacrificed. Jesus is the perfect Son of God. He took the punishment for sin for everyone in the whole world. The Bible says, "Christ also suffered when he died for our sins once for all time" (1 Peter 3:18).

WHY DON'T YOU HAVE TO SACRIFICE ANIMALS TO PAY FOR YOUR SINS?

All Scripture is inspired by God and is useful to teach us what is true and to make us realize what is wrong in our lives. It straightens us out and teaches us to do what is right.
2 Timothy 3:16

YOU CAN PRAY:

Dear God, thank you for making the way for sin to be forgiven through your Son, Jesus. I love you because of what you did for me. In Jesus' name. Amen.

May 7

WHY IS THE OLD TESTAMENT IMPORTANT FOR ME?

All Scripture is inspired by God and is useful to teach us what is true and to make us realize what is wrong in our lives. It straightens us out and teaches us to do what is right.
2 Timothy 3:16

YOU CAN PRAY:
Dear God, thank you that the Old Testament can still help me today. Please help me to obey your laws and stay away from sin. In Jesus' name. Amen.

Some people think it isn't important to read the Old Testament. They think only the New Testament is important. That's not true! The Bible says, "All Scripture is inspired by God and is useful to teach us what is true and to make us realize what is wrong in our lives. It straightens us out and teaches us to do what is right" (2 Timothy 3:16). The whole Bible is important for you!

The Old Testament is helpful for teaching. The Bible says, "Such things were written in the Scriptures long ago to teach us" (Romans 15:4). Reading the Old Testament will train you to live the right way. It will show you how to think and act to please God. He knows what is best for your life. When you live to please him, you will have true happiness on the inside. You can see this as you read about the lives of people in this part of the Bible.

Many of God's laws are in the Old Testament. These laws help you see your sin. God rebukes, or scolds, you by helping you see what you have done wrong. Remembering God's laws can help keep you from sin. The Bible says, "I have hidden your word in my heart, that I might not sin against you" (Psalm 119:11).

WHAT ARE SOME WAYS THE OLD TESTAMENT CAN HELP YOU?

WHAT IS THE NEW TESTAMENT ABOUT?

May
8

The word testament means promise. The New Testament tells about how God kept his promise to send a Savior. This Savior was Jesus. Jesus came from heaven and was born as a baby. He grew up without ever sinning. He was the perfect Son of God. Jesus taught the people about his Father. Then he died on a cross, taking the punishment for sin. The Bible says, "Christ died for our sins" (1 Corinthians 15:3).

Jesus was buried, but he didn't stay dead! On the third day he came alive again. He spent time with many of his followers. He told them to tell people all over the world about him. Jesus said, "Go into all the world and preach the Good News to everyone, everywhere" (Mark 16:15). Then he was taken back up to heaven.

God sent the Holy Spirit to help Jesus' followers. They told people everywhere that Jesus had died for their sin. Many believed in him and were saved. Groups of new believers met together to worship God and serve him. Each of these groups was called a church. The New Testament tells of many new churches that started during the first years after Jesus went back to heaven.

All Scripture is inspired by God and is useful to teach us what is true and to make us realize what is wrong in our lives. It straightens us out and teaches us to do what is right.
2 Timothy 3:16

YOU CAN PRAY:

Thank you, God, for keeping your promise to send a Savior. Help me to be like Jesus' followers and tell other people about him. In Jesus' name. Amen.

WHY IS IT IMPORTANT THAT JESUS' FOLLOWERS TOLD OTHER PEOPLE ABOUT HIM?

May

9

WHY IS THE NEW TESTAMENT IMPORTANT FOR ME?

All Scripture is inspired by God and is useful to teach us what is true and to make us realize what is wrong in our lives. It straightens us out and teaches us to do what is right.
2 Timothy 3:16

YOU CAN PRAY:
Dear God, thank you for sending your Son, Jesus, to die for my sin. Help me to read and obey the New Testament so I can live to please you. In Jesus' name. Amen.

If something could save your life, would you think it was important? What God says in the New Testament can save your life! The New Testament tells how God sent his only Son to earth to die for your sin. When Jesus came back to life, he proved he is the winner over sin and death.

The Bible says, "Believe on the Lord Jesus and you will be saved" (Acts 16:31). You need to trust in Jesus, who died for you! He took the punishment you deserve. When you trust that Jesus is the only one who can forgive you, you will be saved. You can live with God in heaven forever. That is very important news!

Most of the New Testament has been written to people who already believe in Jesus. The New Testament tells us how to live as God's children. It shows us how to love and serve God and how to treat other people. The things written there are still important for you today. If you read and obey them, you will get to know God better. You will be able to live to please him. The New Testament is from God and is important in helping you live for him.

WHAT IS ONE IMPORTANT WAY THE NEW TESTAMENT CAN HELP YOU?

WHAT IS A QUIET TIME?

May
10

Who are your good friends? Do you spend lots of time with them and talk to them often? God wants to be your friend and helper. He is the very best friend you could ever have! The only way to become best friends with him, though, is to spend time with him.

Talking to God in prayer only once in a while isn't enough. Learning about God with other people is good, but you shouldn't stop there. You need to spend time alone with God each day to get to know him well. Even Jesus took time alone to talk to God. The time you set aside to be alone with God is called your quiet time.

When you start your quiet time, ask God to teach you and to help you obey him. Then read God's Word, the Bible, and think about what it means. Spend some time memorizing a Bible verse too. If you don't have a Bible, you can read Bible verses in this book. End your quiet time with prayer. Talk to God about what he has shown you in the Bible and about everything else in your life. Having a quiet time is one way you can "work hard so God can approve you," like our verse says.

WHAT SHOULD YOU DO IN YOUR QUIET TIME WITH GOD?

Work hard so God can approve you. Be a good worker, one who does not need to be ashamed and who correctly explains the word of truth.
2 Timothy 2:15

YOU CAN PRAY:

Thank you, God, that I can talk to you. Thank you for talking to me through the Bible. Help me to spend time alone with you each day. In Jesus' name. Amen.

May
11

SHOULD I HAVE A QUIET TIME?

Josh and Juan were best friends before Josh moved away. They wrote to each other often at first. Juan kept writing to Josh, but Josh quit answering. Soon their friendship wasn't very important to him.

That same thing can happen with you and God. If you don't have a quiet time with him each day, he will become less important to you. Through his Holy Spirit, God will remind you to spend time with him, but what will you do? Will you take time to be with him, or will you ignore him?

When you do spend time with God, you'll get to know him. The Bible says, "Draw close to God, and God will draw close to you" (James 4:8). You will learn what God is really like. You will become close friends and you'll want to know him even better. When you read the Bible, God will teach you things that will help in your life. He will give you the strength you need each day. He will give you the power to obey him so you won't have to be ashamed of the things you do. Will you show God how much you love him by having a quiet time?

Work hard so God can approve you. Be a good worker, one who does not need to be ashamed and who correctly explains the word of truth.
2 Timothy 2:15

YOU CAN PRAY:

Dear God, thank you for being willing to let me know you. Help me to remember each day to spend time alone with you. In Jesus' name. Amen.

HOW CAN HAVING A QUIET TIME HELP YOU?

WHAT DO I NEED TO HAVE A QUIET TIME?

May
12

Are you more likely to do the things you have a set time to do or those you do whenever you happen to think about it? Having a quiet time is important! Set aside a regular time for it each day. Maybe you will need to get up earlier in the morning. Maybe night will be best for you. The important thing is to set a time and stick to it.

Find a place for your time alone with God, where others won't bother you. It is important to be able to think about what God is saying to you in the Bible. You need to be able to talk to him quietly. Let the people around you know you need that time alone each day.

When you have your quiet time, you will need your Bible, some paper, and a pen or pencil. It is also good to use a devotional book like this one. When God shows you something, write it down. Make a list of the things you are praying about. Be sure to write down the answers to your prayers too. Then you will be able to remind yourself of how faithful God is to you.

WHEN AND WHERE WILL YOU HAVE YOUR QUIET TIME?

Work hard so God can approve you. Be a good worker, one who does not need to be ashamed and who correctly explains the word of truth.
2 Timothy 2:15

YOU CAN PRAY:

Dear God, thank you that I can spend time with you. Help me to be faithful in having my quiet time with you each day. In Jesus' name. Amen.

May
13

HOW WILL STUDYING THE BIBLE HELP ME?

Work hard so God can approve you. Be a good worker, one who does not need to be ashamed and who correctly explains the word of truth.
2 Timothy 2:15

YOU CAN PRAY:
Dear God, thank you that your Word is alive and can change me. Help me to be willing to obey what you tell me when I study the Bible. In Jesus' name. Amen.

Learning all you can at school is important. You won't have to be ashamed when you get your grades. Learning will help you prepare for life. Studying the Bible is even more important. It will help you be approved, or pleasing, to God, like our verse says.

Studying the Bible will help you in other ways too. You will find many promises from God that you can believe. They will help you when you are having problems or are afraid. You will learn what God is like. You will see that you can trust him completely.

Studying the Bible and obeying it can change your life! The Bible says, "For the word of God is full of living power" (Hebrews 4:12). It has the power to change you on the inside. It shows you how to get to heaven and how to live here on earth. If you read God's Word and think about it often, your life will be happier. You will learn to make wise choices that keep you from sin. You will have God's peace on the inside, no matter what happens around you. Will you let God's Word change you? Others will see the difference!

WHAT CHANGES DO YOU WANT THE BIBLE TO MAKE IN YOUR LIFE?

HOW IS THE BIBLE A SWORD?

May
14

Can you imagine why the Bible would be called a sword? It doesn't look like one! A sword is long and pointed, with sharp edges. A sword can make deep cuts, slicing things apart. Sometimes God's Word can slice through your thoughts and feelings, cutting apart the good from the bad. The Bible "is sharper than the sharpest knife, cutting deep into our innermost thoughts and desires" (Hebrews 4:12). The Bible will show you what you need to confess to God and let him change in your life.

We learned earlier that a sword is also a weapon. Remember that it's part of the armor that God has given to you. The Bible is your weapon for fighting against Satan. Satan will tempt you to do things you know are wrong. Satan even tempted Jesus! Do you remember what Jesus did? He quoted God's Word and Satan had to leave him. If Satan tries to get you to steal something, you can use the Bible too. You can quote, "Do not steal" (Exodus 20:15). Say this verse aloud or to yourself, then obey it. This is how you resist Satan. He can't stand up to the Bible! Will you use the sword God has given you to fight against Satan?

Work hard so God can approve you. Be a good worker, one who does not need to be ashamed and who correctly explains the word of truth.
2 Timothy 2:15

YOU CAN PRAY:
Dear God, thank you for making the Bible my sword. Help me to learn to use it to fight against Satan's temptations. In Jesus' name. Amen.

WHEN ARE SOME TIMES YOU NEED TO USE THE BIBLE AS A SWORD?

May
15

HOW DO I STUDY THE BIBLE?

The Bible is a very long book, isn't it? It may even seem like too much for you to read. Don't worry, though. God doesn't expect you to read and obey everything in his Word all at once. You need to read a little bit at a time and think about it.

You could start with one of the first four books in the New Testament—Matthew, Mark, Luke, or John. They tell you about Jesus' birth and death. You will also learn many things Jesus did while he was here on earth. The large numbers in the Bible are the chapters. The smaller numbers are the verses. Start with chapter one of the book you choose, and just read a few verses. Most Bibles have titles that tell about different parts of the chapter. It would be a good idea to read one of these parts of a chapter each day. The next day you can start where you left off.

As you read your Bible, God will teach you things. Think about what he says. Then you need to do what he tells you to do. When you obey God's Word, you will be correctly handling the word of truth, like our verse says.

Work hard so God can approve you. Be a good worker, one who does not need to be ashamed and who correctly explains the word of truth.
2 Timothy 2:15

YOU CAN PRAY:
Dear God, thank you that you will teach me when I read the Bible. Help me to remember to stop and think about what you say to me. In Jesus' name. Amen.

HOW CAN READING JUST A LITTLE OF THE BIBLE EACH DAY HELP YOU?

WHAT SHOULD I LOOK FOR AS I STUDY THE BIBLE?

May
16

How will you find out what God wants to teach you in the Bible? Pray and ask for his help first. Then read a few verses and ask yourself these three questions:

1. **What does it say?** Put the ideas in your own words. For the first part of the verse on this page, you might say, "Do everything you can to make God happy."
2. **What does it mean?** If there are words you don't understand, look them up in a dictionary or ask someone what they mean. Are the verses telling you something about God? Is there a promise for you? Do they say something you should or should not do?
3. **What is God saying to me?** How does God want you to use these verses in your own life? Maybe you need to tell God how great he is. Thank him for his promises. Ask him to remind you of them when you are lonely or afraid. Maybe you need to admit that something you are doing is wrong. Learn the verse so you can use it as a sword to help you fight against sinning. Write down what God shows you so you won't forget it.

Work hard so God can approve you. Be a good worker, one who does not need to be ashamed and who correctly explains the word of truth.
2 Timothy 2:15

YOU CAN PRAY:
Dear God, I know you have a lot to teach me. Help me to understand what you want me to see as I read the Bible. In Jesus' name. Amen.

WHAT IS GOD SAYING TO YOU THROUGH YOUR MEMORY VERSE ABOVE?

May

17

HOW CAN I MEMORIZE GOD'S WORD?

Work hard so God can approve you. Be a good worker, one who does not need to be ashamed and who correctly explains the word of truth.
2 Timothy 2:15

YOU CAN PRAY:
Thank you, God, for giving me a mind that can learn. Help me to memorize Bible verses and to use them to fight against sin. In Jesus' name. Amen.

Do you remember your best weapon to fight against sin? It is the Bible. What can you do when you don't have your Bible? If you memorize verses from God's Word, you will always have them with you. They will be ready like a sword to help you fight temptation. The Bible says, "I have hidden your word in my heart, that I might not sin against you" (Psalm 119:11). Start by learning the verses in this devotional book. Then, memorize other special verses God shows you.

Read aloud several times the verse you want to memorize. Think about what it says. Write it down and take it with you to look at often during the day. Say the first part of the verse to yourself over and over until you can do it without looking. Add another part, and do the same thing. Keep adding parts until you can say the whole verse without help. Say it to someone else and tell him or her what it means. Remember to do what the verse says! Learn other verses, but keep reviewing the first ones too. Then, when you need them, God's Spirit can bring them back to your mind.

HOW WILL MEMORIZING PARTS OF THE BIBLE HELP YOU?

May

18

WHAT IS PRAYER?

What would it be like to have a king for your best friend? What if you could talk to the Creator of the universe whenever you wanted to? If you know the Lord Jesus as your Savior, you can do these things! The one, true God is the Creator—the King of kings. He has made a way for you to talk to him! That is called prayer.

You don't have to have a telephone or e-mail to talk to God. Even though you can't see him, he is everywhere all the time. You can talk to him aloud or quietly in your mind. He can always hear you. He wants you to talk to him often. In our Bible verse today, God says, "Ask me and I will tell you." Will he tell you aloud? Probably not, but he will talk to you through the Bible, or he will speak quietly in your heart.

Sometimes people think they have to memorize prayers and say them over and over again. Saying a memorized prayer is fine if you really mean it, but don't stop there. God wants you to talk to him with your own thoughts or words. He is never too busy to listen.

Ask me and I will tell you some remarkable secrets about what is going to happen here.
Jeremiah 33:3

YOU CAN PRAY:

Dear God, thank you for making a way for me to talk to you! Help me to remember to do it often. In Jesus' name. Amen.

WHAT DO YOU WANT TO TALK TO THE CREATOR OF THE UNIVERSE ABOUT?

May

19

WHY SHOULD I PRAY?

God knows everything about you. He knows what you need before you even tell him. Why, then, do you need to pray? One important reason is that God created you to love him and to be his friend. Friends talk to each other. The way you talk to God is through prayer. You can tell him how much you love him and how wonderful he is. You can also tell him what you need.

Another good reason to pray is because you need God's help. Prayer is the way God made for you to ask for his help. The Bible says, "The reason you don't have what you want is that you don't ask God for it" (James 4:2). Maybe you are having trouble at school or don't know what to do about a problem. God has the power to help you, and he can show you what to do. Our verse says, he will "tell you some remarkable secrets about what is going to happen here." God's answer may be something you would never have thought about. Answers to prayer help you remember that God is really the one who gives you everything. They help you remember to depend on him.

Ask me and I will tell you some remarkable secrets about what is going to happen here.
Jeremiah 33:3

YOU CAN PRAY:
Dear God, I need your help every day. Thank you that I can call on you and you will answer. In Jesus' name. Amen.

WHY DO YOU THINK GOD WANTS YOU TO PRAY?

WHY DOES GOD HEAR MY PRAYERS?

May
20

The Bible tells about Elijah, a prophet of the one true God. Elijah was in a contest with 450 prophets of a false god named Baal. First, the prophets of Baal prayed to their god to send down fire from heaven. They screamed and danced for many hours, but no fire came down. Why? Because the god they served wasn't alive! He couldn't even hear them! Then, Elijah prayed to the one true God. Immediately, fire came down from heaven! God was proving that he is the one true God. He showed everyone that he hears and answers prayer!

The one true God is still alive and listening today! That is why he can hear and answer your prayers. The Bible says, "Ask me and I will tell you" (Jeremiah 33:3). God always keeps his promises! When you pray to God as his obedient child, he will hear you. If you have never believed in Jesus, his Son, the first prayer God wants to hear from you is to admit your sin and believe in Jesus, who died to take your punishment. You can talk to God right now. He loves you and is waiting to hear from you!

Ask me and I will tell you some remarkable secrets about what is going to happen here.
Jeremiah 33:3

YOU CAN PRAY:

Dear God, help me never to forget that you are always listening and ready to answer my prayers. In Jesus' name. Amen.

HOW DO YOU KNOW GOD HEARS YOUR PRAYERS?

May
21

WHEN AND WHERE CAN I PRAY?

Jamie and Karl were out on the lake in a small boat. Suddenly, a big motorboat cut right in front of them! Big waves rocked their boat violently, and they tipped over into the water. Jamie couldn't swim well and found himself going under in the waves. "God," he prayed, "help me!" Just then, something bumped into him. It was their boat! It was upside down but floating on the waves. Quickly Jamie grabbed hold of it. Then he saw Karl. "Thank you, God!" Jamie said. He and Karl were able to float with the boat until help came.

Should Jamie have waited to pray until bedtime or until he was at church? No! He did exactly what he should have. He prayed right there where he was when he needed help. God is everywhere all the time, so you, too, can call to him anytime. People in the Bible prayed all times of the day and night wherever they were. The Lord Jesus even prayed to God while he was hanging on the cross. You can talk to God anytime, anyplace. If you are his child, he is always with you and ready to listen.

Ask me and I will tell you some remarkable secrets about what is going to happen here.
Jeremiah 33:3

YOU CAN PRAY:
Dear God, thank you that I can talk to you anytime and anyplace. Remind me to pray often, wherever I am. In Jesus' name. Amen.

NAME SOME TIMES AND PLACES YOU CAN TALK TO GOD.

WHAT SHOULD I PRAY TO GOD ABOUT?

May
22

Do you always have your hand with you? It can remind you who to pray for. Hold it so your thumb points towards you. Your thumb can remind you to pray for the people who are close to you. That might be your family and good friends.

Now turn your hand so the palm faces you. After your thumb comes your pointer finger. It can remind you to pray for the people who point you to the Lord Jesus. That might be your pastor or a teacher. It could be the people who write things to help you learn about God. Then comes your tallest finger. It reminds you to pray for the people who have authority over you. That would include your parents, teachers, and government leaders. Your ring finger is the weakest. It has trouble working by itself. It can remind you to pray for those who are weak. You can pray for the sick, the elderly, or very young children. You could also pray for those who've never trusted Jesus as their Savior.

Last comes your little finger. It helps you remember to put others first and then pray for yourself. The Bible says we should "always be prayerful" (Romans 12:12).

Ask me and I will tell you some remarkable secrets about what is going to happen here.
Jeremiah 33:3

YOU CAN PRAY:
Dear God, thank you for showing me I should pray for others. Help me to think about them more than I think about myself. In Jesus' name. Amen.

WRITE THE NAMES OF THREE PEOPLE YOU SHOULD PRAY FOR.

DOES GOD ALWAYS ANSWER PRAYER?

When you pray about something, will God answer you? He promises to answer if you are his child. God says, "Ask me and I will tell you." God doesn't say, "I *might* tell you" but "I *will* tell you." Does that mean he will always give you what you want? No. God will do what he knows is best for you.

Sometimes in the Bible God gave people what they prayed for. He gave Hannah a baby son when she asked (1 Samuel 1:20). Other times God's answer was "no." Paul wanted God to take away a problem he had (2 Corinthians 12:7-9). God said no. Instead, he helped Paul deal with the problem. The third answer God gave was "wait." Two sisters wanted Jesus to heal their sick brother, Lazarus. The Lord Jesus waited until Lazarus had died. Then, Jesus brought him back to life! People realized that Jesus really was the Son of God (John 11:5, 32, 43-44).

God gives those same answers to prayer today. He may say yes, he may say no, or he may say wait. Your job is to keep praying, believing God will answer your prayers in the way he knows is best for you.

Ask me and I will tell you some remarkable secrets about what is going to happen here.
Jeremiah 33:3

YOU CAN PRAY:
Dear God, help me to trust you to answer my prayers in the way you know is best. Thank you for hearing and answering me. In Jesus' name. Amen.

WRITE ABOUT A TIME WHEN GOD'S ANSWER TO YOUR PRAYER WAS "YES."

SHOULD I HAVE OTHERS PRAY WITH ME?

May
24

How would you feel if you were put in prison for telling others about the Lord Jesus? That's exactly what happened to a man in the Bible named Peter. Peter was thrown into prison. He had four soldiers at a time to guard him. Two of them were even chained to him! Do you think Peter was praying for help? Probably! He wasn't the only one praying, though. Other Christians were praying for Peter too. They knew God was the only one who could help him.

God did one of those "remarkable secrets" our verse talks about. He sent an angel right into that prison. Peter's chains fell off. He and the angel walked out of the prison right past all the guards! God heard and answered the Christians' prayers in a very special way (Acts 12:6-10).

Prayer brings God's power to help you, too. It is very important to pray yourself, but you need to have others pray for you and with you too. That multiplies the power of your prayer. Jesus said, "If two of you agree down here on earth concerning anything you ask, my Father in heaven will do it for you" (Matthew 18:19).

Ask me and I will tell you some remarkable secrets about what is going to happen here.
Jeremiah 33:3

YOU CAN PRAY:
Dear God, thank you for answering prayer. Help me to share my needs with others so they can help me pray. In Jesus' name. Amen.

WHAT DO YOU NEED SOMEONE ELSE TO PRAY WITH YOU ABOUT?

May

25

WHAT DO I NEED TO INCLUDE IN MY PRAYERS?

There are many things you could pray about. Sometimes it is hard to remember them all. The letters in the word *ACTS* can help you.

A stands for adoration. Tell God how much you love and respect him. Praise him for how wonderful and mighty he is. You could even sing your praise to God!

C is for confession. You need to tell God about the wrong things you do. Name your sin and admit it is wrong. God promises to forgive you when you confess your sin. Then your prayer will have "great power and wonderful results," like our verse says.

T is for thanksgiving. If someone gives you a gift or does something nice for you, don't you usually thank that person? God has done a lot for you! Remember to tell God thank you for what you have, who you are, and what he has given you.

S stands for supplication. That means to ask God for things. Talk to God about the things other people need. Pray about the things you want and need too.

Remember what the letters in the word *ACTS* mean when you pray. They will help you talk to God the way you should.

The earnest prayer of a righteous person has great power and wonderful results.
James 5:16

YOU CAN PRAY:
Dear God, you are so good to me! Help me to remember to do more than just ask you for things when I pray. In Jesus' name. Amen.

NAME ONE THING YOU CAN SAY TO GOD FOR EACH LETTER OF THE WORD *ACTS*.

HOW DO I PRAISE GOD?

May
26

How do you feel when someone praises you? Maybe you wrote a great story or did something kind. If others notice and say something about it, you feel good inside. God deserves to be praised far more than you or I do! He is pleased when you tell him how wonderful he is. The Bible says over and over to praise God. In fact, it says, "Let everything that lives sing praises to the Lord!" (Psalm 150:6). Praising God is one way to show how much you love him.

You can praise God by telling him how much you admire him. Talk to him about his greatness, power, wisdom, and love. Praise him for the things he has done, like creating the huge mountains and mighty oceans. Praise him for keeping the stars and planets moving just right. Only our great God could do those things!

The Bible says, "Sing to the Lord a new song" (Psalm 149:1). That is another way to praise God. Maybe you know songs that tell about God's greatness. Sing them to him. You can even make up your own songs to praise God. He is listening and loves to hear your praise!

WRITE THREE THINGS YOU CAN PRAISE GOD FOR TODAY.

The earnest prayer of a righteous person has great power and wonderful results.
James 5:16

YOU CAN PRAY:

Dear God, you are so awesome! Remind me every day to spend time praising you for who you are and what you do. In Jesus' name. Amen.

May
27

HOW DO I CONFESS MY SINS TO GOD?

Kirsten was God's child. She knew she should obey. But she didn't think her mom would let her go to her friend's house, so she said she needed to study at the library but went to her friend's house instead. Later, when she started to pray, things just didn't seem right. She needed to confess her sin to God and to her mother.

As God's child, if you choose to sin, things won't be right between you and God. Your prayer won't be powerful because you haven't acted in a way that is right and good. As soon as you know you have sinned, confess it to God. Admit what you did and agree with God that it was wrong. The Bible says, "But if we confess our sins to him, he is faithful and just to forgive us and to cleanse us from every wrong" (1 John 1:9). You can know God has forgiven you because he always keeps his promises. Make things right with the people you have sinned against too.

Should you keep choosing to sin and asking forgiveness? No! Be willing to stop doing the wrong things. Ask God to help you do what's right.

The earnest prayer of a righteous person has great power and wonderful results.
James 5:16

YOU CAN PRAY:
Dear God, thank you for your forgiveness. Show me when I sin and remind me to confess it to you right away. In Jesus' name. Amen.

WHY IS IT IMPORTANT TO CONFESS YOUR SINS TO GOD RIGHT AWAY?

WHAT SHOULD I THANK GOD FOR?

May

28

Suppose you spent a lot of time doing something really special for a friend. How would you feel if your friend didn't even thank you? You might wonder if he or she cared about you or what you did. God is also disappointed when you don't remember to thank him for the things he does for you.

The most important thing you should thank God for is sending his Son, Jesus, to die on the cross for you. He forgave your sin and is getting a place in heaven ready for you! There are many other things to thank God for as well. Do you know that all the good things you have really came from God? He owns the world and everything in it. Thank him for what he has given you. Thank him for the people he has put into your life to help you.

God gives you the strength you need for each day. When problems come, he is right there helping you. Have you thanked him for his help and strength? The Bible says, "Give thanks to the Lord, for he is good!" (1 Chronicles 16:34). Thanking God should be a big part of your prayer time.

The earnest prayer of a righteous person has great power and wonderful results.
James 5:16

YOU CAN PRAY:
Dear God, please forgive me for not remembering all you do for me. Thank you for loving me and taking care of me in so many ways. In Jesus' name. Amen.

LIST THREE THINGS OR PEOPLE YOU NEED TO THANK GOD FOR.

May
29

HOW SHOULD I PRAY FOR OTHERS?

The earnest prayer of a righteous person has great power and wonderful results.
James 5:16

YOU CAN PRAY:
Dear God, thank you for letting me pray for others! Help me to see their needs and remember to pray for them. In Jesus' name. Amen.

If your friend was hurt in a car wreck, would you know how to pray for him? You could pray that God would heal him, but that is just a start. If the friend has never trusted the Lord Jesus as his Savior, pray that he will. If he has trusted Jesus, pray that he will grow closer to God while he is healing. Ask God to help him show others that he has Jesus in his life by the way he acts.

Maybe a person is tempted to do something wrong. Pray that God would show that person how to escape the temptation. Maybe a friend doesn't get along with his parents. Pray that his actions will show respect and love for them. Ask God to help you be a good listener and helper for your friend.

Sometimes it is hard to know how to pray for the needs of others. Ask God to help them in the way he knows is best. The important thing is to pray for others. Our verse says, "The earnest prayer of a righteous person has great power and wonderful results." Confess your own sins, then put God's power to work in the lives of others through your prayers.

CHOOSE THREE PEOPLE AND WRITE ONE THING YOU COULD PRAY FOR EACH OF THEM.

WHY SHOULD I PRAY FOR THOSE IN CHARGE?

May
30

Think of the people in your life who are in charge. That might include your parents, teachers, government leaders, and others. God chooses who will be in charge. The Bible says, "All governments have been placed in power by God" (Romans 13:1). The things these people do are important! The decisions they make affect many lives. That is why God tells you to pray for them. The Bible says we should pray "for kings and all others who are in authority" (1 Timothy 2:1-2). Those who are in charge need God's help to make wise choices.

Sometimes these people are Christians. Pray that God will show them what to do. Pray that they will depend on God to help them do what is right. Some of the people in charge are not Christians. Pray that they will believe in the Lord Jesus. Ask God to help them make choices that please him. God has more power than any person. He can even work through people who don't know him!

You may think your prayers won't make a difference, but they do! God says that when you live his way, your prayers will be powerful and effective!

WRITE SOMETHING YOU COULD PRAY FOR YOUR PARENTS OR YOUR TEACHER THIS WEEK.

The earnest prayer of a righteous person has great power and wonderful results.
James 5:16

YOU CAN PRAY:
Dear God, thank you that no one can be in charge unless you allow it. Remind me to pray for the authorities in my life every day. In Jesus' name. Amen.

May
31

IS IT OKAY TO PRAY FOR MYSELF?

Is it selfish to talk to God about your own problems? Should you pray for others and ignore your own needs? No! God wants you to pray for others, but he wants you to pray for yourself, too. God loves you so much! He wants to take care of you in every way. When you pray about your own needs, you show God you are trusting him to help you.

Talk to God about physical needs like your health, food, and clothes. Tell him what you are feeling. Sometimes there are things you can't talk to anyone else about. Tell God. You can always trust him to understand and help you. The Bible says, "Give all your worries and cares to God, for he cares about what happens to you" (1 Peter 5:7). When you are worried about something, give it to God. He can take care of it far better than you can!

When you pray for yourself, don't just ask for things. Pray that God will help you fight temptation and live the way he wants you to live. Ask him to help you get to know him better. Those kinds of prayer for yourself will please God.

The earnest prayer of a righteous person has great power and wonderful results.
James 5:16

YOU CAN PRAY:

Dear God, remind me to bring all of my needs and troubles to you. Thank you for loving me and taking care of me. In Jesus' name. Amen.

WHY DOES GOD WANT YOU TO PRAY ABOUT YOUR OWN NEEDS?

THE MEMORY ZONE

Here are some great Bible verses about what you've learned so far. Put a check mark in the box as you memorize each one!

- ❑ **Isaiah 40:8** "The grass withers, and the flowers fade, but the word of our God stands forever."
- ❑ **Romans 15:4** "Such things were written in the Scriptures long ago to teach us. They give us hope and encouragement as we wait patiently for God's promises."
- ❑ **Psalm 119:11** "I have hidden your word in my heart, that I might not sin against you."
- ❑ **Hebrews 4:12** "For the word of God is full of living power. It is sharper than the sharpest knife, cutting deep into our innermost thoughts and desires. It exposes us for what we really are."
- ❑ **Psalm 119:105** "Your word is a lamp for my feet and a light for my path."
- ❑ **Hebrews 4:16** "So let us come boldly to the throne of our gracious God. There we will receive his mercy, and we will find grace to help us when we need it."
- ❑ **Psalm 34:4** "I prayed to the Lord, and he answered me, freeing me from all my fears."
- ❑ **Philippians 4:6-7** "Don't worry about anything; instead, pray about everything. Tell God what you need, and thank him for all he has done. If you do this, you will experience God's peace, which is far more wonderful than the human mind can understand. His peace will guard your hearts and minds as you live in Christ Jesus."

Activity 5: God's Word and Me

GOD'S WORD AND ME

Fill in the blanks to tell more about the Bible and your quiet times with God.

The Bible

It took 1,600 ____________ and 40 ____________ to write the words of the Bible. But ____________ is the author. That's why we call the Bible God's Word.

My Quiet Time

When: ____________

Where: ____________

What I do: ____________

Why my quiet time is important: ____________

____

____

THINKING IT OVER!

God's Word and Me

Write the answers to these questions from your devotionals in the blanks.

1. How can you know the Bible is true?

____

2. What are the two parts of the Bible?

____

3. What is a quiet time?

____

4. What is prayer?

____

5. When and where can you pray?

____

6. What are some things you should include when you pray?

____

If you need help, you can look back in this month's devotionals. The number in ( ) tells you which devotional to check for each question. 1. (1) 2. (4) 3. (10) 4. (18) 5. (21) 6. (25)

JUNE

Witnessing

WHAT IS A WITNESS?

Have you ever seen a witness in a court case? A witness tells the judge or jury what he knows to be true. A Christian witness tells what he knows to be true about Jesus. If you have trusted the Lord Jesus as your Savior, you can be a witness. You can tell others how they can trust him too.

Erin told her friend, Travis, that God loves him. She told him how God sent his Son, Jesus, to die on the cross for his sins and how he came alive again. Travis made an important decision that day. He trusted Jesus to forgive his sins and be his Savior.

Erin is a witness. She knows the truth found in the Bible. Jesus said, "I am the way, the truth, and the life. No one can come to the Father except through me" (John 14:6). Erin wants other people to know the truth about Jesus.

You can be a witness too. First, be sure you have trusted Jesus as your Savior from sin. Then, you can tell others who Jesus is and how he died on the cross for their sins. Encourage them to trust Jesus as their Savior.

And then he told them, "Go into all the world and preach the Good News to everyone, everywhere." Mark 16:15

YOU CAN PRAY:
Dear God, help me to be a true witness for you. In Jesus' name. Amen.

WHAT SHOULD YOU TELL OTHERS IF YOU ARE A WITNESS FOR JESUS?

WHY SHOULD I WITNESS?

Suppose your mom or dad had to go away on a long trip. Would you remember their last words to you? If they gave you some special instructions, would you obey?

Just before Jesus, God's Son, left this earth to go back to heaven, he spoke some last words to his disciples. His words were a command. He said, "Go into all the world and preach the Good News to everyone, everywhere" (Mark 16:15). Jesus told them to go and tell others about him. Do you think they did? Yes! They obeyed Jesus because he had commanded them. They also obeyed because they loved him.

If you know Jesus as your Savior, his command is for you, too. When you go and tell about Jesus, you are being a witness. Jesus wants you to go and tell as many people as you can what he has done for you. Why should you witness? One reason is that God has commanded it. Another reason is that you love Jesus and want to obey him. Jesus wants you to go and tell. Will you obey his command? Will you be a witness for him because you love him?

CAN YOU THINK OF TWO REASONS WHY IT IS IMPORTANT TO BE A WITNESS?

And then he told them, "Go into all the world and preach the Good News to everyone, everywhere." Mark 16:15

YOU CAN PRAY:

Dear God, I love you. I want to obey you every day. Help me to obey your command to go and tell others about you. In Jesus' name. Amen.

June

3

WHAT DO I SAY WHEN I WITNESS?

And then he told them, "Go into all the world and preach the Good News to everyone, everywhere."
Mark 16:15

YOU CAN PRAY:
Dear God, thank you for the Good News I can tell others about how you love them and how Jesus died for their sins and came alive again. In Jesus' name. Amen.

Have you ever wanted to tell someone about Jesus, but you didn't know what to say? Begin by telling about *God.* He is the Creator, who made us special. Tell how God loves us and how he is perfect and lives in heaven.

Then, talk about sin. Sin is when we disobey God. The Bible says, "For all have sinned" (Romans 3:23). We were all born with a desire to sin. Our sin separates us from God. Someday, everyone that is separated from God will be punished forever in a terrible place called hell.

Next, talk about Jesus, God's only Son. Tell how Jesus, who was perfect, died on the cross to take our punishment for sin. He was buried, and three days later he came back to life again. When you believe (trust completely) in Jesus, you can be saved from the punishment of your sin.

Then, you can ask: "Would you like to believe in Jesus today?"

Before you can tell someone else how to believe in Jesus, you need to be sure that you have done so. If you've never told Jesus that you believe he died for you, do that right now. Then you can tell others how to believe in Jesus, just like you did!

WHAT COULD YOU TELL SOMEONE ABOUT GOD, ABOUT SIN, AND ABOUT JESUS?

WHAT IF I'M AFRAID TO WITNESS?

June

4

The Bible tells about a time when God gave a special assignment to the leader of Israel named Moses. His assignment was to tell God's message to the elders of Israel and to Pharaoh, king of Egypt. Moses didn't want to do it. He was afraid. He said to God, "They won't believe me! They won't do what I tell them" (Exodus 4:1).

Have you ever felt like Moses? God has given you a special assignment. You are to tell God's message to other people. You are to be a witness. Like Moses, do you make excuses such as "I'm afraid I might say the wrong thing," or "I'm afraid people will not listen to me," or "I'm afraid people will make fun of me"? God said to Moses, "Who makes mouths? . . . Is it not I, the Lord? Now go, and do as I have told you. I will help you speak well, and I will tell you what to say" (Exodus 4:11-12).

God promises the same to you. He is the one who made you. He will be with you. He will give you the words to say. You don't have to be afraid. Trust God to help you be a witness for him.

WHAT CAN YOU DO IF YOU ARE AFRAID TO WITNESS?

____

____

____

____

____

And then he told them, "Go into all the world and preach the Good News to everyone, everywhere."
Mark 16:15

YOU CAN PRAY:

Dear God, when I'm afraid to witness, help me to remember the promises in your Word and give me courage to tell others about you. In Jesus' name. Amen.

June

5

HOW CAN MY LIFE BE A WITNESS?

When Maria became angry, she often got in trouble with her words. Sometimes she said bad words. Sometimes she said things that were mean or talked back to her parents.

One day Maria heard the Good News about Jesus. She believed in Jesus as her Savior. Then Maria prayed, "Dear Jesus, when I am tempted to sin with my mouth, help me to remember what you did on the cross for me."

God helped Maria control her anger and her words. Soon her friends at school began to see a change in Maria's life. Two of them asked her why she was different. Maria was able to tell them about Jesus. Maria was witnessing, not only by her words but by her changed life.

Your life can be a witness too. If you know Jesus as your Savior, others should see a difference in you. Ask God to help you change those areas that need to be changed. The Holy Spirit, who lives in you, can help you to stop saying bad words you used to say. He can help you to be kind instead of being mean. When others see that your life is different, they will want to know why. Then you can tell them the Good News!

And then he told them, "Go into all the world and preach the Good News to everyone, everywhere." Mark 16:15

YOU CAN PRAY:
Dear God, may my words and my life be a witness for you today. In Jesus' name. Amen.

WHAT ARE SOME THINGS IN YOUR LIFE THAT MAY KEEP YOU FROM BEING A GOOD WITNESS?

WHO CAN I WITNESS TO?

June
6

Did you read the verse at the side of this page? It says that we are to go into all the world and tell the Good News about Jesus to everyone. God has put you in a very special part of his world. He wants you to be a witness for him right now—right where you are.

Think about those people who live around you who do not know Jesus. They could be friends at school or in your neighborhood. Maybe it's a brother or sister or your grandparent. Perhaps even your mom or dad needs to hear about Jesus. Do you know that God might want you to be the one to tell them about him? Maybe God even wants you to be a witness to someone who has been mean to you. That would not be easy, would it?

God didn't promise that being a witness would be easy, but he has promised that he will always be with you. He has promised he will help you to know what to say. God has brought certain people into your life who need to hear about him. He wants to help you to be a witness to those you meet every day.

LIST THREE PEOPLE YOU COULD WITNESS TO.

And then he told them, "Go into all the world and preach the Good News to everyone, everywhere." Mark 16:15

YOU CAN PRAY:

Dear God, I want to pray for the three people on my list. Give me the courage and the words to tell them about you. In Jesus' name. Amen.

June 7

WHERE CAN I WITNESS?

Stephen hated riding the school bus mostly because Anthony rode the same bus. Anthony was a bully. He was always making trouble, especially for Stephen. Stephen talked to his mother about the problem. She suggested that they pray.

Later, Stephen's mother asked him if he would be interested in having a Bible club in their home. Stephen thought that was a great idea. Then, his mother suggested he invite Anthony. She told Stephen to pray and ask God what he should do. Stephen prayed. He knew what God wanted him to do. He asked God for courage to be a witness to Anthony on the school bus.

One day, God gave Stephen that courage. Stephen told Anthony how he had received Jesus as his Savior. Then he invited Anthony to the Bible club. The first day of club, who do you suppose came? Anthony! That day Anthony received Jesus as his Savior.

Like Stephen, you could be a witness on your way to school. Maybe you can tell the Good News to a friend during lunch at school. Perhaps you can be a witness right in your own home. Can you think of other places where you can be a witness?

And then he told them, "Go into all the world and preach the Good News to everyone, everywhere." Mark 16:15

YOU CAN PRAY:
Dear God, help me to think of places where I can be a witness for you; then, help me to do it. In Jesus' name. Amen.

WRITE DOWN THREE PLACES WHERE YOU CAN BE A WITNESS.

DID PEOPLE IN THE BIBLE WITNESS TO OTHERS?

June
8

Here is a W test for you: *Who,* in the Bible, were witnesses? *What* did they say? *Where* did they go to witness?

Who, in the Bible, were witnesses? God used people just like you. He used a young servant girl to tell her master about him. Perhaps she was even your age. Isn't that encouraging! God will use you, if you are willing. The Bible also tells us about a blind man, some followers of Jesus, and two prisoners who were witnesses.

What did witnesses in the Bible say? Perhaps you think they used big, hard words. No, they just told others what they knew about Jesus. One man named Paul told someone, "Believe on the Lord Jesus and you will be saved" (Acts 16:31). Ask God to give you the words to share what you know about him.

Where did they witness? They witnessed wherever God placed them. One was a witness in another country and one was a witness in his home. Another was a witness on a desert road. Two others were witnesses in jail. Where has God placed you so that you can be a witness?

WHY DO YOU THINK GOD USES PEOPLE LIKE YOU TO BE HIS WITNESSES?

But to all who believed him and accepted him, he gave the right to become children of God.
John 1:12

YOU CAN PRAY:

Thank you, Lord, that you are willing to use even me to be a witness for you. In Jesus' name. Amen.

June
9

SHOULD I WITNESS TO PEOPLE IN AUTHORITY OVER ME?

In 2 Kings chapter 5, the Bible tells about an army captain named Naaman. He was sick with a terrible disease that no one could cure. Also, he didn't know the true and living God.

Naaman's country went to war. A young girl was captured and brought to his house to be a servant. This young girl knew the true and living God. She learned about Naaman's disease. She knew her God could help him.

The young girl bravely witnessed to Naaman's wife. She politely told about a prophet of God named Elisha. She knew he could tell Naaman how to be healed by God's power. Naaman went to see Elisha and heard how to be healed. Naaman followed Elisha's instructions. God healed his disease! Naaman now believed in the true and living God.

Was it scary for that girl to witness to someone in authority (in charge) over her? It probably was! But God gave her courage. Are there people in authority over you who need to hear about Jesus? Maybe it's your parents or your teacher. Be polite and respectful when you tell them about Jesus. God will give you courage!

But to all who believed him and accepted him, he gave the right to become children of God.
John 1:12

YOU CAN PRAY:
Dear God, may my words and my actions be a witness to those who are in authority over me. In Jesus' name. Amen.

HOW CAN YOU HAVE COURAGE TO WITNESS TO PEOPLE IN AUTHORITY OVER YOU?

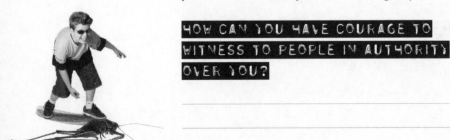

DOES GOD HAVE CERTAIN PEOPLE READY TO LISTEN?

June
10

Philip loved God and told others about him. The Bible says that one day an angel spoke to him. The angel told Philip to go to a certain place on a desert road. Philip obeyed.

Another man was traveling on that same road. This traveler was from Ethiopia. He was an important man in his country. He was the queen's treasurer. This man wanted to worship God.

God made sure that Philip and the Ethiopian man met on that desert road. Philip heard the man reading God's Word. He was reading Old Testament promises about Jesus. Philip asked him if he understood what he was reading. The Ethiopian man said, "How can I, when there is no one to instruct me?" (Acts 8:31).

Philip told the man who Jesus is. He told how Jesus died on the cross for sin and rose again. That day the Ethiopian man believed in Jesus. Philip was a good witness. He obeyed God. God had someone ready to listen to him.

God may have someone ready to listen to you, too. Maybe it's a family member. Maybe it's a friend who needs to hear about Jesus. Maybe it's someone you've never met before. Will you be ready and willing to go where God sends you to tell someone about him?

WHOM DO YOU THINK GOD MAY BE PREPARING FOR YOU TO TALK TO?

But to all who believed him and accepted him, he gave the right to become children of God.
John 1:12

YOU CAN PRAY:
Dear God, may I be ready always to witness for you to anyone, anyplace, and anytime. In Jesus' name. Amen.

June
11

HOW CAN I WITNESS IN HARD TIMES?

"Throw them in jail!" the angry mob probably shouted as they attacked Paul and Silas. The officials ordered them to be beaten many times with a rod. With their backs bleeding, they were thrown in prison. How easy it could have been for them to grumble and complain in that dark prison, but they didn't.

The Bible says that Paul and Silas began praying and singing hymns to God. The other prisoners and the jailer heard them. Paul and Silas were witnesses during their hard time to those around them. It was midnight. Suddenly, an earthquake shook open the jail doors. The jailer was afraid they had escaped, and he was about to kill himself, but Paul called out to him. The jailer asked, "What must I do to be saved?" They witnessed to him, and that night he and his family believed in Jesus Christ (Acts 16:25-31).

Are you going through a hard time in your life? Remember what Paul and Silas did. They prayed and praised God. Their right attitudes were a witness to those around them. What about your attitude? Will you let God use you to be a witness during your hard time?

But to all who believed him and accepted him, he gave the right to become children of God.
John 1:12

YOU CAN PRAY:
Dear God, help me to have a right attitude so that I can be a good witness for you. In Jesus' name. Amen.

HOW CAN GOD USE YOU TO BE A WITNESS DURING A HARD TIME?

SHOULD I WITNESS TO MY BROTHERS AND SISTERS?

June
12

Antonio came from a large family. He had four brothers and two sisters. Their family never went to church. One day a neighbor invited Antonio to a Bible club at her home. There, Antonio heard about Jesus for the first time, and he believed in Jesus as his Savior.

The next week the teacher told the children about a man in the Bible named Andrew. Andrew believed Jesus was the Savior God promised to send. He wanted his brother, Peter, to know him too. Andrew brought his brother to Jesus. The teacher said Andrew was a witness.

Antonio wanted to be like Andrew. He thought about his brothers. The next week he brought his four brothers to club. He wanted them to hear about Jesus. The following week, he brought his two sisters to club!

Andrew was a witness. Antonio was a witness. What about you? Do you have brothers and sisters who need to hear about Jesus? Although it's sometimes hardest to witness to someone in your own family, God can help you do it. Maybe there's no Bible club in your neighborhood, but you can tell your family what Jesus has done for you. God wants you to be a witness.

But to all who believed him and accepted him, he gave the right to become children of God.
John 1:12

YOU CAN PRAY:
Dear God, help me to be like Andrew. Show me how I can be a witness to my brother or sister. In Jesus' name. Amen.

WHAT ARE DIFFERENT WAYS YOU CAN BE A WITNESS TO A SISTER OR BROTHER?

June
13

HOW DO I BEGIN A CONVERSATION ABOUT GOD?

But to all who believed him and accepted him, he gave the right to become children of God.
John 1:12

YOU CAN PRAY:
Dear God, thank you for the opportunities you give to tell others about you. In Jesus' name. Amen.

In Jesus' day, everyone got water from a well. The Bible tells about a woman from Samaria who came to get water from the well. The Lord Jesus began to talk with her. He asked her for a drink of water. They talked about the "living water." He told her he was the "living water" and that he was the one who could forgive her sins (John 4:7-15).

What can we learn from Jesus Christ about witnessing? He showed us to look for everyday opportunities to talk to people about him. Also, Jesus used what the woman was talking about to begin a conversation with her about spiritual things. You can do the same. Maybe a friend at school tells you his parents are getting a divorce. You could be a good listener. Then, at the right time, you could tell him that Jesus loves and cares about him.

Maybe another friend wants you to do something wrong, like stealing something from the store or watching a dirty video. That could be your opportunity. You could tell him why you don't do these things. Then, talk to him about Jesus.

Every day God gives you opportunities to witness. Don't miss out on them!

WRITE AN EVERYDAY OPPORTUNITY YOU COULD USE TO TELL SOMEONE ABOUT JESUS.

DO I HAVE TO KNOW A LOT TO BE A WITNESS?

June
14

The Bible tells us about a man who was blind from birth. As Jesus walked by him, he reached down to the ground and made clay. With the clay, he touched the eyes of the blind man. Jesus then told the man to go wash his eyes. The blind man went immediately and washed, and when he came back, he could see!

The religious leaders, who were called Pharisees, were not happy about what had happened. They even called Jesus a sinner because he healed the man on the Sabbath Day (the day of rest). The man who had been blind said, "I don't know whether he is a sinner. . . . But I know this: I was blind, and now I can see!" (John 9:25). This man did not know a lot about Jesus, but he eagerly told them what he did know. He knew what Jesus had done for him.

What about you? Maybe you don't think you can be a witness because you don't know a lot about Jesus. If Jesus Christ has changed your life, then you have a lot to tell others. Tell them what he has done for you!

DESCRIBE WHAT JESUS HAS DONE FOR YOU.

But to all who believed him and accepted him, he gave the right to become children of God.
John 1:12

YOU CAN PRAY:

Dear God, help me to be willing to tell others what I know about you. In Jesus' name. Amen.

June
15

WILL EVERYONE I WITNESS TO BELIEVE?

These are true stories about a man in the Bible named Paul and a boy in New York named Nathan. The Bible tells us Paul was a witness wherever he went. But not everyone he witnessed to believed. One time Paul witnessed to an important king named Agrippa. After listening to Paul, Agrippa asked, "Do you think you can make me a Christian so quickly?" (Acts 26:28). There is no record that King Agrippa ever became a Christian.

Nathan is eight years old. He wants to be a witness wherever he goes. One day he witnessed to a friend at school. His friend listened for a while. Then he told Nathan that Jesus is just pretend, and he walked away. Nathan was discouraged. Nathan's dad reminded him that all God is asking him to do is to tell his friends the truth about Jesus. They must decide for themselves to believe in Jesus or to reject him.

Have you been discouraged in witnessing? Have people walked away from you? Remember that not everyone you witness to will believe. But God wants you to keep on telling others about him. Don't give up. Trust God and be a faithful witness.

But to all who believed him and accepted him, he gave the right to become children of God.
John 1:12

YOU CAN PRAY:
Dear God, help me to be a faithful witness even if others refuse to believe. In Jesus' name. Amen.

WHAT CAN YOU REMEMBER WHEN YOU ARE DISCOURAGED IN WITNESSING?

WHAT IS THE WORDLESS BOOK?

June
16

Have you seen the Wordless Book? It has no words or pictures. Instead, it has five colors. They are gold, black, red, white, and green. Each color tells a special part of the gospel message—the Good News about Jesus.

Missionaries (Christians who spend their lives telling others about Jesus) have used the *Wordless Book* in many countries to share the gospel with many people. Several years ago, a missionary went to a country where it was difficult to be a witness for Jesus. There were people in that country who hated Christians. Soldiers broke into the home of the missionary. They took all her Bible materials and burned them. She lost everything—well, almost everything. She had a pile of *Wordless Books*. The soldiers picked up a *Wordless Book* and looked at it. Then, they threw it down. Because it had no words, they thought it was not important. They didn't burn one *Wordless Book!* They didn't know how special that little book was!

The Wordless Book has been used to tell many people about Jesus. It is a book you can use to be a witness to others. In the following devotionals, you will learn how to use the *Wordless Book* yourself.

LIST THREE PEOPLE WHO NEED TO HEAR THE MESSAGE OF THE WORDLESS BOOK.

____

____

____

But God showed his great love for us by sending Christ to die for us while we were still sinners.
Romans 5:8

YOU CAN PRAY:

Dear God, help me to learn the message of the *Wordless Book* so I can share it with these three people. In Jesus' name. Amen.

June

17

WHAT CAN I TELL ON THE GOLD PAGE ABOUT GOD?

Each of the five colors of the Wordless Book tells a special part of the gospel. We begin with the gold page. This is what you can tell about God as you witness to a friend:

"This gold page reminds me of a place with a street of gold. It's called heaven and it is God's home. God is the Creator of this world. He made the sky, trees, flowers, birds, and animals. God made everything, and he made you. God loves you. The Bible says, 'For God so loved the world' (John 3:16). That means God loves you. Isn't that good news?

"Because God made you and loves you, he wants you to be a part of his family and be with him in heaven someday. Heaven is a perfect place, and God is perfect. That means he has never thought, said, or done anything wrong. God wants you to be with him in heaven someday, but there's one thing that will never be in heaven and that is sin."

This is the first part of the message you can share with someone. Practice telling the message of the gold page aloud until you can say it smoothly.

But God showed his great love for us by sending Christ to die for us while we were still sinners.
Romans 5:8

YOU CAN PRAY:

Dear God, thank you for loving me. Help me to tell others about your love with the gold page of the *Wordless Book*. In Jesus' name. Amen.

WHAT ARE THREE THINGS YOU CAN TELL A FRIEND ABOUT GOD WHEN YOU LOOK AT THE GOLD PAGE?

WHAT CAN I TELL ON THE DARK PAGE ABOUT SIN?

June
18

Many boys and girls where you live do not know who God is. They don't know that he created them, that he loves them, and that he has a plan for their lives. Perhaps no one has told them that the wrong things they do are called sin and that God hates sin. Turn to the black page in your *Wordless Book*. Here are some important things you can tell a friend about sin:

"Sin is anything you think, say, or do that displeases God. Lying, stealing, or disobeying are things that God calls sin. Having a bad attitude, saying mean and angry words, or destroying someone else's property is also sin. God's Word says, 'All have sinned' (Romans 3:23). That means you and I have sinned. You were born with a want to sin.

"God says that sin must be punished. That punishment is to be separated from God forever in a terrible place of darkness and suffering. But God has a wonderful plan so that you don't have to be punished for your sin."

Be sure to practice telling this part of the message, so you can tell it to a friend.

NAME THREE THINGS GOD TELLS US ABOUT SIN.

But God showed his great love for us by sending Christ to die for us while we were still sinners.
Romans 5:8

YOU CAN PRAY:
Dear God, help me to realize the seriousness of sin. Help me to be able to explain about sin to others. In Jesus' name. Amen.

June

19

WHAT CAN I TELL ON THE RED PAGE ABOUT JESUS?

But God showed his great love for us by sending Christ to die for us while we were still sinners. Romans 5:8

YOU CAN PRAY:

Dear God, help me to learn the message of the red page so I can tell others what Jesus did for them. In Jesus' name. Amen.

The red page of the Wordless Book tells about the Lord Jesus, God's perfect Son, and what he did so our sins could be forgiven. This is what you can say to a friend:

"God loved you and me so much that he didn't want us to be separated from him. In God's perfect plan, he sent his only Son, the Lord Jesus Christ, to be born on earth. Jesus lived a perfect life. He never sinned. When he grew to be a man, he allowed wicked men to put him to death on a wooden cross. This red page reminds me that as Jesus suffered, bled, and died on that cross, he was taking the punishment you and I deserve for our sin. The Bible says, 'Without the shedding of blood, there is no forgiveness of sins' (Hebrews 9:22).

"After Jesus died, he was buried. But Jesus, the all-powerful Son of God, did not stay dead. On the third day he came alive again. Now he is alive in heaven. Because of what Jesus has done for you, you can have your sins forgiven."

You'll want to practice the red page so you can tell your friends about God's wonderful plan to forgive their sins.

HOW DID GOD SHOW HIS LOVE FOR US?

HOW DO I USE THE CLEAN PAGE TO HELP SOMEONE BELIEVE IN JESUS?

June

20

Jesus has the power to forgive sin. That's the Good News of the gospel that you can share on the white page. You can share this verse from the Bible with your friend: "Believe on the Lord Jesus and you will be saved" (Acts 16:31). To explain this verse, remember three key words: Admit, Believe, and Choose. Here's what you can say:

"This verse (read Acts 16:31) means you need to admit you are a sinner. You need to tell God you *believe* (trust completely) in Jesus, who died for you, and that he came alive again. Then, you need to *choose* to let Jesus Christ be your Savior from sin. When you do this, the Lord Jesus promises he will forgive your sin. One day you will go to heaven to be with him. Would you like to believe in Jesus as your Savior?"

If your friend says "yes," you can help him pray, just like you did. If he says "no" or "I want to think about it," don't be discouraged. Pray for him, and remember that God has been pleased with your faithful witness. Practice this white page so you can help your friend believe in Jesus.

WHAT DOES SOMEONE NEED TO DO TO BE SAVED FROM SIN?

But God showed his great love for us by sending Christ to die for us while we were still sinners.
Romans 5:8

YOU CAN PRAY:

Dear God, help me to learn the message of the white page so I can help someone else to believe in Jesus. In Jesus' name. Amen.

June
21

HOW CAN I HELP SOMEONE KNOW HE'S BEEN SAVED?

But God showed his great love for us by sending Christ to die for us while we were still sinners.
Romans 5:8

YOU CAN PRAY:
Thank you, God, that you are the great promise keeper! In Jesus' name. Amen.

Has someone ever made a promise to you, then, at the last minute, he couldn't keep his promise? Our God never breaks a promise. He is a promise keeper!

The verse on the white page that you shared with your friend was Acts 16:31. Do you remember it? That verse is a promise from God. If your friend trusted the Lord Jesus Christ as his Savior, then God made him a promise. God promised in Acts 16:31 that your friend is saved. "Saved" means that God has forgiven his sin. God lives in your friend through his Holy Spirit to help him do right. One day, your friend will go to heaven to be with Jesus. That's a never-to-be-broken promise.

There's another promise you can share with your friend. It's found at the end of Hebrews 13:5 where Jesus says, "I will never fail you." Jesus promises to always be with you. You can talk to him anytime and anyplace. He is there to give you power to do what is right. Look at your hand. You can remember each word of Jesus' promise by your five fingers like this: "Jesus-will-never-leave-you." You can trust God to keep his promise!

WHAT CAN YOU SAY TO SOMEONE TO HELP HIM KNOW HE'S SAVED?

HOW CAN I HELP SOMEONE TO GROW IN CHRIST?

If your friend asked Jesus to forgive his sins and be his Savior, he needs to grow in God's family. This is what you can share on the green page of the *Wordless Book*.

"This green page reminds me of things that grow, like the grass, flowers, and trees. Now that you are part of God's family, he wants you to grow by learning more about him. You have his power and strength to do what is right. When you do something that is sin, God tells you in the Bible what you need to do. He says, 'If we confess our sins to him, he is faithful and just to forgive us' (1 John 1:9). 'To confess' means to name your sin and agree with God that you've done wrong. He will forgive you because that is what he promised to do. Ask him to give you the power and strength to obey him and do what is right.

"There are four things you can do to learn more about the Lord Jesus:

1. **Pray (talk) to God every day.**
2. **Read and obey the Bible.**
3. **Witness by telling others what Jesus has done for you.**
4. **Go to church and Sunday school."**

WHAT ARE SOME THINGS YOU CAN SAY TO HELP SOMEONE GROW IN CHRIST?

But God showed his great love for us by sending Christ to die for us while we were still sinners. Romans 5:8

YOU CAN PRAY:

Dear God, help me to learn how to use the green page of the *Wordless Book* to show others how they can grow in Christ. In Jesus' name. Amen.

June

23

WHO COULD I SHARE THE WORDLESS BOOK WITH?

Stop! The first thing you need to do before you share the *Wordless Book* is to pray. Make a list of people who don't know the Lord Jesus as Savior. Pray for each one by name. Ask God to make them ready to hear the gospel. If you don't have your *Wordless Book* with you, look around to see if you can find the colors in something else—maybe even your clothes!

Katie is nine years old. She has just learned how to use the *Wordless Book*. She began praying for the first person on her list, her cousin, Lisa. One day Katie showed Lisa her *Wordless Book*. She asked her if she had ever seen a book like that. Lisa said, "No." Katie asked Lisa what makes this book different from other books. Lisa looked at it carefully and said, "It has no words or pictures." Katie said, "But it has colors, and the colors tell the most wonderful true story from the Bible. Do you want to hear it?" Lisa said, "Sure!" Katie shared the *Wordless Book* with her, and Lisa trusted Jesus as her Savior! Now, Katie is praying for the next person on her list. What about you? Have you made your list?

But God showed his great love for us by sending Christ to die for us while we were still sinners.
Romans 5:8

YOU CAN PRAY:

Thank you, God, for the *Wordless Book*. Help me to share it with the people on my list. In Jesus' name. Amen.

WRITE A PRAYER TO GOD FOR ONE FRIEND WHO NEEDS TO HEAR ABOUT JESUS.

HOW DO I GIVE A TESTIMONY?

June
24

"Sara, would you be willing to give your testimony at church next Sunday night?" Pastor Carson asked. Giving a testimony means telling others how you came to trust the Lord Jesus as your Savior and what he means to you. Sara was a little scared about being asked to share her testimony, but when she thought about her wonderful Savior, she was willing to do it. She had never given a testimony before. Sara's Sunday school teacher helped her prepare.

They prayed and asked God for help, and then her teacher suggested she write her testimony. Sara wrote what her life was like before she trusted Jesus Christ as her Savior. Then she wrote where and how she made the decision to believe in him. Sara thought it would be important to include a Bible verse. She wrote out the verse, John 1:12. The last thing Sara wrote was how much Jesus means to her. She wrote about how he helps her to say no to sin and to obey God.

Sara then practiced saying what she had written. Now she was ready to share her testimony at any time with others. What about you? Would you be ready to share your testimony?

WRITE TWO IMPORTANT THINGS YOU WOULD WANT TO INCLUDE IN YOUR TESTIMONY.

If you are asked about your Christian hope, always be ready to explain it. But you must do this in a gentle and respectful way.
1 Peter 3:15-16

YOU CAN PRAY:
Dear God, help me to prepare my testimony and be willing to share it with others. In Jesus' name. Amen.

June

25

SHOULD I GIVE MY FRIEND A TRACT?

"A paper missionary"—that's what Carlos' Sunday school teacher called a tract. His teacher said that one way to be a witness for Jesus was to give tracts. Tracts are pieces of paper that tell people about sin and their need to trust the Lord Jesus as their Savior. Carlos' teacher set out some tracts and challenged the Christian kids to give one to a friend.

Carlos prayed for the courage to give his friend Luis the tract. Then he prayed that Luis wouldn't throw it away. Luis wanted Carlos to play street ball with some of the other kids. After the game, Carlos asked Luis if he wanted some lemonade. As they went into the kitchen, Carlos quietly prayed, "God, help me." Just before Luis left, Carlos ran to get his Bible. He took out the tract and told Luis to read it sometime. To Carlos' surprise, Luis sat down and read it. Luis asked, "Who is Jesus?"

For Carlos, giving a tract to Luis was one way of introducing him to Jesus. Do you know someone you could share a tract with? If you don't have a tract to share, maybe you could make one of your own!

If you are asked about your Christian hope, always be ready to explain it. But you must do this in a gentle and respectful way.
1 Peter 3:15-16

YOU CAN PRAY:
Dear God, help me to use tracts as a witness to others. In Jesus' name. Amen.

WHY SHOULD I GIVE MY FRIEND A TRACT?

HOW CAN I TELL THE GOSPEL WITH MY HAND?

June
26

You can use your hand to share the gospel with others. Here's how! Hold your hand up, point your thumb to yourself and say, "God loves me. God says in the Bible, 'I have loved you, my people, with an everlasting love' (Jeremiah 31:3)."

Then go to your pointer finger and say, "I am a sinner. The Bible says, 'For all have sinned' (Romans 3:23). My sin separates me from God."

Point to your tallest finger and say, "Jesus, God's perfect Son, died and came alive for me. The Bible says, 'Christ died for our sins, just as the Scriptures said. He was buried, and he was raised from the dead on the third day' (1 Corinthians 15:3-4). Jesus paid the payment for my sin."

Go on to the next finger and say, "I believe in the Lord Jesus as my Savior. The Bible says, 'Believe on the Lord Jesus and you will be saved' (Acts 16:31). I believe Jesus died for me."

Point to your little finger and say, "I am saved. The Bible says, 'All who believe in God's Son have eternal life' (John 3:36). I know that I will live forever with God."

Learn these Bible verses and practice sharing the gospel with your hand!

WHAT ARE THE FIVE IMPORTANT TRUTHS YOU CAN SHARE ON YOUR HAND?

If you are asked about your Christian hope, always be ready to explain it. But you must do this in a gentle and respectful way.
1 Peter 3:15-16

YOU CAN PRAY:
Dear God, help me to learn the important truths and verses I can share on my hand so that I will always be ready to be a witness. In Jesus' name. Amen.

June
27

WHERE COULD I INVITE MY FRIEND TO COME HEAR THE GOSPEL?

If you are asked about your Christian hope, always be ready to explain it. But you must do this in a gentle and respectful way.
1 Peter 3:15-16

YOU CAN PRAY:
Thank you, God, for places where I can invite my friends to hear the gospel. In Jesus' name. Amen.

Can you think of three places where you could take a friend to hear the gospel? Sunday school should be on the top of your list. If your church has a children's program, you could invite a friend to go with you. In the summer, a great place to bring a friend is to vacation Bible school. Another great place is a Christian camp. Some churches have programs especially for kids during their missionary conference. Sometimes churches will have children's rallies or fairs.

Is there a Bible club in your neighborhood? If not, maybe your family could start one! What a great witness that would be. Is there a Christian radio program in your area? You could invite a friend to listen with you.

Maybe you live in a place where people are not allowed to openly worship God and talk about the gospel. Perhaps people are even punished for following the Lord Jesus Christ. Pray and ask God to help you find ways to share about him with your friends. Even if you can't invite them to a special place to hear the gospel, you may be able to share with them from your own life.

WHERE COULD YOU INVITE A FRIEND TO HEAR THE GOSPEL?

IS MY LIFE A GOOD WITNESS TO OTHERS?

June
28

Witnessing is not just the words that you say. God says that the light of his love should shine through your life. Then others will be drawn to him (Matthew 5:16). Are your actions and attitudes a good witness to those around you, or do they keep others from wanting to believe?

Todd is a Christian. He's usually fun to be around. However, at home, whenever Todd doesn't get his way, he has a bad attitude. He becomes mean and angry. He makes his family miserable. What kind of a witness is Todd to his family? God can use your good attitudes and actions to show your family how the Lord Jesus controls your life. But bad attitudes or selfish behavior can ruin your witness.

Marissa was always inviting her friend Tina to Sunday school. She wanted Tina to hear about Jesus Christ. One day at school during a test, Marissa looked at someone else's paper for an answer. When she turned around, Tina was watching her. What kind of witness was Marissa's life?

If you want to be a good witness to your family and friends, remember that your actions and attitudes speak louder than your words. What kind of witness is your life?

HOW CAN YOUR LIFE BE A GOOD WITNESS?

If you are asked about your Christian hope, always be ready to explain it. But you must do this in a gentle and respectful way.
1 Peter 3:15-16

YOU CAN PRAY:

Dear God, help me to be a good witness for you by my actions and attitudes. In Jesus' name. Amen.

June

29

HOW CAN I HELP OTHERS GO WITH THE GOSPEL?

If you are asked about your Christian hope, always be ready to explain it. But you must do this in a gentle and respectful way.
1 Peter 3:15-16

YOU CAN PRAY:
Dear God, thank you for missionaries who take the gospel to many places. Help me to pray and give so that missionaries can go. In Jesus' name. Amen.

You can't witness to everybody in the world! However, there is a way you can share the gospel with people you will never meet. You can help to send a missionary. A missionary is a Christian whose life's work is telling others about the Lord Jesus. Some missionaries work in their own country. Others go to foreign countries.

How can you help missionaries to go with the gospel? First, pray for them. Ask God to send people that he chooses to be missionaries. When you pray for missionaries, think of the many needs they may have. Just like you, missionaries need food, clothing, and a place to live. They need medicine when they are sick. They need fuel for their cars. They need safety in dangerous places. Missionaries also need encouragement to face loneliness or other difficulties. They need courage to tell others about Jesus.

Another way you can help missionaries to go is to give money. You could give some of the money you have earned as an offering to the missionaries at your church. When you give your money to help missionaries, you are giving to God! What are you doing to help missionaries to go with the gospel?

WRITE THREE THINGS YOU CAN DO TO HELP MISSIONARIES GO WITH THE GOSPEL.

COULD I BE A MISSIONARY SOMEDAY?

June
30

Many missionaries knew when they were children that God wanted them to do that work. How did they know? They spent time with God each day to read his Word and pray. They attended church where they could learn more about God. Perhaps they read missionary stories. They were faithful witnesses right where they lived. Little by little, God put a strong desire in their hearts to do his work as full-time missionaries. Perhaps he even gave them a deep concern for a particular place or people.

Someday, God may ask you to be a missionary. You can prepare now by learning all you can about God. Read his Word and pray. Go to church whenever you can. Also, you can pray for and give to missionaries. Read missionary stories. Most importantly, be a faithful witness where God has placed you.

Don't worry that God will ask you to do something you don't like or something you can't do. If God wants you to be a missionary, he will give you the desire and the ability to do it. Ask God to give you a willing heart to obey him. Maybe one day God will ask you to be a missionary!

HOW MIGHT YOU KNOW THAT GOD WANTS YOU TO BE A MISSIONARY?

If you are asked about your Christian hope, always be ready to explain it. But you must do this in a gentle and respectful way.
1 Peter 3:15-16

YOU CAN PRAY:

Dear God, please help me to know if you want me to be a missionary someday, and then please give me a willing heart to obey you. In Jesus' name. Amen.

Activity 6: Witnessing

I CAN SHARE THE WORDLESS BOOK

Fill in the blanks below then practice sharing the story with a friend.

God __________ you. He wants you to be with him in heaven someday. (John 3:16)

All have __________ . You deserve God's punishment for sin. (Romans 3:23)

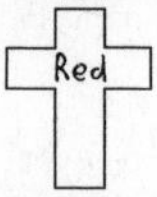

Jesus __________ on a cross and rose again to pay for your sin. (1 Corinthians 15:3-4)

Believe on __________ to save you from your sin. (Acts 16:31)

Grow to be more like Jesus: pray, read and obey the Bible, witness, go to church.

I'm asking God to help me witness to these people . . .

____

THINKING IT OVER!

Witnessing

Write the answers to these questions from your devotionals in the blanks.

1. What is witnessing?

____

2. Why should you witness about Jesus?

____

3. How can the things you do be a witness for God?

____

4. Who can you witness to?

____

5. How can you witness if you are going through hard things?

____

6. What is a missionary?

____

If you need help, you can look back in this month's devotionals. The number in ( ) tells you which devotional to check for each question. 1. (1) 2. (2) 3. (5) 4. (6) 5. (11) 6. (29)

JULY

Worshiping God

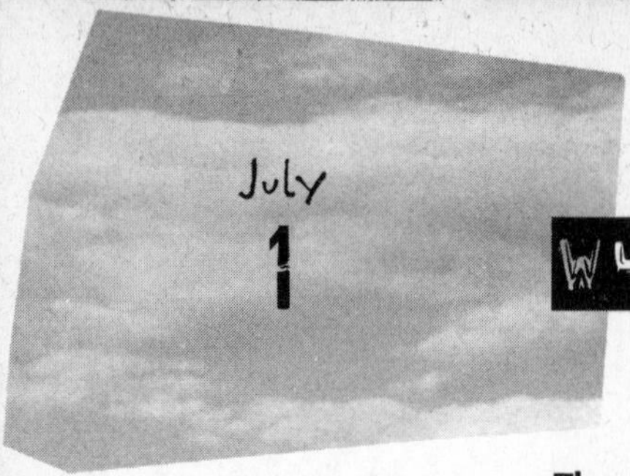

WHAT IS WORSHIP?

Draw close to God, and God will draw close to you.
James 4:8

YOU CAN PRAY:
Dear God, you *are* worth it! Help me to love and worship you more each day. In Jesus' name. Amen.

The young boy worked hard almost every afternoon, shining shoes for the people who passed by. No one ever paid him much, only a few cents for a good shine, but the boy didn't complain. He wanted to buy a bicycle! No matter how hard he had to work, it was worth it!

What is "worth it" to you? Take a look at how you spent your time last week, and you'll get a pretty good idea. Did you spend most of your time with friends? Watching TV? Playing on the computer? How much time did you spend with God? Did you *worship* him?

What is worship? Some people think worship is only what Christians do at church on Sundays, but worship is much more! Worship is showing God he is "worth it" to you. You can worship God as you sing songs, pray, and give money at church. You can also worship when you do ordinary things like obeying your parents. However, just doing those things isn't worship. Worship is doing those things in a way that shows God you think he's awesome. It's something you can and should do every minute of your life!

WHAT WILL YOU DO TO SHOW GOD HE IS WORTH IT TO YOU?

WHO CAN WORSHIP GOD?

July

2

On the outside, some things look almost the same. For example, how can you tell the difference between a raw egg and a hard-boiled one? Or between a dry orange and a juicy one? Sometimes you can only tell the difference by looking on the inside.

When God looks at those who worship him, he looks on the inside—he looks at their hearts. Only those who have received Jesus as their Savior can truly worship him. True worshipers are those who know that Jesus is the one and only way to God the Father.

What does God see when he looks at your heart? Does he see someone who is forgiven of their sins? Or does he see someone who needs to become his child? The Bible says, "But to all who believed him and accepted him, he gave the right to become children of God" (John 1:12). To become a child of God, you must have your sin forgiven. You can pray right now and believe in Jesus, who died and rose again for you.

If you have already received Jesus, you are God's child. The Holy Spirit lives in you. Now you can truly worship God as part of his family!

ARE YOU IN GOD'S FAMILY? HOW DO YOU KNOW?

Draw close to God, and God will draw close to you.
James 4:8

YOU CAN PRAY:

Dear God, I'm so glad I'm your child. Thank you for sending your Holy Spirit to always live inside me. In Jesus' name. Amen.

July
3

WHY SHOULD WE WORSHIP GOD?

Draw close to God, and God will draw close to you.
James 4:8

YOU CAN PRAY:
Dear God, help me to love and worship you more each day. In Jesus' name. Amen.

The candle was sad. Everything else in the house seemed useful, but not him. He had tried everything from propping open a door to stirring a pot of soup, but everything he did failed. Then, one dark day the master of the house struck a match and applied it to the little candle's wick. Instantly, a small flame took hold and filled the house with light! *Wow!* thought the candle. *Now I know what I was made for!*

Do you know what you were made for? The Bible teaches that God made you for himself—he made you to love, worship, and glorify him. His Word says, "Whatever you eat or drink or whatever you do, you must do all for the glory of God" (1 Corinthians 10:31). Although this world is full of things to enjoy, God wants you to enjoy him most of all.

The Bible says, "Draw close to God, and God will draw close to you" (James 4:8). You can come near to God by obeying his Word, the Bible, and spending time with him. God wants you to come near and worship him. God wants you to know him as a Father and a special friend, but God won't force you to come. It's your choice, and it's the best choice you'll ever make.

WHAT ONE THING WILL YOU DO RIGHT NOW TO COME NEAR TO GOD?

WHERE IS GOD?

Have you ever looked up to see the stars so high in the sky? God created each one—even the stars billions of light-years away! Isn't that amazing? You could never live long enough to visit just one of those faraway stars, but God can! In fact, God is there right now, just as he is here with you.

The Bible teaches that God is omnipresent. "I can never escape from your spirit! I can never get away from your presence!" (Psalm 139:7). He is there and here and everywhere else all at once! God is caring for hungry people in a distant country. He's also guiding presidents, and God is taking care of you.

Nothing is too big or too small for God to pay attention to. You may think you're not very important, but to God you are. He's been with you every second of your life! He's always been there loving you just as he is loving you now.

The next time you look at the stars, think about how God is omnipresent. You can be in only one place at a time, but God is everywhere, all the time! The more you realize that God is omnipresent, the more you'll want to worship him.

AS GOD WATCHES OVER YOU TODAY, WHAT'S ONE THING HE'D LIKE TO SEE YOU DOING?

Draw close to God, and God will draw close to you.
James 4:8

YOU CAN PRAY:
Dear God, I praise you for being omnipresent. It's good to know you always watch over me. In Jesus' name. Amen.

July 5

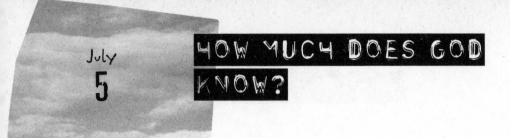

HOW MUCH DOES GOD KNOW?

Can you keep a secret? When someone tells you to be quiet about something, can you do it? Even if you're good at keeping secrets, there is always someone who knows. That someone is God!

God is not only omnipresent (everywhere), he is also omniscient (om-NISH-ant). God is all-knowing! God knows everything. He knew when and where you would be born. He knew who your parents would be. He knows easy things like your name and how old you are. He knows difficult things like how many hairs you have on your head. He even knows private things like your thoughts and your feelings.

Nothing can ever surprise God. He knows what will happen long before it does. He knows the future! The Bible says God knew how you would live every day of your life "before a single day had passed" (Psalm 139:16). God is there guiding and loving you as you live through each one!

Aren't you glad you don't need to hide things from God? You can come to him in worship and be who you really are. The more you realize that God is omniscient, the more you'll want to worship him.

Draw close to God, and God will draw close to you.
James 4:8

YOU CAN PRAY:
Dear God, I praise you for being omniscient. I'm glad you know everything there is to know. In Jesus' name. Amen.

WRITE DOWN TWO THINGS YOU'RE GLAD GOD KNOWS ABOUT YOU.

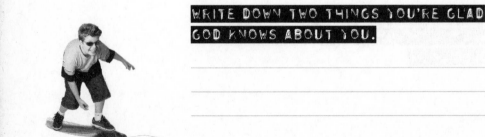

HOW MUCH CAN GOD DO?

July
6

Have you ever thought of what you could do if you had more power? What if you were stronger or quicker? What if you could stay awake all the time and never have to sleep? What if you could do *anything* you wanted to do?

Power can sometimes be a bad thing. Some people use their power to break the law or hurt others, but power can also be a good thing. Think of how God made this world in just six days. He made all the mountains, streams, animals, and people. Now that's power! The Bible teaches that God is *omnipotent* (om-NIP-oh-tent). He is all-powerful. He has power to do absolutely anything! And because God is good, he will never use his power to do wrong.

You can worship and thank God in every situation because he has power to help you. The Bible says, "If God is for us, who can ever be against us?" (Romans 8:31). God has power to help you make right choices. He has power to help you be joyful even in hard times. The more you realize that God is omnipotent, the more you'll want to worship him.

WHAT'S ONE WAY GOD HAS SHOWN HIS POWER IN YOUR LIFE?

Draw close to God, and God will draw close to you.
James 4:8

YOU CAN PRAY:

Dear God, I praise you for being omnipotent. Thank you for always using your power for good. In Jesus' name. Amen.

AM I A FRIEND OF GOD?

Draw close to God, and God will draw close to you.
James 4:8

YOU CAN PRAY:
Dear God, I want to be your friend. Help me to love you more than anyone or anything else. In Jesus' name. Amen.

How can you tell if someone is your friend? That person likes to spend time with you, to talk to you, and to listen to you. He says good things about you to others. You are important to him. Did you know that God wants you to be his friend? What does it mean to be a friend of God?

The Bible tells about a man named Abraham. He once worshiped false gods—gods that weren't real. Then, one day the true God spoke to him. Abraham believed in God and chose to obey him. Abraham was changed from a sinful man who didn't know God to one who knew him in a special way. The Bible says Abraham was a friend of God (Isaiah 41:8).

Maybe you're like Abraham. There was a time when you didn't know or worship God, but now you do. Would others say you're a friend of God? Do you love spending time with God each day? Do you say good things about him to others? Is he more important to you than anything else? When you know God as your friend, you'll want to worship him.

The Bible says, "Draw close to God, and God will draw close to you" (James 4:8). Come near to God today and be his friend!

WHAT'S ONE THING YOU WILL DO TO BE A FRIEND OF GOD?

CAN I WORSHIP GOD WHEN I'M ALL ALONE?

July 8

Do you remember what worship is? Worship is showing God he is "worth it" to you. You were made to worship God. He is omnipresent (everywhere), omniscient (all-knowing), and omnipotent (all-powerful)! He is more awesome than you could ever imagine, yet he loves you and wants to be your friend.

Can you worship God on your own? Yes! The Bible says, "Christ also suffered when he died for our sins . . . that he might bring us safely home to God" (1 Peter 3:18). Because Jesus died for your sins and rose again, you can talk directly to God through prayer. You can worship him even when no one else is there.

It's good to sing praise songs while someone plays music, but you can also sing to God all by yourself. You can even write your own songs like David did. He wrote many of the psalms (poems or songs) in the Bible! We can learn a lot from David's life. He loved and worshiped God in almost everything he did. In fact, the Bible says David was "a man after [God's] own heart" (1 Samuel 13:14).

Do you want to love and worship God that way? Today is a great day to start!

Draw close to God, and God will draw close to you.
James 4:8

YOU CAN PRAY:

Dear God, I love the time we spend together! Thank you for always being there. In Jesus' name. Amen.

WHAT'S ONE WAY YOU CAN WORSHIP GOD AS YOU'RE ALONE WITH HIM RIGHT NOW?

July
9

CAN I WORSHIP GOD TOGETHER WITH OTHER PEOPLE?

Draw close to God, and God will draw close to you.
James 4:8

YOU CAN PRAY:
Dear God, thank you for my brothers and sisters in Christ. Help us to burn brightly together for you. In Jesus' name. Amen.

Have you ever wondered why people go to church? God is everywhere, and you can worship God on your own. So why do you need to go to church and meet with other people? Wouldn't it be better to just worship by yourself?

God does want you to worship by yourself. But God also wants you to worship with other Christians. Worshiping together honors God as our King and Lord. It shows that we belong to him. God's Holy Spirit brings us together as brothers and sisters in Christ.

Worshiping God together also makes us stronger on the inside. We need each other. The Bible says, "Let us not neglect our meeting together . . . but encourage and warn each other" (Hebrews 10:25). Your Christian life is like a flaming branch. On its own, that branch will quickly burn out. But put that flaming branch with others, and the fire will burn longer and brighter. Spending time with others who believe in Jesus will help your life burn long and bright for God. Besides, others who believe in Jesus can be the best friends you'll ever have!

WHY DOES GOD WANT YOU TO WORSHIP WITH OTHER CHRISTIANS?

HAVE I TOLD GOD EVERYTHING?

July
10

Candace mixed the cookie dough together in a big bowl. She added flour, sugar, and eggs. She added all the other ingredients that make cookies so yummy. But she forgot to do one important thing before she began. She forgot to clean the bowl!

Sometimes you and I try to worship God that way. We forget to clean the bowl! We do all the right things we should do in worship, but we forget to make sure our lives are clean before we begin. Just like cookie dough mixed in a dirty bowl, unclean worship is not very good.

How can you make sure your life is clean? God gives the answer in his Word. He says, "But if we confess our sins to him, he is faithful and just to forgive us and to cleanse us from every wrong" (1 John 1:9).

Before you worship God, confess (agree with God about) the wrong things you've done. Thank him for his forgiveness. Ask him to help you not to do those things again. When you do that, God promises to forgive your sin and make your life clean again. You'll be ready to worship him in all the right ways—and with a clean life!

For God is Spirit, so those who worship him must worship in spirit and in truth.
John 4:24

YOU CAN PRAY:

Dear God, I know I have done things that are sinful. Thank you for your forgiveness. Help me to live my life for you. In Jesus' name. Amen.

WHY IS IT IMPORTANT TO CONFESS YOUR SINS TO GOD BEFORE YOU WORSHIP HIM?

July 11

WHAT IS THE RIGHT ATTITUDE FOR WORSHIP?

For God is Spirit, so those who worship him must worship in spirit and in truth.
John 4:24

YOU CAN PRAY:
Dear God, help me to honor you every day and to worship you with the right attitude. In Jesus' name. Amen.

How do you behave when you're with a very important person like the principal of your school or the pastor of your church? You're probably very careful to show respect in what you say and do. If you show respect for important people, how much more should you show respect for God? He is most important of all!

Did you know that God invites you to meet with him anytime? It's an incredible gift God gives you as his child. How should you come to God in worship? What should your attitude (your way of thinking and acting) be? The Bible says, "God is Spirit, so those who worship him must worship in spirit and in truth" (John 4:24). Because God is Spirit and you can't see him, it's easy to forget that he is right there with you. But he is always there. He is real and he is powerful. He deserves your reverence (honor and respect).

The Bible says, "The Lord is in his holy Temple; the Lord still rules from heaven" (Psalm 11:4). The next time you pray to God, remember that you are approaching the King who rules all of Creation. Honor him in your thoughts and the words you say.

HOW COULD YOU SHOW HONOR TO GOD?

DOES GOD WANT MY WORSHIP?

July
12

Someone has said, "Love makes the world go around." There's a lot of truth to that! Love is all around us and it's the one thing that gives meaning to life. Think of the love between family members and friends. Think of the love we feel for pets or things we do and places we live. Each of these forms of love is different.

Above all these loves is a special love reserved only for God. Because God made you and knows all about you, your love for him can be the deepest love you'll ever know. The way you show that love is through worship.

Does God really want your worship? Yes! God loves you as a perfect Father. He watches over you every second of your life. It's true that God can have anything he wants. He made all things and can do all things, but you are a special treasure to him. He wants your love and worship more than anything in the world. That's why one of the Bible writers named King David wrote these words: "Come, let us worship and bow down. Let us kneel before the Lord our maker" (Psalm 95:6). God longs for your worship.

For God is Spirit, so those who worship him must worship in spirit and in truth.
John 4:24

YOU CAN PRAY:

Dear God, I do love you. Thank you for inviting me to worship you. In Jesus' name. Amen.

WHY DOES GOD WANT YOUR WORSHIP?

July
13

CAN I HAVE A CONVERSATION WITH GOD?

Having a conversation with someone means talking and listening. Conversations can be wonderful, especially when you talk with a good friend. The best friend you could ever talk to is God!

You can talk to God through prayer. You don't have to use special words. You don't even have to speak aloud—you can just think the words, and God will hear them. If you're too upset to talk, you can even cry to God. He will always hear you and understand. No matter what you say, he will never stop loving you. He knows all about you and always knows how to help.

You can listen to God through his Word and his Holy Spirit. As you read the Bible, you'll learn about things that happened long ago. God will use those stories to tell you what he wants you to do today. As you make decisions each day, God will use his Holy Spirit to guide you. He won't speak to you with a voice you can hear, but he will help you to know deep inside when you should do something and when you should not. Have you had a conversation with God lately? Ask God to help you be a good talker and listener today!

For God is Spirit, so those who worship him must worship in spirit and in truth.
John 4:24

YOU CAN PRAY:
Dear God, help me to talk with you more and learn to listen as you talk to me. In Jesus' name. Amen.

WHY IS IT IMPORTANT TO BOTH TALK AND LISTEN TO GOD?

HOW DO I KNOW THE TRUTH?

If someone told you that all apples are red, would you believe him? Of course not! You can see for yourself that there are also yellow apples and green ones. But sometimes it's harder to know what's true and what isn't. How can you find out?

The first thing you must know is that all truth comes from God. The Bible says that God "cannot lie" (Titus 1:2). Everything he has written in his Word is true. In fact, God *is* truth! The Lord Jesus Christ, God the Son, said, "I am the way, the truth, and the life" (John 14:6).

The second thing you must know is that all lies come from God's enemy, Satan, the "father of lies" (John 8:44). Satan won't try to tell you that all apples are red, but he will try to make you believe God doesn't love you. He will try to lead you away from God and get you to sin.

You need to know God's truth. As you read God's Word, really think about what you're reading. Repeat in prayer to God what he has shown you. As God's truth begins to fill your mind, you'll have no more room for lies.

WHAT IS ONE TRUTH YOU'VE LEARNED TODAY THAT YOU COULD PRAY BACK TO GOD?

For God is Spirit, so those who worship him must worship in spirit and in truth.
John 4:24

YOU CAN PRAY:
Dear God, you are the truth. Thank you that I can trust you to never lie. In Jesus' name. Amen.

July

15

HOW CAN GOD AND I HAVE FUN TOGETHER?

For God is Spirit, so those who worship him must worship in spirit and in truth.
John 4:24

YOU CAN PRAY:
Dear God, thank you that you know all about fun. Help me to share my good times with you. In Jesus' name. Amen.

What does God know about fun? Lots! God is a spirit and he doesn't do some of the things you do, but God does know about fun. Remember that he's the Creator! He's the one who made laughter, good times, and fun! He wants you to enjoy life and the good things he has given you.

When you're alone and want a friend to play with, remember that God is right there with you. Talk to him and ask him to help you have fun right where you are. Then, find something to do and keep sharing that time with God. He loves just watching you grow and explore and learn new skills. He understands you and he loves to hear you laugh.

When you spend time with friends, you can have even more fun when you let God join you. Yes, God is right there with you. But you let him join you when you think about him and talk about how wonderful he is. There's a special joy you can share with other Christians just by being together. Talking about God as you work or play makes your time together that much more special.

WHAT WILL YOU DO TO HAVE FUN WITH GOD?

HOW DO I WORSHIP GOD?

Have you ever wanted to do something, but you just didn't know how? Maybe worship is like that to you. You're not quite sure how to do it.

The most important thing to remember about worship is that it's not what you do but why you do it. Worship is showing God he is "worth it" to you. When you set aside a special time to worship God, the first thing you must do is be sure you're doing it for the right reasons.

The next thing you must do is confess your sins. Your obedience is more important than your worship to God. When you confess your sins, God will forgive you and gladly welcome your worship from a clean life.

After that, you can read or remember verses from God's Word, pray, sing praise songs, or give to God in some other way. If you are worshiping with other Christians, there will be an order you follow so everyone worships together. When you're worshiping alone, you can really make the time personal and special. However you choose to worship, always be sure you are really worshiping God. Be sure you are letting him know he is worth it to you.

Come, let us worship and bow down. Let us kneel before the Lord our maker, for he is our God.
Psalm 95:6-7

YOU CAN PRAY:

Dear God, help me to show just how special you are to me. In Jesus' name. Amen.

WRITE THREE THINGS YOU CAN DO THE NEXT TIME YOU WORSHIP GOD.

WHAT IS PRAISING GOD?

Have you ever wondered what it means to praise God? Praising God is telling how much you appreciate him and the great things that he does. Praising God may sound difficult, but it's really one of the easiest things to do. You can praise God with prayers, songs, poems, or even by drawing pictures. You could praise him every moment of your life and still never run out of good things to say! The more you get to know God, the more you love him and realize he is good in every way.

Even though praising God is easy, it's something we need to practice. One simple way you can start praising God more is to use the alphabet. Tell God one thing you love about him, using each letter. You could say, "Thank you, God, for **a***lways* being there for me. You are **b***eautiful* in every way. I love the way you **c***are* for me. You **d***o* so many things for me each day." Then, continue with the rest of the letters.

The Bible says, "How good it is to sing praises to our God!" (Psalm 147:1). Take time right now to find out!

Come, let us worship and bow down. Let us kneel before the Lord our maker, for he is our God.
Psalm 95:6-7

YOU CAN PRAY:

Dear God, I think you're amazing! Help me to think of new ways every day to praise you. In Jesus' name. Amen.

CHOOSE THREE LETTERS AND WRITE WHAT YOU LOVE ABOUT GOD, USING EACH LETTER.

WHY SHOULD I PRAISE GOD?

July
18

Have you ever done something without knowing why you were doing it? Praising God should never be that way. Praising God isn't just something you do because you should. It isn't something you do so that God will do something for you. Praising God is a way of worshiping him. God commands us to praise him. He is worthy of all of your praise. But you should also praise God to show how much you love him.

The Bible says, "Come, let us sing to the Lord! . . . Come, let us worship and bow down. Let us kneel before the Lord our maker, for he is our God" (Psalm 95:1, 6-7). Praise comes from a joyful heart. It's easy to be joyful when you think of who God is and all he has done for you. The Lord is the one who created you. He is God and he rules heaven and earth. He is the perfect one who suffered and died on the cross for your sins and then rose again. What a great God he is! When you praise God, remember who he is and give him the worship he really deserves.

Come, let us worship and bow down. Let us kneel before the Lord our maker, for he is our God.
Psalm 95:6-7

YOU CAN PRAY:

Dear God, I praise you for being my God. Help me to always give you the praise you deserve. In Jesus' name. Amen.

WHAT ARE THREE REASONS WHY YOU SHOULD PRAISE GOD?

July
19

WHAT CAN I GIVE TO GOD?

Many people love the Christmas song about a little drummer boy. He was too poor to give a gift just right for the newborn King, but he did have one thing to give—his talent! The boy played his drum the best that he could. He knew that would please Jesus.

As God's child, what should you give? The Bible teaches that every good gift you have comes from God. Your money, clothes, home, family, friends—every good thing you have—comes from God. God wants you to give back some of what he gives as a way to show him you love and trust him.

You can give some of your money in the offering of your church. Instead of asking your parents for money, think of ways you can earn some money to give to God. You can also give time to God by helping at church or helping a neighbor. You can give your talents by singing or playing a musical instrument in a worship service or using some other skill for God.

There are so many ways you can give to God. Take time to thank him for all he has given and then joyfully give back to God in worship!

Come, let us worship and bow down. Let us kneel before the Lord our maker, for he is our God.
Psalm 95:6-7

YOU CAN PRAY:
Dear God, thank you for giving me so many good things. Help me to joyfully give back to you. In Jesus' name. Amen.

WRITE TWO OR THREE THINGS THAT YOU WILL GIVE TO GOD.

DOES GOD LIKE MUSIC?

July
20

Did you know that the Bible is filled with songs?
Whenever God's people wanted to praise him and celebrate, they sang songs to him. At other times, they sang sad songs as a way to express their feelings. Many of their songs are included in the Bible. In fact, a whole book of the Bible, the book of Psalms, is filled with such songs.

Does God like music? Yes! The Bible says, "Sing new songs of praise to him; play skillfully on the harp and sing with joy" (Psalms 33:3). God wants his people to use their skills to worship him with music.

Music was alive even before Creation. When God created the world, "the morning stars sang together and all the angels shouted for joy" (Job 38:7). God uses beautiful words to describe a similar celebration in nature: "The mountains and hills will burst into song, and the trees of the field will clap their hands!" (Isaiah 55:12). In heaven the songs continue as God's people sing praises to him.

God is the creator of music and he loves songs that honor him. When you sing songs that give praise to Jesus, you can be sure God is listening with joy.

WRITE YOUR OWN SHORT SONG OF PRAISE TO GOD.

Come, let us worship and bow down. Let us kneel before the Lord our maker, for he is our God.
Psalm 95:6-7

YOU CAN PRAY:
Dear God, help me to honor you in the music I sing and listen to. Teach me to praise you in song. In Jesus' name. Amen.

July

21

HOW CAN I PRAY?

Do you sometimes not know what to say when you pray? You want to talk to God, but you don't know how! One thing to remember is to be yourself. Talk to God in your own words and not someone else's. You don't need big fancy words or rhyming prayers. God wants to hear what *you* have to say.

Earlier in this book, you learned how to use the word ACTS to help you know how to pray. Can you remember what each letter stands for? (Go back and read the devotional for May 25 if you need help.) The **A** in *ACTS* stands for ______________________________ . Tell God how you love, honor, and respect him. Praise God for who he is and what he does. The **C** stands for ______________________________ . Tell God about the wrong things you have done and agree with him that they are sins. The **T** stands for ______________________________ . Express your gratitude to God for all the good things he does for you. The **S** stands for ________________________ . Ask God to provide for your needs and for the needs of others.

God is your heavenly Father. He wants you to talk to him about everything that concerns you. He delights in meeting your needs.

Come, let us worship and bow down. Let us kneel before the Lord our maker, for he is our God.
Psalm 95:6-7

YOU CAN PRAY:

Dear God, thank you that I can just talk to you as my Father and my best friend. In Jesus' name. Amen.

WHY SHOULD YOU TALK TO GOD IN YOUR OWN WORDS?

IS GOD ALWAYS RIGHT HERE?

July 22

Where is God? Some say he's up in heaven. Some people who know the Lord Jesus say he lives inside them. Some say God is very far away. All of those answers are right! God is omnipresent—he is everywhere at once.

If you know Jesus Christ as your Savior, you know God in a special way. The Bible teaches that God the Holy Spirit lives inside you! God has given you a special promise. In the Bible God says, "I will never fail you" (Hebrews 13:5). No matter what happens or what you do, God promises to always be with you.

Here's another promise to think about. The Bible also says, "The Lord is my helper" (Hebrews 13:6). Not only is God always with you, he is always there to help! He wants you to depend on him to guide your life. He wants you to let him help you with big things and small things. He is able to always give the help you need.

When you remember that God is always with you, it makes a big difference. You can know that he's always there to help, and you can worship him wherever you go.

Come, let us worship and bow down. Let us kneel before the Lord our maker, for he is our God.
Psalm 95:6-7

YOU CAN PRAY:
Dear God, thank you that you will never leave me. Thank you for always being there to help. In Jesus' name. Amen.

WHAT WILL YOU DO DIFFERENTLY TODAY BECAUSE YOU KNOW GOD IS WITH YOU?

July
23

WHY DOES GOD SOMETIMES SEEM FAR AWAY?

Come, let us worship and bow down. Let us kneel before the Lord our maker, for he is our God.
Psalm 95:6-7

YOU CAN PRAY:
Dear God, thank you that you are always with me. In Jesus' name. Amen.

If God is always with you, why does he sometimes seem far away? One reason may be sin. When you sin, you hurt your relationship with God. You are still his child, but God wants you to confess your sin to him and thank him for his forgiveness.

Do you remember God's promise about confessing sin? The Bible says, "But if we confess our sins to him, he is faithful and just to forgive us and to cleanse us from every wrong" (1 John 1:9). You need to agree with God that you have sinned and ask him to help you do what is right. When you do that, God promises to forgive your sin and make you clean. Then your relationship with God will be close again.

God may also seem far away when you are discouraged or sick. You may not understand how God is working in your life. Even in times like these, you can know that God is still with you and is caring for you.

The next time God seems far away, remember his promise to be with you always (Matthew 28:20). Tell God how you feel and ask him to help you to trust him.

WHAT CAN YOU DO WHEN GOD SEEMS FAR AWAY?

WHAT IS THE BODY OF CHRIST?

July
24

When the Lord Jesus lived on earth, he had a human body. He lived in that body and did many great things. Now that Jesus lives in heaven, he does great things through a different kind of body called the body of Christ.

A body can sometimes be a group of people. When we talk about the body of Christ, we're not talking about Jesus' human body. We're talking about a group of people who represent Jesus Christ. These people are Christians—men, women, boys, and girls who have trusted Jesus as Savior.

In the Bible, the body of Christ is compared to a human body so we can understand it. In a human body, the head does the thinking and tells the other body parts what to do. In the body of Christ, Jesus is the "head" or leader. He is the one who guides the people who make up the "parts" of his body. These people do different things, but they are all part of one group.

If you're a Christian, you're in the body of Christ! Have you ever thought of that? You belong to Jesus, your "head," and every other Christian is part of the body with you.

But if we are living in the light of God's presence, just as Christ is, then we have fellowship with each other, and the blood of Jesus, his Son, cleanses us from every sin.
1 John 1:7

YOU CAN PRAY:

Dear God, thank you that I'm part of your body. Help me to do what you say. In Jesus' name. Amen.

HOW SHOULD CHRISTIANS IN THE BODY OF CHRIST TREAT EACH OTHER?

July

25

AM I IN THE BODY OF CHRIST?

Now that you know what the body of Christ is, you need to know if you're part of it!

The Bible teaches that "all have sinned" (Romans 3:23). When you steal, tell a lie, or do some other wrong thing, you sin. God is holy (sinless) and he must punish sin. That punishment is separation from God forever.

The only person who never sinned was Jesus Christ, God the Son. Because he loves you, he was willing to pay for your sin. He did it by letting himself be hung on a cross, where he suffered, bled, and died. His body was buried in a tomb, but three days later he came back to life. Today he's alive in heaven, and he wants you to join him someday.

The only way you can be forgiven and know you are going to heaven is to trust Jesus as your Savior. Tell God that you're sorry for your sin and believe Jesus died for you. Ask the Lord Jesus to come into your life and be your Savior. God promises to forgive your sin and help you live for him. When you trust Jesus as your Savior, you become part of the body of Christ.

But if we are living in the light of God's presence, just as Christ is, then we have fellowship with each other, and the blood of Jesus, his Son, cleanses us from every sin.
1 John 1:7

YOU CAN PRAY:

Dear God, thank you that I can be part of the body of Christ by trusting in your Son as my Savior. In Jesus' name. Amen.

WHAT DID JESUS DO SO THAT YOU COULD BE PART OF THE BODY OF CHRIST?

WHERE IS THE BODY OF CHRIST?

July
26

When you trust the Lord Jesus as your Savior, you become part of the body of Christ. Sometimes the body of Christ is called the church. All Christians (those who have trusted the Lord Jesus Christ as Savior) are also part of this body. This large group of Christians lives all over the world. On earth you will never meet most of these Christians, but you belong to the same group.

Each person in the body of Christ needs to be part of a local church. Some Christians meet in buildings called churches. Others meet in homes or in other buildings. Where you meet isn't as important as what you do when you're together. The main reason to get together with others in the body is to worship God. The body also gets together to learn more about God and his Word, to encourage each other, and to help each other become more and more like Jesus. God's plan is for you to be an active part of the local church.

Isn't it great to know there are Christians not only where you live but all around the world? What a wonderful privilege it is to be part of the body of Christ!

But if we are living in the light of God's presence, just as Christ is, then we have fellowship with each other, and the blood of Jesus, his Son, cleanses us from every sin.
1 John 1:7

YOU CAN PRAY:
Dear God, thank you for Christians all over the world that make up the body of Christ. In Jesus' name. Amen.

WHY DO YOU NEED TO BE PART OF A LOCAL CHURCH?

IS THERE A RIGHT WAY TO WORSHIP IN THE BODY OF CHRIST?

But if we are living in the light of God's presence, just as Christ is, then we have fellowship with each other, and the blood of Jesus, his Son, cleanses us from every sin.
1 John 1:7

YOU CAN PRAY:
Dear God, help me learn to worship with others in the body of Christ. I want to always honor you. In Jesus' name. Amen.

In a family, people are joined together in a special relationship. The people in the family can be loud or quiet, careful or clumsy, loving or selfish. They can be different in so many ways and yet be part of one family.

The body of Christ is like that. We all belong to the Lord Jesus Christ and yet we are different. One important way we are different is in our worship. Some Christians worship together in a loud and joyful way while others are quiet. Some like to move around while others like to be still. Some worship several hours while others have a shorter worship time. With so many differences, is there a right way to worship?

The answer is yes! Worship that pleases God comes from a person whose heart is right with him. The Bible says we are to worship God "in spirit and in truth" (John 4:24). Whenever an obedient Christian gives honor and praise to God through the Lord Jesus, he is worshiping in the right way. The way someone else worships might look wrong to you, but God knows that person's heart attitude.

HOW CAN YOU WORSHIP GOD THE RIGHT WAY?

CAN I DO ANYTHING SPECIAL IN THE BODY OF CHRIST?

July
28

When you trusted Jesus as your Savior, God gave you some skills called spiritual gifts. You read about them earlier in this devotional book. God wants you to use these gifts to serve him and others in the body of Christ.

If you have the gift of serving, you enjoy helping others. If you have the gift of *giving* you like to give your money, time, or talents to help meet needs. The gift of *mercy* helps you comfort others who are hurting. If you enjoy studying God's Word and sharing what you've learned with others, you may have the gift of *teaching.* If you like to organize projects and get others involved, you may have the gift of *leading.*

Each of these gifts is important. What if everyone in the body of Christ had the gift of leading? What if no one had the gift of giving or mercy? God is very wise to give different gifts to different people. He wants all of us to use our gifts. If you don't know what your spiritual gifts are, ask God to show you. As you begin serving God, you'll soon find what God has gifted you to do.

WHAT SPECIAL THING CAN YOU DO TO HELP THE BODY OF CHRIST?

But if we are living in the light of God's presence, just as Christ is, then we have fellowship with each other, and the blood of Jesus, his Son, cleanses us from every sin.
1 John 1:7

YOU CAN PRAY:

Dear God, thank you for giving me spiritual gifts to serve you. Help me to find out what they are. In Jesus' name. Amen.

July

29

HOW CAN I USE MY GIFTS?

But if we are living in the light of God's presence, just as Christ is, then we have fellowship with each other, and the blood of Jesus, his Son, cleanses us from every sin.
1 John 1:7

YOU CAN PRAY:

Dear God, help me to find the best ways I can use my gifts to serve you. In Jesus' name. Amen.

Do you know what your spiritual gifts are? If you're a new Christian, you probably don't! But you can find out. The best way to find out is by serving God. Your spiritual gifts are often things you enjoy and do well. Let's think about some of the spiritual gifts and how they might be useful in your church.

If you have the gift of serving, maybe you help set up chairs for a meeting or clean up when it is over. If you have the gift of giving, you enjoy bringing your offering to church—especially when there is a special project. If you have the gift of mercy, you may want to visit someone who is sick, just to sit and keep him company. If you have the gift of teaching, you might decide to teach a Sunday school class. If you have the gift of leading, you enjoy being in charge of projects like organizing a special get-together for your class.

Whatever way you choose to use your spiritual gifts, be sure you use them with love. As you use your gifts to help others, you'll be serving God well and having a great time while doing it.

WRITE HOW YOU COULD USE ONE OF YOUR SPIRITUAL GIFTS IN YOUR CHURCH.

July
30

WHAT IS FELLOWSHIP?

The Bible says that as Christians we can have fellowship with God and one another. Do you know what fellowship is and how you can have it?

Fellowship is a lot like friendship. It means caring about someone and talking with him. It means spending time together because you want to. Like friendship, fellowship comes from having something in common. What do Christians have in common? The Lord Jesus Christ. Because we know Jesus, we can all have a special love for God and each other.

Making friends can be hard because others may not always accept you. However, as a Christian you are already accepted because Christ accepts you! His love in you and other Christians allows you to have fellowship with God and one another. It's like having friends wherever you go. God is a friend who will never leave you, and other Christians can also be your closest friends.

As you worship God today, think about your fellowship with him. The God who made you wants to have a special friendship with you. He loves you more than anyone ever could! He's multiplied his love by giving you fellowship with other Christians.

WHY DO YOU THINK FELLOWSHIP WITH GOD AND OTHER CHRISTIANS IS IMPORTANT?

But if we are living in the light of God's presence, just as Christ is, then we have fellowship with each other, and the blood of Jesus, his Son, cleanses us from every sin.
1 John 1:7

YOU CAN PRAY:

Dear God, thank you for the fellowship I can have with you and with my brothers and sisters in Christ. In Jesus' name. Amen.

July
31

WHY DO I NEED FELLOWSHIP?

As a Christian, you have received many good gifts from God. He's given you so many good things that it's easy to miss out on some. One gift we sometimes forget is fellowship. We don't realize what a wonderful gift it is!

The Bible says, "As iron sharpens iron, a friend sharpens a friend" (Proverbs 27:17). When we fellowship with other Christians, they make us stronger and better. If we're not careful, many things in life can turn us away from God. We need fellowship with other Christians to keep us strong in him.

Friends who aren't Christians can sometimes lead you astray. The Bible says, "Bad company corrupts good character" (1 Corinthians 15:33). People who aren't Christians may not do many bad things, but because they don't believe in Jesus Christ, they look at the world in a different way. They depend on money, things, and other people to make them happy. As a Christian, you know that the Lord Jesus is the true source of happiness.

God knows you need fellowship to be strong as a Christian. Good fellowship with other Christians begins in fellowship with him. Take time today just to enjoy your friendship with God. Worship him!

But if we are living in the light of God's presence, just as Christ is, then we have fellowship with each other, and the blood of Jesus, his Son, cleanses us from every sin.
1 John 1:7

YOU CAN PRAY:
Dear God, thank you for your gift of fellowship! Help me to enjoy my fellowship with you and other Christians. In Jesus' name. Amen.

WHY DO YOU NEED FELLOWSHIP?

THE MEMORY ZONE

Here are some great Bible verses about what you've learned so far. Put a check mark in the box as you memorize each one!

- ❑ **Psalm 34:3** "Come, let us tell of the Lord's greatness; let us exalt his name together."
- ❑ **James 3:9-10** "Sometimes [the tongue] praises our Lord and Father, and sometimes it breaks out into curses against those who have been made in the image of God. And so blessing and cursing come pouring out of the same mouth. Surely, my brothers and sisters, this is not right!"
- ❑ **1 Corinthians 10:31** "Whatever you eat or drink or whatever you do, you must do all for the glory of God."
- ❑ **Hebrews 10:25** "And let us not neglect our meeting together, as some people do, but encourage and warn each other, especially now that the day of his coming back again is drawing near."
- ❑ **Psalm 11:4** "But the Lord is in his holy Temple; the Lord still rules from heaven. He watches everything closely, examining everyone on earth."
- ❑ **Psalm 33:1, 3** "Let the godly sing with joy to the Lord, for it is fitting to praise him. . . . Sing new songs of praise to him; play skillfully on the harp and sing with joy."
- ❑ **Proverbs 27:17** "As iron sharpens iron, a friend sharpens a friend."
- ❑ **Revelation 7:12** "Amen! Blessing and glory and wisdom and thanksgiving and honor and power and strength belong to our God forever and forever. Amen!"

Activity 7: Worshiping God

I LOVE TO WORSHIP GOD

Write a prayer of worship below, using the letters to form words describing God. Then fill in the remaining blanks with thoughts that express your love.

Dear God,
You are . . .

A ______________________ B ______________________

C ______________________ D ______________________

E ______________________ F ______________________

G ______________________ H ______________________

I'm so glad you're my God because ______________________

____

Thank you for ______________________

____

In Jesus' name. Amen.

THINKING IT OVER!

Worshiping God

Write the answers to these questions from your devotionals in the blanks.

1. Who can truly worship God?

____

2. What does it mean that God is omnipresent?

____

3. What does God use his power for?

____

4. How does worshiping God with others help you?

____

5. What are some ways you can worship God?

____

6. What does it mean to be in the body of Christ?

____

If you need help, you can look back in this month's devotionals. The number in ( ) tells you which devotional to check for each question. 1. (2) 2. (4) 3. (6) 4. (9) 5. (16) 6. (24)

AUGUST

Obeying God

August
1

WHO SHOULD I OBEY?

I will hurry, without lingering, to obey your commands.
Psalm 119:60

Chad was watching TV. His mom came into the room, stopped a minute, and said, "I don't want you to watch that program, Son." Chad changed the channel. Did he obey? Yes! However, as soon as Mom left the room, he switched back to see the rest of the program. Ooops! The Bible says, "You children must always obey your parents, for this is what pleases the Lord" (Colossians 3:20).

Emily listened as her coach explained a new rule. "That is just so dumb," Emily muttered. Later, she chose to break the rule. Is this a good idea? The Bible says, "Obey your leaders and submit to their authority" (Hebrews 13:17, NIV). Leaders include teachers and coaches. Leaders may be camp counselors, the police—even the president. You have lots and lots of leaders.

The greatest Leader we have is God himself. He asks us to obey him. Then he gives us the power to do what he says. King David wrote, "Give me understanding and I will obey your law; I will put it into practice with all my heart" (Psalm 119:34). When you obey the leaders God gives you, you are obeying one of God's commands. Will you choose to do it today?

YOU CAN PRAY:
Dear God, I want to obey your commands. Help me to listen to my parents and my other leaders, and help me to do what they say. In Jesus' name. Amen.

LIST SOME OF THE PEOPLE GOD WANTS YOU TO OBEY.

WHY SHOULD I OBEY GOD?

August
2

It is easy to make a l-o-n-g list of what God wants you to do: Be nice to people. Pray. Tell the truth. Tell others about Jesus. Obey your parents.

What a list! Can you add other things? The hard part is to hasten (or hurry) and not delay (wait) to do those things. God wants you to pay attention to what the Bible says. Then he wants you to choose to obey cheerfully.

When you fail to obey God, you cannot expect him to answer your prayers. You cause unhappiness for yourself and probably for other people. Most of all, you disappoint the God who loves you and sent Jesus to be your Savior.

Why should you obey God? In the Bible Jesus says, "If you love me, obey my commandments" (John 14:15). The main reason you should obey God is because you love him. Tell God you want to obey him. Ask God to give you the power to obey him. What will happen when you obey God's commands? The Bible says, "You know these things—now do them! That is the path of blessing" (John 13:17). Obeying God will bring you joy in your life here on earth. Obeying God will bring you rewards in heaven.

I will hurry, without lingering, to obey your commands.
Psalm 119:60

YOU CAN PRAY:

Dear God, I need your strength to obey all of your commands today. Help me to choose to obey you and do what is right. In Jesus' name. Amen.

WHAT ARE SOME OF GOD'S COMMANDS THAT ARE HARD FOR YOU TO OBEY?

August
3

HOW DO I OBEY GOD'S COMMANDS?

I will hurry, without lingering, to obey your commands.
Psalm 119:60

YOU CAN PRAY:
Dear God, I love you and want to obey your commands. Please show me what you want me to do, and help me to obey quickly. In Jesus' name. Amen.

Chris heard about a really great job. It would help him earn the money he needed for a new racing bike. However, he was disappointed to learn that he would have to work every Sunday morning when he normally goes to church. Now Chris would have to make a choice. He loves God and really wants to obey him.

If you love God, you'll want to obey him too. First you need to know what God's commands are. As you read his Word each day, try to understand what he is saying to you. You may even want to memorize Bible verses so that you will remember his commands. Also, you need to listen carefully whenever someone is teaching from the Bible. When you discover a command in God's Word, ask him to help you obey it right away. Your love for God will be seen in your quick obedience to his commands.

In his quiet time, Chris discovered Hebrews 10:25, which says, "Let us not neglect our meeting together." Chris realized that he needed to put God first. He decided not to take the job so that he could be in God's house on Sunday mornings. Chris was quick to obey God's command.

HOW CAN YOU OBEY GOD'S COMMANDS?

IS IT MY FAULT?

"But, Mom," Steve pleaded, "I've got to head for the park now. They've probably already started choosing teams. If I don't get there soon, I'll be left out."

Mom looked at Steve. She didn't say anything. She didn't have to. Steve's mom never changed her mind about room cleaning. Not ever! Steve was accountable for this job. That meant it had to be done. Sometimes he tried to shift the blame for not doing a job by saying something like, "I didn't do it because my teacher gave us too much homework." Homework or not, Steve needed to do his jobs.

You are accountable for some jobs too. Being accountable means you are responsible for your thoughts and actions. When you get lazy or you choose to disobey and leave a job undone, whose fault is it? It is your fault! Most important, the Bible says that each of us will have to answer to God (Romans 14:12). God tells you in the Bible what he wants you to do. He expects you to obey him. He gives you the power to do what is right. Don't blame others when you fail to do what you're supposed to do. You are accountable!

I will hurry, without lingering, to obey your commands.
Psalm 119:60

YOU CAN PRAY:
Dear God, help me to remember that I'm accountable to you. Give me the strength to obey you quickly and with a right attitude. In Jesus' name. Amen.

IF YOU REMEMBER PSALM 119:60, HOW WILL IT HELP YOU?

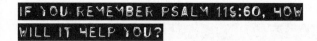

August
5

WHAT HAPPENS IF I DON'T OBEY GOD?

I will hurry, without lingering, to obey your commands.
Psalm 119:60

YOU CAN PRAY:
Dear God, don't let me be like Jonah. I want to obey you. Thank you for loving me and for helping me to do the right things. In Jesus' name. Amen.

Jonah loved God. God told Jonah to go to Nineveh. Very bad people lived in Nineveh, but God still loved them. Jonah was to tell them how they could have their sins forgiven.

Jonah knew God's command. Did he "hurry, without lingering, to obey"? No! He hurried and ran the other way. By disobeying God, Jonah caused problems for other people. He also got into big trouble. He was swallowed by a big fish. God kept him inside that fish for three days. Jonah sure had time to think about what a bad plan it was to disobey God.

Disobeying God is a bad plan for you, too. When you choose to do something wrong, you grieve the Holy Spirit. Because you love God, you shouldn't want to grieve his Spirit. Also, disobeying God makes you feel sad inside. You do not feel like talking to God or reading the Bible. You may get into trouble. Plus, you miss the real happiness that comes from choosing to obey God.

Jonah was sorry he did not obey God. When you choose to disobey, another person will not always know, but God will know. God knows everything. You will know too, and, like Jonah, you will be sorry.

WHY IS IT SUCH A BAD IDEA TO DISOBEY GOD?

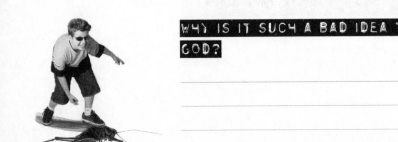

WHAT HAPPENS IF I DO OBEY GOD?

August
6

Just think! In heaven, we will get to meet David. We learn quite a lot about him in the Bible. He was a shepherd. He played the harp. He killed the giant Goliath. He was a king. God inspired him to write many of the psalms in the Bible.

David really loved God and chose to obey him. David said, "I have tried my best to find you—don't let me wander from your commands" (Psalm 119:10). What a great prayer!

When you choose to obey God, he says your life will be longer and happier. Also, you will get to know God and worship him better. Other people will notice that you are honest, kind, and loving, and that you work hard. They will notice that you're full of joy! They will want to know why you are so different. Obeying God makes it possible for you to tell people that Jesus, your Savior, has changed your life.

So many people worry. Obeying God gives you peace in your heart. David had peace in his heart, even when he faced that giant. Why? Because he did not delay to obey God's commands. Will you choose to obey God, today and every day?

WHY ARE PSALM 119:60 AND PSALM 119:10 GOOD VERSES TO REMEMBER?

I will hurry, without lingering, to obey your commands.
Psalm 119:60

YOU CAN PRAY:
Dear God, I want to be like David and seek you with all my heart. Don't let me stray from your commands. In Jesus' name. Amen.

August
7

WHEN I OBEY GOD, WILL GOOD THINGS ALWAYS HAPPEN?

I will hurry, without lingering, to obey your commands.
Psalm 119:60

YOU CAN PRAY:
Dear God, help me to choose to obey you even when bad things happen. I do trust you, God. Thank you for promising to help me. In Jesus' name. Amen.

Isn't it nice when people say good things about you? Imagine God saying something good about you! Here is what God said about a man named Job: "He was blameless, a man of complete integrity" (Job 1:1). Job was a man who obeyed God with all his heart.

Since Job loved God and chose to obey him, did that mean good things always happened to Job? No! His animals were stolen. His servants were killed. His 10 children died in a storm. Wow! Job lost everything. He didn't know why God let all those bad things happen. But God gave Job the strength to get through those problems.

When you choose to obey God, even in the hard times, others see the special strength God gives you. Problems could turn you away from God. Instead, God uses problems to help you trust him more and more. God promises he will never leave you (Hebrews 13:5). Remembering that will help you when bad things happen.

It would be great if everything would always be wonderful for those who choose to obey God. But things won't always be great—they weren't for Job. Job learned that God would get him through very bad days. You need to learn that too.

WHAT CAN YOU DO WHEN BAD THINGS HAPPEN?

WHY DOES GOD OPPOSE PRIDE?

Kevin couldn't resist. He raced around the block, the metal on his new bike sparkling. Knowing people were watching, he jumped the curb and pedaled faster. He heard Josh call, "Hey, Kev! Wait up! Let me see your bike," but Kevin stuck his nose in the air and rode right by. Kevin was proud of his new high-powered wheels. He circled and rode past Josh a second time. *Josh will never have a bike this great,* he thought. *Plus, I'm the best rider!*

Do you like people to notice you? "Look what I did!" "Watch me!" "See what I have!" "I'm so-o-o good!" God opposes you when you have those proud thoughts. Why? Because you call attention to yourself and not to your God. You take all the credit for what God has helped you to do or to get. God hates pride!

Pride is thinking too highly of yourself. It's right to be pleased when you get good grades, score the winning point, or have something new. Thank God for it, but don't be proud. Proud people expect others to praise them. They act bossy and even rude. Jesus did not have a "notice me" attitude. Neither should you.

God sets himself against the proud, but he shows favor to the humble.
James 4:6

YOU CAN PRAY:
Dear God, forgive me for the times I've acted proudly. Thank you for what you have given me and for what you help me to do. In Jesus' name. Amen.

WHY IS IT WRONG TO BRAG ABOUT SOMETHING YOU OWN OR SOMETHING YOU CAN DO?

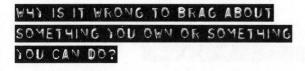

August
9

WHAT DOES IT MEAN TO BE HUMBLE?

It's hard to believe! Jesus was with his disciples. Read what happened: "He got up from the table, . . . wrapped a towel around his waist, and poured water into a basin. Then he began to wash the disciples' feet and to wipe them with the towel" (John 13:4-5).

Jesus, God the Son, washing feet! At that time, people wore sandals. Roads were very dusty. When anyone came to visit, a servant had to wash feet. Was this a great job? No! Did servants like to do it? No! Did someone ask Jesus to wash feet? No!

Jesus chose to do this job to show he was not too proud to be a servant. Jesus had a humble heart. A humble person cares more about others than he cares about himself. He does not have a problem with pride. To be humble, like Jesus, you must be willing to help someone who has a need. Even if no one says, "Thanks!" or "Great job!" Even if no one notices you. It's hard! We want people to praise us and give us prizes.

God will help you. Look for ways to serve others. Don't expect everyone to pay attention to you. Follow the example of Jesus.

God sets himself against the proud, but he shows favor to the humble.
James 4:6

YOU CAN PRAY:
Dear God, help me to learn how to serve you with a humble heart. Help me to be a humble servant to someone today. In Jesus' name. Amen.

WHO CAN YOU SERVE TODAY, AND WHAT CAN YOU DO FOR THEM?

AM I PROUD OR HUMBLE?

Would you like to have a name like Nebuchadnezzar (Neb-you-kad-NEZ-ur)? Imagine learning to spell it. Whew!

Nebuchadnezzar was a king. He made a huge gold statue of himself. Everyone had to bow down and worship his statue. King Nebuchadnezzar was proud. Pride is a serious sin. The Bible says, "Pride leads to disgrace, but with humility comes wisdom" (Proverbs 11:2).

Proud King Nebuchadnezzar was disgraced. For seven years, he became like an animal. He crawled on the ground and ate grass (Daniel 4:33). Really! God tells us about Nebuchadnezzar to show us he hates pride.

If you brag about what you can do or what you have, you have a pride problem. God wants you to be humble, not proud. God made you. Without God, you cannot do any good thing. Give God the credit for all you have and all you can do. Look for ways to help people. Be happy when others win a game. By choosing to be humble, you may get to tell others about your wonderful Savior.

Humbly honoring God will fill your life with blessings. Pride can destroy you. Look what happened to Nebuchadnezzar.

WHEN PEOPLE COMPLIMENT YOU, HOW CAN YOU HUMBLY ANSWER THEM?

God sets himself against the proud, but he shows favor to the humble.
James 4:6

YOU CAN PRAY:

Dear God, I want to quietly help others even if no one notices me. When people say something nice about me, help me to give you the credit. In Jesus' name. Amen.

August
11

WHAT IS A LAZY PERSON?

Are you lazy? A lazy person waits and waits to start doing his work. This makes other people angry or sad. Do you do this?

A lazy person sits and sits, thinking about this and that. He should be listening to the teacher or studying a lesson. Do you do this?

A lazy person hurries through his work. He does such a bad job that he has to do it over. Do you do this?

Lazy Christians do not work to learn more about God. They do not memorize Bible verses. They do not read the Bible and pray. What about you?

Lazy people are not willing to work hard or to get jobs done on time. They think only about themselves and what they want. They forget about people who are counting on them. Worst of all, they forget about God. The Bible says, "Lazy people are soon poor" (Proverbs 10:4).

Don't be lazy! Work with all your heart. Because you belong to God, he will help you with whatever you do. He wants you to choose to do your jobs right away. This will please other people. Best of all, this will please God.

Work hard and cheerfully at whatever you do, as though you were working for the Lord rather than for people.
Colossians 3:23

YOU CAN PRAY:
Dear God, I don't want to be lazy. Help me to do my very best on each of my jobs. I choose to work for you. In Jesus' name. Amen.

WHAT ARE THREE THINGS YOU KNOW YOU SHOULD DO THIS WEEK?

WHAT IS A DILIGENT PERSON?

August
12

Your parents probably tell you things like, "Do your homework. Clean your room. Practice the piano." Can you add to that list? It is tempting to say, "Not now" or "I don't feel like it." A diligent person starts working right away. A diligent person works hard to finish a job and do it well.

Proverbs 13:4 says, "Lazy people want much but get little, but those who work hard will prosper and be satisfied." Lazy people want many things. They do not get them because they do not work for them. Diligent people often get what they want because they work hard.

Diligent people get busy clearing the dishes off the table instead of sitting and pouting about it. Diligent people get up on time instead of being too late to even make their bed. Diligent people take care of their clothes instead of throwing them on the floor. It doesn't take very long to do these jobs. Be diligent!

Choose to work to please God, not just other people. Do not complain about what you have to do. Do the very best you can because God wants you to. When you're tempted to be lazy, remember Colossians 3:23. Then smile and get started!

Work hard and cheerfully at whatever you do, as though you were working for the Lord rather than for people.
Colossians 3:23

YOU CAN PRAY:

Dear God, I want to be a diligent person. When I am tempted to be lazy, help me to remember Colossians 3:23. In Jesus' name. Amen.

WHAT ARE SOME JOBS GOD HELPED YOU TO DO DILIGENTLY THIS WEEK?

August
13

WHAT WILL HAPPEN IF I AM DILIGENT?

Work hard and cheerfully at whatever you do, as though you were working for the Lord rather than for people.
Colossians 3:23

YOU CAN PRAY:
Dear God, help me to be diligent in everything I do today. Help me to work with all of my heart to please you. In Jesus' name. Amen.

God tells lazy people they should watch ants. Really! No one says to ants, "Do this!" or "Go there!" Ants just do what they are supposed to do. Because they work hard all summer, they have the food needed for winter. No one says to ants, "Great job!" or "Let me pay you!" Ants work and work even though no one pays attention to them. The Bible says, "Take a lesson from the ants, you lazybones. Learn from their ways and be wise!" (Proverbs 6:6).

If you are diligent, you may not get any money for your hard work. People may not even notice. But God will know! Remember that whatever you do, you are working for the Lord. God is pleased when you do your work with all your heart. He will see that your needs are met.

You can become a better Christian by being diligent. Learn new Bible verses. Review verses you already know. Read God's Word every day. Take time to pray. You should not wait for someone to tell you to do this. Just be diligent and do it.

Diligent people see jobs that need to be done and they do them. Remember that's what ants do!

WHY DOES GOD TELL US TO STUDY THE ANTS?

WHY IS IT IMPORTANT TO MAKE RIGHT CHOICES?

August
14

Julie's teacher asked, "How many brothers and sisters do you have?"

Julie said, "Three," but in her mind she added, Sort of. Julie and her older brother have the same dad. Her mom never married their dad. Then there is Andy. Julie's mom never married Andy's dad either. Later, Julie's mom got married and had a child named Brenda. Now her mom and Brenda's dad are divorced.

Julie's mom has filled her life with wrong choices. Julie is determined to ask God to show her which man to marry. Julie wants to fill her life with right choices so she can serve the Lord.

Making right choices means obeying God's Word. You have to make choices many times each day: Will I obey my mom? Will I read my Bible? Will I work hard in school? Will I tell the truth? Wrong choices make you feel sad and sometimes scared. Wrong choices disappoint God.

Make right choices day by day. This will help you make right choices for very important things later in life, like "Who will I marry?" The wrong choice—all wrong choices—will cause problems for you and for many other people. Julie could tell you that is true.

WHY IS IT SO IMPORTANT TO CHOOSE THE RIGHT PERSON TO MARRY?

Choose today whom you will serve. . . . But as for me and my family, we will serve the Lord.
Joshua 24:15

YOU CAN PRAY:

Dear God, I need your help to make right choices today, and I need your help for the big decisions I'll have to make later. In Jesus' name. Amen.

August
15

HOW CAN I KEEP FROM MAKING THE WRONG CHOICES?

Choose today whom you will serve. . . . But as for me and my family, we will serve the Lord.
Joshua 24:15

YOU CAN PRAY:
Dear God, help me to obey your Word and listen to the Holy Spirit so I won't make bad choices. In Jesus' name. Amen.

Suppose when you needed to make a choice, you could say, "Should I watch this TV program?" If God liked your choice, a special light would turn green—Go! If not, the light would be red—Stop!

This would be so-o-o great. "Should I invite Sean to my house?"—Green! "Should I visit this Web site?"—Red! "Should I eat spinach?"—Red . . . well, maybe green!

Some choices are very important: Whom should I choose for friends? How will I act when others make fun of me? Paying attention to God's Word and deciding to obey it every time will help you make right choices.

When you don't know what God wants you to do, ask a godly Christian to help you. A godly person reads and obeys the Bible, prays, and goes to church. He talks about the Lord Jesus Christ. Others notice he lives to please God.

There is no "right choice" light, but God does give you the Holy Spirit to live inside you. The Spirit guides your thoughts and helps you make right choices. When God shows you what to do, be sure you obey. Knowing what to do and choosing not to do it would be a very bad choice.

WHAT ARE THREE THINGS YOU CAN DO TO HELP YOU MAKE RIGHT CHOICES?

WHAT IF I MAKE THE WRONG CHOICE?

August
16

Sometimes wrong choices are mistakes. Sometimes wrong choices are on purpose. King David made a wrong choice on purpose. He wanted to marry Bathsheba. She was already married. David told the commander of his army to put her husband up front on the battlefield so he would be killed. Then David married Bathsheba. Perhaps David thought he could get away with choosing to sin.

Nathan, a prophet of God, knew what David had done. He showed David the terribleness of his sin. David confessed his sin to God. God forgave David, but he also punished him. David and Bathsheba's first baby died.

When you choose to do wrong, don't think, "So what? I'll confess my sin to God. He will forgive me." Bad things happen because of sin. When you choose to disobey your parents or your teacher, you may have to stay in your room or miss an important game. Sin ruins your chance to talk to people about Jesus because they will not trust what you say.

Don't think you can sin on purpose and get away with it. It didn't work for David, and it will not work for you. Confess your sin to God and do what's right.

WHAT HAPPENS IF YOU CHOOSE TO DO WRONG?

Choose today whom you will serve. . . . But as for me and my family, we will serve the Lord.
Joshua 24:15

YOU CAN PRAY:
Dear God, thank you for reminding me that wrong choices will cause trouble in my life. Help me to make right choices. In Jesus' name. Amen.

August
17

WHAT IS GODLY COUNSEL?

Joash was seven years old when he became the King. When he was given the crown, "the people clapped their hands and shouted, 'Long live the king!' " (2 Kings 11:12). How could little Joash know what to say and do to lead so many people? What a lot of pressure! He needed help from wise people who loved God.

You are not the king of a country, but you, too, have lots of pressure. How do you know what to say? How do you know what to do? Like Joash, you need godly counsel.

Godly counsel—help in knowing what to do—comes from people in your life who know God's Word better than you do. In Proverbs 22:17, God says, "Listen to the words of the wise." To know people who love the Lord Jesus Christ is a great gift from God. God may give you parents, teachers, pastors, Sunday school teachers, and older Christians to teach you. There are books written by godly people that can help you know what to do.

Because Joash listened to godly counsel, he became a wise king. Will you listen to those who can help you become wise?

Listen to the words of the wise.
Proverbs 22:17

YOU CAN PRAY:

Dear God, help me to listen to godly counsel so I can become a wise person. In Jesus' name. Amen.

WHO ARE SOME PEOPLE WHO COULD GIVE YOU GODLY COUNSEL?

WHY IS GOOD COUNSEL IMPORTANT?

August
18

God chose Moses to be a leader. People knew that God spoke to Moses. Therefore, when they had arguments or questions, people came to him for good counsel. Day after day, from morning until evening, people lined up to talk to him. Moses was getting tired.

Jethro, his father-in-law, told Moses this was too much for him to do alone. Jethro said, "Let me give you a word of advice" (Exodus 18:19). He told Moses to assign other godly men to help him. Moses listened to Jethro's good counsel and followed his advice. With other men now helping him, Moses' job became easier.

It is wise to listen to what good counselors say. They can stop you from making mistakes. They can explain things in the Bible you don't understand. They can help you make right decisions like choosing good friends or joining the right club.

Even as you become wiser, there will still be things for you to learn. Moses was a leader, but he needed good counsel. Proverbs 9:9 says, "Teach the wise, and they will be wiser." Keep studying God's Word. Obey what it says. Then, someday you will be able to give good counsel to many people.

WHAT ARE SOME THINGS YOU COULD LEARN FROM A GOOD COUNSELOR?

Listen to the words of the wise.
Proverbs 22:17

YOU CAN PRAY:
Dear God, I praise you for people who can give me good counsel. Help me to listen to them and to your Word. In Jesus' name. Amen.

August

19

HOW CAN I TELL BAD COUNSEL FROM GOOD COUNSEL?

Listen to the words of the wise.
Proverbs 22:17

YOU CAN PRAY:
Dear God, please help me to decide if people are giving me bad or good counsel. Then help me to choose to do what is right. In Jesus' name. Amen.

"Come on," Jed yelled. "Follow the leader." As Jed jumped on his bike, Randy followed and tried to trace Jed's path. Down the sidewalk. Across the street. Down one driveway and up the next.

Both boys stopped at a busy intersection to catch their breath. That was as far as either boy was allowed to ride. But Jed started walking his bike across the highway saying, "Let's keep going!" Randy wanted to follow, but he knew it was a bad idea because God tells us in Ephesians 6:1 to obey our parents.

Like a bad idea from a friend, bad counsel does not feel right. God's Holy Spirit lives inside you to help you know if the counsel someone gives you is right or wrong. The Spirit reminds you of things you have heard from God's Word. Good counsel always agrees with God's Word. The more of God's Word you learn, the easier it will be for you to tell bad counsel from good counsel.

The right thing to do may not always be the most fun. Randy knew that. He may have wanted to follow Jed, but he decided to go home. Will you ask God to help you know and do what is right?

HOW DOES THE HOLY SPIRIT HELP YOU DECIDE IF COUNSEL IS GOOD OR BAD?

WHY DO PEOPLE COMPLAIN?

August
20

Do you ever say things like, "This is a dumb assignment; I don't see why we have to do it." "You never choose me. It's my turn." "Are we having *that* for dinner again? I hate it!" "Do this! Do that! Why do I have to do so much work?" "How come he gets to go, but I don't?"

Complain! Complain! Complain! When you complain, you forget God is in control. You forget God loves you. You forget God promised to give you whatever you need. Complaining shows you are selfish. Complaining makes you unhappy, and other people do not want to be around you. It is impossible to complain and please God at the same time. Why? Because God says, "Always be joyful" and "No matter what happens, always be thankful."

Each time you are tempted to complain about food, homework assignments, clothes, jobs, or anything else, stop and see if you can say something good instead. Be happy you have something to eat. Be thankful if you are well and can go to school, do your work, or play a game. Ask God to help you say words that show you really believe God is good.

Always be joyful. Keep on praying. No matter what happens, always be thankful, for this is God's will for you who belong to Christ Jesus.
1 Thessalonians 5:16-18

YOU CAN PRAY:
Dear God, please help me to stop complaining and to be thankful instead. In Jesus' name. Amen.

WRITE SOMETHING YOU'VE COMPLAINED ABOUT THAT TURNED OUT TO BE GOOD.

August 21

WHAT DOES GOD THINK ABOUT COMPLAINING?

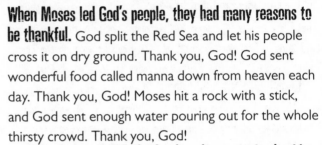

Always be joyful. Keep on praying. No matter what happens, always be thankful, for this is God's will for you who belong to Christ Jesus.
1 Thessalonians 5:16-18

YOU CAN PRAY:
Dear God, help me to be thankful and to stop complaining. In Jesus' name. Amen.

When Moses led God's people, they had many reasons to be thankful. God split the Red Sea and let his people cross it on dry ground. Thank you, God! God sent wonderful food called manna down from heaven each day. Thank you, God! Moses hit a rock with a stick, and God sent enough water pouring out for the whole thirsty crowd. Thank you, God!

"Thank you, God!" That's what those people should have said over and over and over. Do you know what they did instead? They complained, saying, "We need more water! We're tired of manna! We need a new leader."

They even complained about God. Because of this sin, God sent snakes to punish them—many poisonous snakes that bit people! Many people died. Moses prayed and God answered by making a way for them to be forgiven for their sin of complaining (Numbers 21:5-9).

The Bible says, "In everything you do, stay away from complaining and arguing" (Philippians 2:14). Notice it says, "In *everything* you do." When you complain, you forget God promised to give you whatever you need. God is in control and he loves you. Be joyful, give thanks, and stop complaining!

WHY DO YOU THINK THAT COMPLAINING IS A SIN?

HOW CAN I BE THANKFUL?

August
22

"I hate my clothes!" Rachel shouted. "What's wrong with them?" Stacy asked. "I think you always look nice." Rachel frowned at her friend. "They're all so old!" she exclaimed. "I never have anything new. I just get my sister's old clothes when she grows out of them. I know my parents don't have a lot of money, but I want new clothes like everybody else!"

Like Rachel, when you complain about something, you act like God doesn't know what he is doing. Don't think that way! Stop for a moment and think about God. Remember that God is love, and he loves you. God is wise, and he knows what is best for you. God is powerful, and he can help you.

Give thanks to God for all the great things he has done for you. The Bible says, "Always give thanks for everything to God the Father" (Ephesians 5:20). Sing a song to praise him instead of complaining. Say the words "I will" and then quote 1 Thessalonians 5:16-18. Do this whenever you feel like complaining about your clothes, your family, the weather, schoolwork, or whatever. You can be thankful if you will choose to be.

Always be joyful. Keep on praying. No matter what happens, always be thankful, for this is God's will for you who belong to Christ Jesus.
1 Thessalonians 5:16-18

YOU CAN PRAY:
Dear God, help me to be thankful today instead of complaining. In Jesus' name. Amen.

HOW CAN YOU REMEMBER TO BE THANKFUL INSTEAD OF COMPLAINING?

August
23

WHAT IS GOSSIP?

Don't use foul or abusive language. Let everything you say be good and helpful, so that your words will be an encouragement to those who hear them. Ephesians 4:29

YOU CAN PRAY:
Dear God, please help me not to gossip about other people. Help me always to use words that build up others. In Jesus' name. Amen.

During a break at vacation Bible school, Rachel carried her snack to the picnic table where Kirsten was sitting. As soon as she sat down, she lowered her voice and whispered, "Did you hear that Marcia failed her Bible memory test?" Kirsten whispered back, "She did? I thought she was smart."

Rachel said, "She's lazy. Look! She's coming this way! Her hair is a mess today." Kirsten added, "And she's wearing that awful pink shirt."

Does this sound like talk that would please God? Are Rachel and Kirsten saying words that would build up Marcia? No! This is what Ephesians 4:29 calls "foul or abusive language." This is gossip.

Gossip should never come out of your mouth. Gossip is saying unkind (and often untrue) things about other people. Gossip is sin. You can try to stop others when you hear them gossip. For example, if Rachel told you about Marcia's bad test you could say, "What could we do to help her with the next test?" When someone says unkind words about another person, you could say, "It isn't right to talk that way." Then, change the subject. Do everything you can to stop gossip.

WHY DO YOU THINK GOD CALLS GOSSIP A SIN?

WHAT DOES GOSSIP DO?

August
24

Dave and Tim were best friends until last summer. Dave made the soccer team. Tim didn't. Tim was angry, hurt, and jealous. So Tim said some words to other people he never should have said.

Tim told Dustin, "The only reason Dave made the soccer team is because his dad is friends with the coach." He told Sarah, "Dave will ruin the soccer team. He's too fat to run fast." Soon Dave heard what Tim was saying about him. Then he was hurt and angry. Dave and Tim were no longer friends. The Bible says in Proverbs 16:28, "Gossip separates the best of friends."

People who gossip tell your secrets. Tim told Dave that he felt so bad about not making the team that he cried. Should Dave tell others about that? No! Proverbs 11:13 says, "A gossip goes around revealing secrets, but those who are trustworthy can keep a confidence."

God hears the words you say when you gossip. He knows the harm you have done. One day God will ask, "Why did you say that?" God says in Matthew 12:36, "And I tell you this, that you must give an account . . . of every idle word you speak." Remember that, and you will not gossip.

Don't use foul or abusive language. Let everything you say be good and helpful, so that your words will be an encouragement to those who hear them.
Ephesians 4:29

YOU CAN PRAY:

Dear God, help me to be careful about the words I say and to remember that you are always listening. In Jesus' name. Amen.

HOW MIGHT GOSSIP HURT YOUR FRIENDSHIPS?

August
25

HOW CAN I BUILD UP OTHERS?

Do you know what your name means? A man in the Bible had a name with a very special meaning. His name was Barnabas, and his name meant "son of encouragement." Isn't that a great name? The Bible tells us that Barnabas did just what his name says—he built up other people by encouraging them.

We first meet Barnabas in the New Testament, right after Saul (later called Paul) became a Christian. People were afraid of Saul. In Acts 9:26-27 we learn that Barnabas took Saul to other believers, told them Saul was now a Christian, and said they didn't need to be afraid of him anymore. Barnabas encouraged Paul when they traveled together. Barnabas encouraged people to listen to God's Word and believe it. Barnabas encouraged people to live for the Lord.

Are you an encourager like Barnabas? You can be! Encourage people by saying things like: "You did a great job!" "Thanks for working so hard!" "I like being on your team!" "God loves you and so do I." "I'm glad I know you!" "You are a great friend!"

The Lord Jesus Christ living in Barnabas helped him to build up others. He can do the same for you!

Don't use foul or abusive language. Let everything you say be good and helpful, so that your words will be an encouragement to those who hear them. Ephesians 4:29

YOU CAN PRAY:

Dear God, help me to build up others by encouraging them. In Jesus' name. Amen.

WHAT WILL YOU SAY TO BUILD UP SOMEONE TODAY?

WHAT DOES IT MEAN TO MISUSE GOD'S NAME?

August
26

Storm clouds fill the sky. It is getting darker and darker. The wind is really blowing. You watch out the window. All of a sudden, you see a twisting funnel-shaped cloud. You yell, "Oh, God, it's a tornado!"

However, in saying, "Oh, God," you are not even thinking about the true and living God. You are not talking to the one who has the power to make storms and to stop them. You are misusing God's name.

Maybe you are watching a TV program. A family is having a big argument. In anger, one person spits out the words "Jesus Christ." The words are not said with love or respect. The words are not used to help those listening think of our wonderful Savior. This person is misusing the name of the Lord.

When you misuse the name of the Lord, you say "God" and "Lord" and "Jesus Christ" as empty words, even angry words. God is real! God the Son, the Lord Jesus Christ, suffered and died for us. Now Jesus is alive! It is very, very wrong to use names of God as just words. You should feel sad whenever you hear someone do this.

Do not misuse the name of the Lord your God. The Lord will not let you go unpunished if you misuse his name.
Exodus 20:7

YOU CAN PRAY:
Dear God, your name is wonderful. Help me to honor your name and to never misuse it. In Jesus' name. Amen.

WHY IS IT WRONG TO MISUSE GOD'S NAME?

August
27

WHY SHOULD I BE CAREFUL ABOUT MY WORDS?

The Bible has much to say about speaking. Read the verses on this page carefully. Read them more than once.

"Harsh words stir up anger." (Proverbs 15:1)

"Some people make cutting remarks, but the words of the wise bring healing." (Proverbs 12:18)

"And so blessing and cursing come pouring out of the same mouth. . . . This is not right!" (James 3:10)

"Those who control their tongue will have a long life; a quick retort can ruin everything." (Proverbs 13:3)

"If you claim to be religious but don't control your tongue, you are just fooling yourself, and your religion is worthless." (James 1:26)

Words are powerful. Your mouth can praise God or misuse his name. What you say can help people or hurt them. The words you use can tell people how they can become a Christian. People listen to what you say. When you, as a Christian, misuse God's name, people will not forget it. They may never believe you when you try to tell them that the Lord Jesus wants to be their Savior. It may not seem fair, but people remember the bad things you say longer than the good things, so be careful with your words!

Do not misuse the name of the Lord your God. The Lord will not let you go unpunished if you misuse his name.
Exodus 20:7

YOU CAN PRAY:
Dear God, help me to remember that my words can hurt people or help them. Help me to speak only the words that please you. In Jesus' name. Amen.

WHY ARE YOUR WORDS IMPORTANT TO GOD?

HOW CAN I HAVE "WISE" LIPS?

August 28

Mandy likes to talk a lot! She talks about what she did yesterday and what she wants to do tomorrow. She talks about people and places. She talks about sports, homework, her computer, TV programs, church, vacations, things she likes, and things she doesn't like.

Do people who talk so much have "wise" lips? Proverbs 10:19 says, "Don't talk too much, for it fosters sin. Be sensible and turn off the flow!" Why would God say to be quiet? Because every time you speak it is possible you will say something untrue, unkind, or unimportant. Also, when you talk so much, people may stop listening. The Bible says, "Let your words be few" (Ecclesiastes 5:2).

Queen Esther wanted to speak to the king. She had a plan to save God's people from being killed (Esther 4–5). She had to think and pray so she would say exactly the right words. She had "wise" lips. How can you have "wise" lips? The Bible says, "Take control of what I say, O Lord" (Psalm 141:3).

Be careful what you say. Use words to help people. Use God's name in a right way. Remember this: Pray more! Listen more! Talk less!

HOW CAN LISTENING, INSTEAD OF TALKING, HELP YOU TO HAVE "WISE" LIPS?

Do not misuse the name of the Lord your God. The Lord will not let you go unpunished if you misuse his name.
Exodus 20:7

YOU CAN PRAY:

Dear God, help me to know when to talk and when to be quiet. I want to have "wise" lips. In Jesus' name. Amen.

August
29

WHAT DOES IT MEAN TO BE LOYAL?

Naomi, her husband, and their two sons left their home in Bethlehem and traveled to Moab. While living there, Naomi's husband died. Her sons got married, choosing Ruth and Orpah. Then, both sons died. What a sad time it must have been.

Naomi decided she would return to Bethlehem. Ruth and Orpah started out with her. Naomi told the two women to go back to their homes (Ruth 1:6-14).

Orpah went home, but Ruth said to Naomi, "I will go wherever you go and live wherever you live. Your people will be my people, and your God will be my God" (Ruth 1:16). Ruth was loyal to Naomi and to her God.

Loyalty is being faithful to those who deserve your love and support. Christians are to be loyal to God first of all. Also, Christians should be loyal to family and friends, except when those people choose to disobey God over and over.

When you are loyal to a person, you stand up for him when someone is mean to him. You say good things about him. You help him when he is in trouble. That's what Ruth did. Because of her faithful loyalty, she was blessed richly. Will you follow the wonderful example of Ruth?

The trustworthy will get a rich reward.
Proverbs 28:20

YOU CAN PRAY:
Dear God, please help me to be loyal to my family and friends. Mostly, help me to be loyal to you. In Jesus' name. Amen.

HOW CAN YOU SHOW LOYALTY TO A FRIEND THIS WEEK?

HOW CAN I BE LOYAL TO GOD?

August
30

The trustworthy will get a rich reward.
Proverbs 28:20

YOU CAN PRAY:

Dear God, thank you for loving me. Even when it is hard, I want to be loyal to you. In Jesus' name. Amen.

Jason was a Christian. He wanted to be loyal to God. Matt sat right behind him at school. He poked Jason with a pencil, sneered at him, and whispered, "Don't get mad, Jason. If you're a Christian, you'll forgive me!" Then he poked him again and laughed.

What would you do if someone like Matt teased you because you are a Christian? It takes strength greater than your own to stay loyal to God. God can give "grace to help us when we need it" (Hebrews 4:16).

Loyal Christians read the Bible and pray each day. They go to church faithfully. It is easier to stay loyal to God when you spend time with other Christians. Christian friends help each other live for God. The real test of your loyalty to God is your obedience to him.

It will be hard for you to be loyal to God if you have close friends who do not love and serve God. That's why Jason did not choose Matt for a close friend. But Jason and his friends pray for Matt. That pleases God. Be loyal to God and obey him with all of your heart.

HOW CAN YOU SHOW GOD YOU ARE LOYAL TO HIM?

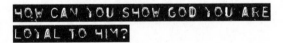

WHY IS IT IMPORTANT TO BE FAITHFUL?

The trustworthy will get a rich reward.
Proverbs 28:20

YOU CAN PRAY:

Dear God, help me to faithfully use my money, time, and talents to serve you. I want to be someone others can depend on. In Jesus' name. Amen.

When you know you should do something, but you don't feel like doing it, what do you say to yourself? "I'm too-o-o tired!" or "I want to do something else" or "This is the right thing to do and God will help me do it!"

When you tell yourself something like that last thought, you are learning to be faithful. Faithfulness means staying true to God in your thoughts, words, and actions. What does Proverbs 28:20 say? Being faithful to God brings his blessing—joy—to your life!

When you say you are a Christian but you are not faithful, people don't trust you. They don't want to be like you. They don't want to hear the important things you should be telling them about God.

When you are faithful, people can see God has made a difference in your life. You use your money wisely. You use your time to help other people. You study the Bible and go to church. You use your talents (the things you do well) to serve God.

There is great joy in choosing to obey God. When you trust God to help you be faithful, you will be blessed richly. God says so!

WHY IS IT HARD, SOMETIMES, TO BE FAITHFUL?

THE MEMORY ZONE

Here are some great Bible verses about what you've learned so far. Put a check mark in the box as you memorize each one!

- ☐ **Psalm 119:34** "Give me understanding and I will obey your law; I will put it into practice with all my heart."
- ☐ **Hebrews 13:17** "Obey your spiritual leaders and do what they say. Their work is to watch over your souls, and they know they are accountable to God. Give them reason to do this joyfully and not with sorrow. That would certainly not be for your benefit."
- ☐ **James 1:22** "And remember, [God's message] is a message to obey, not just to listen to. If you don't obey, you are only fooling yourself."
- ☐ **Proverbs 11:2** "Pride leads to disgrace, but with humility comes wisdom."
- ☐ **Philippians 2:14-15** "In everything you do, stay away from complaining and arguing, so that no one can speak a word of blame against you. You are to live clean, innocent lives as children of God in a dark world full of crooked and perverse people. Let your lives shine brightly before them."
- ☐ **Psalm 119:9** "How can a young person stay pure? By obeying your word and following its rules."
- ☐ **Philippians 4:8** "Fix your thoughts on what is true and honorable and right. Think about things that are pure and lovely and admirable. Think about things that are excellent and worthy of praise."
- ☐ **Psalm 141:3** "Take control of what I say, O Lord, and keep my lips sealed."

Activity 8:
Obeying God

I CHOOSE TO OBEY

Find the false statement below and cross out the letter in front of it. Use the remaining letters to fill in the blanks.

V I will have joy.

H Good things will always happen.

O God will reward me.

L My life will be happier.

Obeying God shows that I ___ ___ ___ E him.

When it's hard to obey God I . . .

____

____

____

THINKING IT OVER!

Obeying God

Write the answers to these questions from your devotionals in the blanks.

1. Why should you obey God?

____

2. What will people notice if you are obeying God?

____

3. Why should you work hard and carefully?

____

4. Where can you get help to make right choices?

____

5. What should you do instead of complaining?

____

6. What will you do if you are loyal to someone?

____

If you need help, you can look back in this month's devotionals. The number in ( ) tells you which devotional to check for each question. 1. (2) 2. (6) 3. (12) 4. (15) 5. (20) 6. (29)

SEPTEMBER

Living for God

September
1

WHAT DOES GOD SAY ABOUT RESPECTING LIFE?

Thank you for making me so wonderfully complex!
Psalm 139:14

YOU CAN PRAY:
Dear God, thank you for making me in your image. Help me to respect my life and the lives of those around me. In Jesus' name. Amen.

Has anyone ever told you, "You look just like your dad" or "You have your mother's smile"? Why is that? You were born with certain qualities that make you like your parents.

Just as there are family likenesses, God, the Creator, made all people in his likeness. The Bible says, "God created people in his own image" (Genesis 1:27). How are you made in God's image? You have a personality. You can think about things. You can feel emotions like joy and sadness. You can make choices. God also made you with a soul that will live forever. These are a few of the wonderful ways God has made you. God created the entire universe but only people were made in his image.

All life is important, or valuable, to God, but, because you are made in God's image, you have a special value to him. No animal or plant is made in his image like you are. In the Bible God commands, "Do not murder" (Exodus 20:13). Each person's life is important to God. No one has the right to take another person's life. God wants you to honor him by respecting and protecting life.

WHY DOES GOD WANT YOU TO RESPECT LIFE?

HOW DID PEOPLE IN THE BIBLE RESPECT LIFE?

September
2

"Kill all the baby boys born to the Israelites!" ordered angry Pharaoh, the king of Egypt (see Exodus 1:22). Two Israelite nurses hurried from Pharaoh's presence. They understood his order, but they wanted to obey God.

The Israelites were slaves in Egypt. Pharaoh was afraid they would join his enemies and fight against him. That's why he wanted the boys killed. Pharaoh had no respect for human life, but the two nurses did. They protected the lives of the baby boys.

All human life is important to God. When does life begin? Life starts when God begins to form a baby inside the mother's body. God values unborn babies. The Bible says God forms every detail of their bodies even before they are born into this world (Psalm 139:13).

When a doctor performs an abortion (killing a baby before or while he is being born), he is killing a life God created. Only God has the right to give life and to take it away. Leaders of many countries have made laws that allow unborn babies to be killed. Pray that the leaders of all countries will obey God. Pray that they will want to respect and protect human life.

WRITE A THANK-YOU PRAYER TO GOD FOR THE LIFE HE HAS GIVEN YOU.

Thank you for making me so wonderfully complex!
Psalm 139:14

YOU CAN PRAY:
Dear God, thank you for creating me. Please help me to protect and respect human life. In Jesus' name. Amen.

September
3

HOW CAN I RESPECT LIFE?

Thank you for making me so wonderfully complex!
Psalm 139:14

YOU CAN PRAY:
Dear God, help me to say "no" to violent games, TV shows, and music. Help me to honor you by honoring life. In Jesus' name. Amen.

Do you enjoy playing video games? Some of them are lots of fun, but there are some video games that are violent. They encourage you to "kill" others to win the game. You might think that it's not so bad—it's only a game. However, the more you play those kinds of games, the less violence bothers you.

Violence is on TV, in movies, in music—even in cartoons! Some people who listen to a lot of music that talks about killing start thinking about hurting others or even themselves. Some people who watch movies that show people killing or being killed go and try to copy what they've seen. Some kids have taken guns to school to hurt and kill others.

God hates this violence. He says, "Do not murder" (Exodus 20:13). Taking someone's life—or even your own life—is sin. No one has the right to take away life. God wants you to respect life, including your own.

Be careful what you listen to and what you watch. Don't fill your mind with thoughts of killing. Turn off the violent TV shows or video games. Listen to music that celebrates life. You honor God when you honor life.

WHAT ARE THREE THINGS YOU CAN DO TO SHOW YOUR RESPECT FOR LIFE?

WHAT DOES GOD SAY ABOUT RESPECTING AUTHORITY?

September
4

Jason threw paper wads at the girls sitting in the bus seats ahead of him. The bus driver told him to stop, but as soon as the bus driver wasn't looking, Jason started causing trouble again.

Keshia's teacher told her not to push in line in front of others. Keshia rudely talked back to her teacher.

Jason and Keshia weren't showing respect for those in authority over them.

Do you show respect to those in authority over you? Or do you talk back to them or disobey them? The Bible says, "Obey the government, for God is the one who put it there" (Romans 13:1). God's plan is for you to respect your leaders by speaking kindly to them and obeying. God puts people in authority over you for your good. They are there to help you keep the rules so you will be safe. They help you make right choices so that everyone can get along.

Those who are rude or do not obey authority are punished. When you are rude or disobey, you cause problems for yourself and others. If you've been rude or disobedient, confess that sin to God. Ask him to help you respect those in authority over you.

LIST SEVERAL PEOPLE YOU NEED TO BE MORE RESPECTFUL TO.

Thank you for making me so wonderfully complex! Psalm 139:14

YOU CAN PRAY:

Dear God, please forgive me for the times I've been rude or have disobeyed those in authority. Help me to show respect to them. In Jesus' name. Amen.

September
5

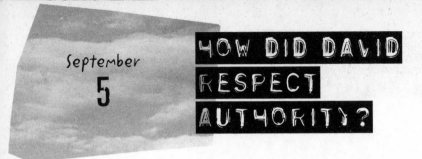

HOW DID DAVID RESPECT AUTHORITY?

God promised a young man named David that someday he would be king of Israel. Until then, he would have to patiently respect the authority over him—King Saul.

One day, the women praised David as being a better soldier than Saul. Saul was jealous. Later, as David played his harp, hate and jealousy took control of Saul's mind. He threw his spear at David, but God saved David's life. From that time on, Saul chased David. He wanted to kill him!

David knew that God had planned for him to be king. He could have turned against Saul. But David respected Saul's authority over him. Once Saul entered a cave. He didn't know that David and his soldiers were hiding in the back. David's men wanted to kill Saul, but David refused. He cut a piece of cloth from Saul's robe to show that he could have killed him. Later, David felt guilty about cutting the king's robe. He respected the king's authority even though Saul was disobeying God.

Like David, you can show respect for authority. Be patient and wait for God to work out his plan. When the time was right, God honored David. He was made king of Israel. God will honor you, too, as you respect those in authority.

Thank you for making me so wonderfully complex!
Psalm 139:14

YOU CAN PRAY:
Dear God, help me to respect authority even when it's hard. In Jesus' name. Amen.

HOW WAS DAVID ABLE TO RESPECT KING SAUL?

HOW CAN I RESPECT AUTHORITY?

September
6

In the Bible, God gave 10 commandments, or rules. His commandments show you how to respect authority. The most important person who has authority over you is God. His first commandment says, "Do not worship any other gods besides me" (Exodus 20:3). Nothing should be more important than God. He deserves first place. Give God first place by spending time with him each day in prayer and Bible reading. Give him the first day of the week by going to church on Sunday.

Even God's name deserves respect. In another commandment God says, "Do not misuse the name of the Lord your God" (Exodus 20:7). Using God's name as a curse word is disrespectful. Remember that God is holy. Use his name with respect.

God has placed different people in authority in your life. Probably the first one you think of is your mom or dad. One of God's commandments says, "Honor your father and mother" (Exodus 20:12). One of the best ways to honor your parents is to obey them with a right attitude. God has put himself and other people in authority over your life. Ask him to help you respect them.

NAME TWO WAYS YOU CAN HONOR YOUR PARENTS.

Thank you for making me so wonderfully complex! Psalm 139:14

YOU CAN PRAY:

Dear God, thank you for my parents. Help me to respect them by obeying with a right attitude. In Jesus' name. Amen.

September
7

WHAT DOES IT MEAN TO COVET?

"Give me your vineyard!" King Ahab demanded. (A vineyard is a garden where grapes are grown.) The vineyard belonged to a man named Naboth. It had been owned by his father and grandfather.

"No," Naboth replied, "I will not give you my vineyard."

King Ahab was furious. He stomped back to his palace, lay on his bed, faced the wall, and refused to eat any food. He pouted because he couldn't get his own way. King Ahab coveted Naboth's vineyard. *Coveting* is a strong desire to have something that doesn't belong to you. The king coveted Naboth's vineyard so much, he later had Naboth put to death! Coveting can lead to terrible things.

But God knew what was in King Ahab's heart. After Naboth was put to death, King Ahab went to the vineyard to claim it as his own. God sent his prophet, Elijah, to meet him there. Elijah told the king that God was going to punish him for his terrible actions.

The Bible says, "Beware! Don't be greedy for what you don't have" (Luke 12:15). God is warning you not to want what isn't yours. Rather, be thankful to God for what you have. Put God first and you will have all that you need.

Yet true religion with contentment is great wealth.
1 Timothy 6:6

YOU CAN PRAY:
Dear God, show me ways that I am coveting. Help me to be satisfied with what you have given me. In Jesus' name. Amen.

WHAT SHOULD YOU DO WHEN YOU ARE TEMPTED TO COVET?

WHAT DOES GOD SAY ABOUT CONTENTMENT?

September
8

Here are some steps from the Bible to help you be content:

- **Be prayerful.** Ask God first if you should buy or ask for something. God will help you to know what is right. "Pray about everything. Tell God what you need, and thank him for all he has done" (Philippians 4:6).
- **Be patient.** God will give you what you need, when you need it. "His peace will guard your hearts and minds as you live in Christ Jesus" (Philippians 4:7).
- **Be content.** If God says no, remember that his answer is best for you. "I have learned how to get along happily whether I have much or little" (Philippians 4:11).
- **Be trusting.** God will provide for your needs. "And this same God who takes care of me will supply all your needs from his glorious riches" (Philippians 4:19).

Being content with what you have will give you great joy and peace in life.

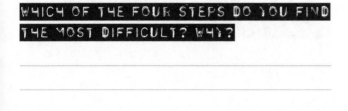

WHICH OF THE FOUR STEPS DO YOU FIND THE MOST DIFFICULT? WHY?

Yet true religion with contentment is great wealth.
1 Timothy 6:6

YOU CAN PRAY:

Dear God, thank you for meeting all my needs. In your strength I will be content. In Jesus' name. Amen.

September
9

HOW CAN I BE CONTENT?

One of the richest men in the world was asked, "How much money does it take to be happy?" His answer was, "A few more dollars." He was saying he never has enough. He always wants more.

Many Christians often have the same problem of wanting more. The Bible says, "Be satisfied with what you have. For God has said, 'I will never fail you' " (Hebrews 13:5). Contentment is being satisfied with what you have. When you are not content, you are really saying that God is not taking care of you.

If you've trusted in Jesus as your Savior, he promises he will never, never leave you. He will be with you at home, at school—wherever you are. He will meet your needs. With Jesus you can be content just the way you are—just how you look, just where you live, and with just what you have.

Whenever you are not content, stop and thank God for what you already have. Thank him that he is with you and will meet all of your needs. Our verse says, "Yet true religion with contentment is great wealth." When you have Jesus, you have all you need—and more! Are you content today?

Yet true religion with contentment is great wealth.
1 Timothy 6:6

YOU CAN PRAY:
Dear God, thank you for giving Jesus to be with me all the time. Help me to be content in him. In Jesus' name. Amen.

LIST THREE THINGS THAT YOU CAN THANK GOD FOR.

WHAT DOES GOD SAY ABOUT GREEDINESS AND STEALING?

September
10

Markia loved strawberries. One night her mom served strawberries for dessert. When the bowl was passed to her, Markia filled her dish with strawberries. She left only a few for her brother and sister. Markia was being greedy. She wasn't content to take a few and share the rest. She wanted them all for herself.

Greed is a strong desire to have all that you can get. When you are greedy you are thinking only of yourself. The Bible says, "Dishonest money brings grief to the whole family" (Proverbs 15:27).

Keith was in a store when he saw some apples in a basket by the door. He waited till the store owner was busy, and then he walked over to the basket. Keith took an apple and put it inside his shirt. He walked out without paying for the apple. Keith was stealing.

God's eighth commandment says, "Do not steal" (Exodus 20:15). Stealing is taking something that doesn't belong to you. You should use your hands to work and earn money to buy what you need. You shouldn't take things from someone else.

Greediness and stealing are selfish desires that will keep you from being content.

WHAT SHOULD YOU DO WHEN YOU ARE TEMPTED TO BE GREEDY OR TO STEAL?

Yet true religion with contentment is great wealth.
1 Timothy 6:6

YOU CAN PRAY:
Dear God, help me to be a godly example to others by being content with what I have and by not being greedy. In Jesus' name. Amen.

September
11

WHAT HAPPENED WHEN ACHAN WAS GREEDY?

Yet true religion with contentment is great wealth.
1 Timothy 6:6

YOU CAN PRAY:

Dear God, thank you for reminding me not to steal or be greedy. Help me to be content with what I have. In Jesus' name. Amen.

"Hurrah! Victory is ours! God has given us victory over Jericho." God helped the army of Israel defeat the large city of Jericho. But when they went to fight the much smaller city of Ai, Israel lost the battle. Joshua, the leader, came with deep sadness before the Lord. God told Joshua the problem. "Israel has sinned" (Joshua 7:11). Someone had stolen treasure from Jericho.

God had given clear instructions. All treasure taken from Jericho was to be given to the Lord's house. Anyone keeping treasure for himself would bring God's punishment. During the battle of Jericho, a man named Achan became greedy. He took some valuable things and buried them in his tent. God showed Joshua that Achan was the guilty one. Achan admitted what he had done. Achan, his family, and all that he owned were destroyed—all because of greed (Joshua 7).

If you allow greed in your life, you may have to face a terrible punishment. Think of how many other people may also be affected by your greed. You will be setting a bad example for others to follow. Some may even decide not to receive Jesus as their Savior because of what they see in you.

HOW MIGHT YOUR GREED AFFECT OTHER PEOPLE?

HOW CAN I AVOID BEING GREEDY?

September
12

Greed is a strong desire to have something for yourself. The opposite of being greedy is being content—being satisfied with what God has given you. Only God can help you to be content. Thank God for forgiving your sins and giving you all the good things you have. When you are content, you'll want to give instead of always wanting to get things for yourself.

You can give God your time by praying and reading your Bible. You can give part of your allowance to God in your church offering. You can give your talents and abilities to serve God. Maybe you can sing a song in the worship service or draw a picture to decorate the church. Giving to God is a great way to keep from being greedy.

God can also help you to give to others instead of being greedy. You can share your toys. You can allow others to get in line in front of you. You can give others first choice at dessert.

Ask God to show you how you can help meet the needs of others. Let God help you to be content. Give to God and others, and you won't have time to be greedy!

HOW CAN YOU GUARD AGAINST BEING GREEDY?

Yet true religion with contentment is great wealth.
1 Timothy 6:6

YOU CAN PRAY:

Dear God, help me to be content and to give to you and to others so I can guard against being greedy. In Jesus' name. Amen.

September
13

WHAT DOES GOD SAY ABOUT PATIENCE?

Wait is one of the hardest words to obey. But God uses waiting to teach you patience. Patience is being able to wait calmly, even through hard or boring times. God sometimes allows hard things to happen to his children to help them learn to be patient. It can be a hard lesson to learn!

The Bible says, "Dear brothers and sisters, whenever trouble comes your way, let it be an opportunity for joy. For when your faith is tested, your endurance has a chance to grow" (James 1:2-3). Hard times in your life will test your faith in God. You might want to say to God, "Help me get better now!" or "Help me get a new bike soon!" Will you be patient and keep living for God even if he says, "Wait"?

As a Christian, you can wait patiently on the Lord knowing your life is in God's control. "Wait patiently for the Lord. Be brave and courageous. Yes, wait patiently for the Lord" (Psalm 27:14). When you show patience by waiting on the Lord, you will grow stronger. Next time you face a hard time, let God use it to teach you to be patient.

Be quick to listen, slow to speak, and slow to get angry.
James 1:19

YOU CAN PRAY:
Dear God, thank you for the hard times in my life. Help me to patiently wait for you to work and to trust your plan. In Jesus' name. Amen.

WRITE HOW GOD HAS BEEN TEACHING YOU TO BE PATIENT.

HOW DID GOD REWARD JOB'S PATIENCE?

September
14

Job was a rich man. He had 7000 sheep, 3000 camels, 500 oxen, and 500 donkeys. Job and his wife had seven sons and three daughters.

Most importantly, Job had faith in God. Job's relationship with God was more important to him than anything. But God allowed hard times in Job's life. One day, all Job's oxen, donkeys, and camels were stolen by enemies, and his sheep were killed in a fire. His children were eating in a house when a strong wind came and the house fell, killing them all. Job's sadness was more than you can imagine, yet Job did not sin by blaming God (Job 1:14-19).

Next, God allowed Job to get painful sores all over his body (Job 1:7). Job's wife told Job to "curse God and die" (Job 2:9). Life couldn't get much worse. Yet Job did not sin in what he said. Job lost everything except his faith in God. His friends and family discouraged him, but Job was patient. He believed that God was in control.

The Bible says that God finally rewarded Job's patience. He gave back to Job twice what he owned. He also gave Job more children. God had given him even more than he had before (Job 42:12-13).

Be quick to listen, slow to speak, and slow to get angry.
James 1:19

YOU CAN PRAY:
Dear Lord, help me to be patient in hard times, and help me to always be faithful to you. In Jesus' name. Amen.

HOW DID JOB REMAIN FAITHFUL TO GOD THROUGH ALL OF HIS HARD TIMES?

September

15

HOW CAN I BE PATIENT?

"I wish I had my own dog," Tom thought. He daydreamed about playing catch in the yard and wrestling in the grass with his dog. He had asked his parents, but they said they couldn't afford to keep a dog. Tom didn't complain. He just kept praying and hoping. Finally, after a long time, Tom's parents agreed that he could get a dog. Tom's patience was rewarded!

Sometimes God or your parents may say "no" or "wait" when you ask for something like a dog, bike, or game. At times like these you must "be still in the presence of the Lord, and wait patiently for him to act" (Psalm 37:7). Don't fuss and complain. Keep praying and trusting God to do what is best.

Maybe you are asking God for something much more serious, like healing for a friend who is dying or help in a serious family problem. Being still and waiting patiently for God is difficult. Remember that God knows the future. Part of being patient is knowing God will do what is best for you. You may have to wait for years. Patience is trusting God to do what is best in his time.

Be quick to listen, slow to speak, and slow to get angry.
James 1:19

YOU CAN PRAY:
Dear God, help me to wait patiently and trust you to answer my prayers in your perfect time. In Jesus' name. Amen.

HOW HAS GOD REWARDED YOUR PATIENCE?

WHAT DOES GOD SAY ABOUT ANGER?

September
16

What kinds of things make you angry? Are you angry when your little brother wrecks your room or your sister wears your clothes? Maybe you're angry when your parents say "no" to something you want to do.

Anger can cause many problems. Anger can make you say or do things that you will feel badly about later. It can cause you guilt and shame. It can ruin your friendships. People don't like to be with an angry person. It can even ruin your health! It is normal to feel angry sometimes, but anger that is uncontrolled is sin. God's desire is for you to live at peace—with him, with yourself, and with others. That isn't always easy to do!

A good rule to follow is this: "Don't let the sun go down while you are still angry" (Ephesians 4:26). In other words, don't let anger control your life. If you've been letting anger control you, admit it to God and ask his forgiveness. If you are angry at another person, talk to that person. Try to work out the problem. You might even have to apologize. Remember our Bible verse: "Be quick to listen, slow to speak, and slow to get angry" (James 1:19).

Be quick to listen, slow to speak, and slow to get angry.
James 1:19

YOU CAN PRAY:
Dear God, please help me to be patient with others and slow to become angry. In Jesus' name. Amen.

HOW CAN ANGER HURT YOUR LIFE?

September
17

IS IT EVER RIGHT TO BE ANGRY?

Parents had brought their children to the Lord Jesus so he could hold them and pray for them. When the disciples saw the children coming, they tried to keep them away. Jesus became angry with the disciples. He commanded them to let the children come to him (Mark 10:13-16).

Another time, Jesus entered the temple (place of worship). He found people there who were buying and selling animals, exchanging money, and cheating others. They had used God's holy temple for their own greedy plans. Jesus pushed them out and turned over their tables. He shouted, "The Scriptures declare, 'My Temple will be called a place of prayer for all nations,' but you have turned it into a den of thieves" (Mark 11:17).

In both of these situations, Jesus was angry at sin. You, too, should be angry at sin. Be angry if someone offers you drugs. You should be angry when you hear God's name used as a swear word. Being angry doesn't mean that you sin. God's Word tells us, "Don't sin by letting anger gain control over you" (Ephesians 4:26). We should be angry at sin, but we should not let that anger control us. Ask God to give you a right attitude, especially when it comes to anger.

Be quick to listen, slow to speak, and slow to get angry.
James 1:19

YOU CAN PRAY:
Dear God, thank you for teaching me about the right kind of anger. Help me not to let my anger turn into sin. In Jesus' name. Amen.

WHY SHOULD YOU BE ANGRY AT SIN?

HOW CAN I HAVE SELF-CONTROL?

September

18

Self-control means letting God work through you to control your thoughts, feelings, and actions, rather than letting those things control you. Jesus showed us the way to live a self-controlled life. As a child, the Lord Jesus had self-control to obey his parents (Luke 2:41-51). As a man, Jesus showed self-control by refusing to sin when tempted by Satan (Luke 4:1-13). Even when he was dying, Jesus showed self-control when he forgave those who crucified him (Luke 23:34).

Self-control is part of the fruit of the Spirit that you learned about earlier in this devotional book (read March 23 again). Through the power of the Holy Spirit you can have self-control. Allow the Holy Spirit within you to control what you think, say, and do. Stay away from people and places that tempt you to lose your self-control.

Each morning give God control of yourself. You might say, "God, I give you my mouth to speak the truth. I give you my hands to help others. I give you my mind to think pure thoughts. I give you my eyes to read your Word." Developing self-control takes hard work. Trust and allow the Holy Spirit to work in you.

IN WHAT AREAS OF YOUR LIFE IS IT HARDEST FOR YOU TO HAVE SELF-CONTROL?

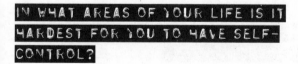

Be quick to listen, slow to speak, and slow to get angry.
James 1:19

YOU CAN PRAY:

Dear God, help me to give you every part of my life to be controlled by the Holy Spirit. In Jesus' name. Amen.

September
19

WHAT DOES GOD SAY ABOUT KINDNESS?

Would other people describe you as a kind person? Kindness is treating others with love and respect. Kindness is love in action. Think about how kind Jesus was when he lived on the earth. Even though people didn't deserve it, he treated them with kindness. He was kind to the poor, to the sick, to children, and to elderly people. He was kind to his friends and to his enemies. He even showed kindness to people that others hated.

The greatest demonstration of Jesus' love and kindness was when he died on the cross for your sins and mine. He willingly suffered, bled, and died a cruel death so that we could be forgiven. He was even kind to those who put him to death.

Because Jesus has shown such kindness to us, as his children, we should show the same kindness to others. Show kindness at home by helping around the house without being asked. Show kindness at school by being friends with someone that no one else seems to like. Show kindness in your neighborhood by helping an elderly person to clean up the yard or take out the trash. Look for ways to show God's kindness to others.

HOW CAN YOU SHOW KINDNESS TO SOMEONE THIS WEEK?

Be kind to each other, tenderhearted, forgiving one another, just as God through Christ has forgiven you.
Ephesians 4:32

YOU CAN PRAY:
Dear God, help me to show your love and kindness to others. In Jesus' name. Amen.

HOW WAS ABRAM KIND TO LOT?

September

20

Abram (later called Abraham) was a wealthy man. God had told him to leave his home and go to a new country to live. God promised Abram that his family would become a great nation and have a land to call home (Genesis 12:1-2).

Traveling with Abram and his wife, Sarai (later called Sarah), was his nephew, Lot. Abram and Lot both had many animals and servants. When they arrived in the new country, they found that the land did not have enough food and water for all the animals. Their servants argued about this problem (Genesis 12:5, 13:6-7).

Abram told Lot that they would have to separate so that their herds would have enough food and water. God had already given the land to Abram, but Abram made a kind, generous offer to Lot. He allowed Lot to have first choice. Lot chose the best land, with clean wells and rich soil. Abram took what was left. He could have kept the best land, but he decided to show kindness by giving the best land to Lot (Genesis 13:8-11).

Abram shows us a great example of being kind to family members. It's not always easy, but God can help you to do it!

Be kind to each other, tenderhearted, forgiving one another, just as God through Christ has forgiven you.
Ephesians 4:32

YOU CAN PRAY:
Dear Lord, thank you for my family. Help me to show kindness to each member, even when it's hard. In Jesus' name. Amen.

HOW CAN YOU SHOW KINDNESS TO A MEMBER OF YOUR FAMILY?

September

21

HOW CAN I BE KIND TO OTHERS?

Be kind to each other, tenderhearted, forgiving one another, just as God through Christ has forgiven you.
Ephesians 4:32

YOU CAN PRAY:
Dear God, help me to show your kindness to others in my thoughts, words, and actions. In Jesus' name. Amen.

Showing kindness to others involves your thoughts, words, and actions. Do you think of others before yourself? Think of the letters **J-O-Y**: **J**esus first, **O**thers second, and **Y**ourself last. That's what it means to "be humble, thinking of others as better than yourself" (Philippians 2:3).

Our words are also important in showing kindness. People may say, "Words will never hurt me," but words *do* hurt. Some children will remember for a whole lifetime the mean names they are called. Think before you speak. If you don't have anything good to say, don't say anything at all. Look for something kind to say.

Finally, showing kindness to others involves actions. Look for ways you can help others. Help a classmate who is not doing well in school. Help a neighbor rake the leaves. Help your mom by watching your little brother or sister. Help a sick friend by making him a card.

Showing kindness can help you show others you are a Christian. You may be able to tell them about the great kindness the Lord Jesus has shown to you. As you show kindness to others you are showing the love of Jesus to them.

LIST THREE WAYS YOU WILL BE KIND TO OTHERS THIS WEEK.

WHAT DOES GOD SAY ABOUT FORGIVING OTHERS?

September
22

Forgiveness means letting go of your anger and your desire to get even with someone who has hurt you. True forgiveness comes from God. Ever since sin entered the world through the first people, Adam and Eve, individuals have needed God's forgiveness. Jesus Christ, God the Son, died on the cross to make the way for us to be forgiven for our sins. Those who trust in Jesus as their Savior are forgiven—made clean from their sins. If you have trusted the Lord Jesus as your Savior, you can thank him that he has forgiven you.

Once you have received God's forgiveness, he wants you to forgive others who have hurt you. Our verse says, "Be kind to each other, tenderhearted, forgiving one another, just as God through Christ has forgiven you" (Ephesians 4:32). You need to forgive others because God has forgiven you. Maybe someone has said or done something mean to you. Don't hold on to your anger toward that person. Think of all the sinful things God has forgiven in your life. Then, choose to forgive the one who has hurt you. Even if that person never apologizes for what he did, you can forgive him because God has forgiven you.

Be kind to each other, tenderhearted, forgiving one another, just as God through Christ has forgiven you.
Ephesians 4:32

YOU CAN PRAY:

Dear God, thank you for your forgiveness. Help me to forgive others as you have forgiven me. In Jesus' name. Amen.

WHY SHOULD YOU BE WILLING TO FORGIVE OTHERS?

September
23

HOW DID JOSEPH TREAT HIS BROTHERS?

Be kind to each other, tenderhearted, forgiving one another, just as God through Christ has forgiven you.
Ephesians 4:32

YOU CAN PRAY:
Dear God, thank you for teaching me about Joseph. Help me to forgive completely. In Jesus' name. Amen.

If anyone had a good reason to hate his brothers it was Joseph. We learned earlier in this book about how Joseph's brothers threw him into a pit, made plans to kill him, and finally sold him into slavery. With God's help and blessing, Joseph became the second most powerful leader in Egypt. When a terrible famine (lack of food) came to the land, people came from miles around to buy food in Egypt.

One day as Joseph was giving out the food, he saw his 10 older brothers standing before him. He knew them, but they didn't recognize him because he now looked and spoke like an Egyptian. Joseph could have taken revenge on his brothers, but he didn't. Joseph forgave them. He even thanked God for sending him to Egypt. Joseph realized that God had used his brothers to work out God's perfect plan. Joseph forgave his brothers completely. He invited his father, his brothers, and their families to come live in Egypt where he could take care of them (Genesis 50:16-21).

Like Joseph, you need to learn to forgive others as God has forgiven you. Only God can give you the strength inside to forgive.

HOW IS JOSEPH'S FORGIVENESS OF HIS BROTHERS LIKE GOD'S FORGIVENESS OF YOU?

HOW CAN I FORGIVE THOSE WHO HURT ME?

September
24

Courtney cried quietly, alone in her room. The older kids on the school bus had been teasing her again. Courtney was hurt and angry.

Eldon was shocked. He had heard his parents argue late at night, but he never expected his dad to pack a suitcase and leave. Now Eldon felt it was his fault. Eldon was hurt and angry.

Every person has had hurt feelings. Sometimes the hurt is physical like being hit or kicked. Often with the hurt comes anger toward the person who caused the hurt. Remembering God's forgiveness can help you forgive those who have hurt you. It is only by God's strength that you can truly forgive.

Pray for the person who has hurt you. Ask God to change him. Think of something kind you can do for him. This may be hard. God doesn't say, "Just be kind to your friends." He tells you to be kind to friends *and* enemies.

Remember the forgiveness Jesus had for those who nailed him to the cross and watched him die. He said, "Father, forgive these people, because they don't know what they are doing" (Luke 23:34). Ask God to help you forgive in the same way.

HOW CAN YOU FORGIVE THOSE WHO HURT YOU?

Be kind to each other, tenderhearted, forgiving one another, just as God through Christ has forgiven you.
Ephesians 4:32

YOU CAN PRAY:

Dear God, I have been hurt by others. With your help I now forgive them. [Say their names to God.] In Jesus' name. Amen.

September

25

WHAT DOES GOD SAY ABOUT BEING HONEST?

We are careful to be honorable before the Lord, but we also want everyone else to know we are honorable.
2 Corinthians 8:21

YOU CAN PRAY:
Dear God, help me to think and live honestly so that my life will glorify you. In Jesus' name. Amen.

Have you ever heard the phrase "Honesty is the best policy"? Although it is not in the Bible, it is a good phrase to remember when you are faced with a choice.

The Bible says, "We are careful to be honorable before the Lord, but we also want everyone else to know we are honorable" (2 Corinthians 8:21).

There are times when you can make an honest choice or you can make a dishonest choice. There are people who may tell you it's okay to be dishonest as long as you don't get caught. The truth is you *do* get caught—every time. God knows all your actions and even your thoughts! The Lord Jesus Christ sees all you do.

You are also to do right "in the eyes of men." Be honest. Others are watching you. If you are dishonest, others may not believe you when you witness to them about Jesus.

Honesty is so important to God that he even wants your thoughts to be honest. The Bible says, "And now, dear brothers and sisters, . . . fix your thoughts on what is true and honorable and right. Think about things that are pure and lovely and admirable. Think about things that are excellent and worthy of praise" (Philippians 4:8). Remember that God is watching, and others are watching too. Think and act honestly.

HOW CAN OTHERS TELL THAT YOU'RE AN HONEST PERSON?

WHAT HAPPENED WHEN JACOB WAS DISHONEST?

September
26

The Bible tells about two men, Esau and Jacob, who were twins but were very different. Esau, born first, liked to hunt and be outside. Jacob worked near their home and liked to cook.

One day, their father, Isaac, wanted to give Esau a special blessing because Esau was born first. Jacob decided to trick his father into giving him the blessing instead. With the help of his mother, Rebekah, Jacob prepared a meal. Then Rebekah tied goat skins on Jacob's neck and hands. Dishonest Jacob carried the meal into his father's tent. He gave his father the food, pretending to be his brother.

Isaac was probably over 100 years old. He could not see well. Isaac reached out and touched his son's hands—they were hairy like Esau's hands. *This must be Esau,* thought Isaac. Isaac ate the food and blessed his son. Jacob had tricked his father!

When Esau arrived, he was furious at what Jacob had done. "I will kill Jacob," Esau said (Genesis 27:41).

Jacob had to go away for many years. Later, Jacob's wife's father was dishonest to him many times. Often what you do to others will eventually be done to you. Many sad things happened in Jacob's family—all because of dishonesty.

HOW MIGHT YOUR DISHONESTY AFFECT OTHER MEMBERS OF YOUR FAMILY?

We are careful to be honorable before the Lord, but we also want everyone else to know we are honorable.
2 Corinthians 8:21

YOU CAN PRAY:

Dear Lord, help me to be honest with my family and my friends. In Jesus' name. Amen.

September
27

HOW CAN I BE HONEST IN ALL THINGS?

We are careful to be honorable before the Lord, but we also want everyone else to know we are honorable.
2 Corinthians 8:21

YOU CAN PRAY:
Dear God, please help me to be honest for you, even in small things. In Jesus' name. Amen.

Daryl and his brother, David, loved to play games. Since Daryl was older, he would keep the score for their games. David wasn't very good with math, so he was happy to let Daryl keep score. One afternoon, when Daryl was losing, he thought about adding extra points to his score. David wouldn't know. What should he do? Does it really matter? It's just a game.

Ashley went to the grocery store to buy some items for her mom. She paid for the groceries, but when the cashier gave her the change, Ashley noticed that he had given her 25 cents too much. What should Ashley do? Does it really matter? It's only 25 cents.

Yes, it does matter to God. He wants your words, thoughts, and actions to be honest. Remember that God knows all you do. He knows if you change the score of the game or if you keep the extra change. Even small things matter to him.

When others see your honesty in small ways, often they will trust you with bigger jobs and responsibilities. Think honestly and then act honestly. God will be pleased when you do.

WHY IS IT IMPORTANT TO BE HONEST, EVEN IN SMALL THINGS?

WHAT DOES GOD SAY ABOUT BEING AFRAID?

September
28

King David knew what it was to feel afraid. He had many scary experiences in his life. As a shepherd boy, he had to protect his sheep from wild animals. As a young man, David fought against a giant who had been terrorizing all of Israel.

Later, as an adult, David led his army into many battles, and his life was often threatened. However, in all of these scary experiences, David knew what to do about his fear.

"I will not be afraid," David wrote, "for you are close beside me" (Psalm 23:4). In another psalm, David wrote, "But when I am afraid, I put my trust in you" (Psalm 56:3). David often reminded himself that wherever he went, God was there. God was always with him.

- **It's natural to feel afraid sometimes.** However, if you have trusted Jesus as your Savior, you can be sure that God is with you all the time. He has promised in his Word, "I will never fail you" (Hebrews 13:5). He is with you every moment of every day, everywhere you go. When you are afraid, do what David did. Remember that God is with you, and put your trust in him.

But when I am afraid, I put my trust in you.
Psalm 56:3

YOU CAN PRAY:
Dear God, thank you that you are with me all the time. Help me to trust you when I am afraid. In Jesus' name. Amen.

WHAT DID DAVID DO WHEN HE FELT AFRAID?

September
29

WHAT DID JESUS' DISCIPLES DO WHEN THEY WERE AFRAID?

But when I am afraid, I put my trust in you.
Psalm 56:3

YOU CAN PRAY:

Dear God, thank you for being with me. Help me to trust you when I am afraid. In Jesus' name. Amen.

"Row for your life! The waves are going to sink us!" Jesus' disciples were terrified. They never imagined that their day with Jesus would end in such fear.

The Lord Jesus Christ had been teaching along the shore of the Sea of Galilee. When evening came, he and his disciples got into a small boat to cross to the other side of the lake. As they started out, Jesus was soon asleep in the boat.

Then a strong storm began to blow. The waves came over the sides of the boat, and the disciples tried to keep the boat from sinking. Fearing for their lives, the disciples woke Jesus and cried, "Teacher, don't you even care that we are going to drown?" (Mark 4:38). Jesus got up and spoke to the wind and waves. "Quiet down!" (Mark 4:39). Immediately the wind and the waves stopped. All was still.

Jesus said to his disciples, "Why are you so afraid? Do you still not have faith in me?" (Mark 4:40). The disciples were beginning to see that Jesus, God the Son, had great power over all things. Jesus wanted them to learn that they could trust him when they were afraid. That's a lesson Jesus wants you to learn too!

WRITE ABOUT A TIME YOU WERE AFRAID AND JESUS HELPED YOU HAVE COURAGE.

WHAT SHOULD I DO WHEN I AM AFRAID?

September
30

What makes you afraid? Perhaps things like darkness or storms scare you. Maybe you're afraid of being home alone or having to give a report in front of the class. Sometimes serious problems make you afraid, like illness or your parents getting divorced.

Whether it's caused by something small or something great, fear can be a terrible problem. Being afraid can even affect your body, making you ill. Fear is a natural thing that God has built into your body to help you escape from danger. But when fear takes control of you, it becomes a problem.

God's solution to fear is trust in him. Nothing that happens is ever a surprise to God. He is in control of all things. Here is a special promise from God that you can remember when you are afraid: "Be strong and courageous! Do not be afraid or discouraged. For the Lord your God is with you wherever you go" (Joshua 1:9). God is with you, no matter what. Tell him about the thing that is making you afraid. Say this verse to yourself and believe what it says. Trust in God when you are afraid. He will never let you down!

WHAT WILL YOU DO THE NEXT TIME YOU ARE AFRAID?

But when I am afraid, I put my trust in you.
Psalm 56:3

YOU CAN PRAY:

Dear God, when I am afraid, help me to remember that you are with me. Help me to trust in you. In Jesus' name. Amen.

Activity 9:
Living for God

I CAN LIVE FOR GOD WITH ALL OF ME

Fill in the blanks with the ways you can live for God.

My mind can think about God.

My eyes can ______________________.

My mouth can ______________________.

My heart can ______________________.

My hands can ______________________.

My feet can ______________________.

THINKING IT OVER!

Living for God

Write the answers to these questions from your devotionals in the blanks.

1. Why do people have special value to God?

____

2. How does God want you to treat those in authority?

____

3. What can you do when you are not content?

____

4. Why should you show kindness to others?

____

5. What does God want you to do when someone hurts you?

____

6. What should you remind yourself of when you are afraid?

____

If you need help, you can look back in this month's devotionals. The number in ( ) tells you which devotional to check for each question. 1. (1) 2. (4) 3. (9) 4. (19) 5. (22) 6. (28)

OCTOBER

Trusting God

October 1

WHAT IS GOD'S PROVIDENCE?

And we know that God causes everything to work together for the good of those who love God.
Romans 8:28

YOU CAN PRAY:
Dear God, thank you for your providence. Help me to trust you in all that happens in my life. In Jesus' name. Amen.

Have you ever put a picture puzzle together? When you spread out all the pieces, it's quite a mess! However, each piece has a special place. When all the pieces are in the right place, you see a beautiful picture!

God has a plan for your life, and that plan has many pieces to it. There are many good things that God has planned for you. He also allows hard things to happen in your life. Like a great puzzle, God is putting all of these things together in his special way. This is called God's providence (PROV-uh-dense). Providence means that God always cares for his people and controls all that happens in their lives. The Bible says, "And we know that God causes everything to work together for the good of those who love God" (Romans 8:28).

At times you may not understand the reason something happens to you, but nothing is ever a surprise to God. You can praise God for his providence even when you can't see how the puzzle will turn out. Each day, look for ways that God is at work. God always knows and does what is best. Thank him today for his providence.

HOW HAVE YOU SEEN GOD'S CARE AND CONTROL IN YOUR LIFE?

DOES GOD HAVE A PURPOSE FOR MY LIFE?

October
2

"Why am I here?" Many people have asked that question. Is there a reason that God put you on this earth? The answer is yes! God does everything for a reason. People keep life going on our planet, but there's so much more than just living.

In his perfect plan, God made you special. There's no one else like you, even if you have a twin! Your personality, the way you think about things, what makes you laugh or cry—all these things make you different from others. God purposely made you this way. You are one of a kind!

God also has a purpose (plan) for what he wants you to become. He wants your life to glorify (honor) him. In the Bible God says, "For I know the plans I have for you. . . . They are plans for good and not for disaster, to give you a future and a hope" (Jeremiah 29:11). God has good plans for your life. In his providence, he allows only what is best. Even when hard things happen, remember that God has a purpose—a plan—that he is working out for your good and his glory.

And we know that God causes everything to work together for the good of those who love God.
Romans 8:28

YOU CAN PRAY:

Dear God, thank you for making me special. Thank you that you have a good purpose for my life. I trust you to work out your plan for me. In Jesus' name. Amen.

WRITE THREE THINGS ABOUT YOU THAT MAKE YOU DIFFERENT FROM A FRIEND.

WHAT WAS GOD'S PURPOSE FOR JOSEPH?

And we know that God causes everything to work together for the good of those who love God.
Romans 8:28

YOU CAN PRAY:

Dear God, thank you for the good plans you had for Joseph. Please help me to trust and obey you like he did. In Jesus' name. Amen.

Do you remember Joseph? He grew up with 10 older brothers! Joseph's father loved him most of all. He even gave Joseph a beautiful robe. But Joseph's brothers were jealous.

One day, the brothers were in a field taking care of their father's sheep when they saw Joseph coming. They took his beautiful robe and threw Joseph into a deep hole in the ground. Later, they sold Joseph as a slave. Joseph went through many more hard times. He even had to go to prison in Egypt for something he didn't do.

While Joseph was in prison, the king had a strange dream. God gave Joseph wisdom to understand the dream. The king rewarded Joseph by giving him an important job. God told Joseph to save lots of grain because soon there would be no food to eat. Joseph obeyed and many people were saved from starving.

God had good plans for Joseph's life, even though his life was sometimes hard. God's purpose was for Joseph to learn to trust and obey him. Joseph's hard times prepared him for the important work that God had for him to do. Joseph followed God's plan and his life glorified God.

WRITE DOWN TWO WAYS YOU SEE GOD'S PROVIDENCE IN JOSEPH'S LIFE.

HOW DID JOSEPH RESPOND TO HARD TIMES?

October
4

Imagine being hated by your family. Imagine being sold as a slave. Imagine being put into prison for something you didn't do. Those hard things happened to Joseph in the Bible.

How did he respond? Did he get angry with God? Did he want to get even with his brothers? No! Even though it was hard, Joseph trusted and obeyed God. He worked hard and did the best that he could. After much suffering, Joseph became an important man in Egypt.

One day his brothers came to buy grain. They didn't recognize Joseph, but he recognized them. Joseph had the power to punish them. However, instead of punishing them, Joseph forgave his brothers! He said, "God turned into good what you meant for evil" (Genesis 50:20). Joseph took care of his family the rest of his life.

Joseph saw that everything that had happened was part of God's plan. God had cared for Joseph and worked out his purpose. Although people may have evil plans, God's good plans can never be ruined. Joseph responded to his hard times with forgiveness and trust in God's providence. How do you respond to your hard times?

HOW SHOULD YOU RESPOND TO HARD TIMES IN YOUR LIFE?

And we know that God causes everything to work together for the good of those who love God.
Romans 8:28

YOU CAN PRAY:

Dear God, thank you for taking the bad things in my life and making them turn out for good. Help me to forgive and to trust in you. In Jesus' name. Amen.

October
5

WHAT WAS GOD'S PURPOSE FOR ESTHER?

Esther was good at keeping secrets. She was a young girl who lived a long time ago in Persia. The Bible tells how she was chosen to be the queen. Queen Esther had a secret that not even the king knew. Her cousin, Mordecai, had warned her not to tell anyone that she was Jewish.

A proud man named Haman worked for the king. He liked to have people bow down to honor him. Mordecai refused to bow to anyone but God. Haman was angry. He learned that Mordecai was Jewish. Haman made a terrible law. On a certain day, all of the Jewish people would be killed.

Mordecai told Esther about the law. He wanted her to get help from the king, but Esther was afraid. If she went to the king without being invited, he could have her killed. Esther told Mordecai she couldn't do it. Mordecai sent a message back to her telling her that God may have made her queen for such a time as this.

God had a special purpose in allowing Esther to become queen. She was in just the right place to save the Jewish people. Would Esther trust God's plan for her? Would you?

And we know that God causes everything to work together for the good of those who love God.
Romans 8:28

YOU CAN PRAY:

Dear God, thank you that you have a special place for me. Help me to have courage to trust your plan. In Jesus' name. Amen.

WHAT WOULD YOU DO IF YOU WERE ESTHER?

HOW DID ESTHER RESPOND TO HARD TIMES?

October
6

Esther was having a hard time. She wanted to help her people, but she was afraid to go to the king. Esther knew the true and living God. She believed that God let her be the queen for a special reason. Esther trusted God's plan for her.

She sent this message to Mordecai: "Go and gather together all the Jews of Susa and fast for me" (Esther 4:16). To fast means to go without eating. Usually when people fasted in the Bible, they used that time to pray. After three days, Esther would go to the king to plead for her people. She knew that she could trust God's plan for her, even if it meant that she would die.

After three days of fasting, Esther went before the powerful king. To her relief, the king welcomed her! She told him Haman's evil plan. The king had Haman put to death. The old law couldn't be changed, but a new law was made. The Jewish people could defend themselves from their enemies. God used Esther to save the Jewish people.

How did Esther respond to hard times? She did the two best things anyone could do—she prayed and she trusted God! Will you remember to pray and trust God when you have hard times?

WRITE DOWN A HARD TIME IN YOUR LIFE WHEN YOU NEED TO PRAY AND TRUST GOD.

____

____

And we know that God causes everything to work together for the good of those who love God.
Romans 8:28

YOU CAN PRAY:
Dear God, thank you that I can pray and trust you in any situation. Help me to remember that whenever I have a hard time. In Jesus' name. Amen.

October
7

WHAT IS GOD'S PURPOSE FOR ME?

You may not live in a palace like Joseph or Esther. Maybe you live in an apartment in a crowded city. Maybe you live with a stepparent and lots of brothers and sisters. Wherever you live or whatever your family is like, God has a purpose for you.

Ricardo trusted Jesus as his Savior when he was eight years old. He lived in a scary neighborhood. There were gangs and drugs and guns. Ricardo knew that joining a gang would not honor God.

Sometimes Ricardo wondered, "Does God have a purpose for me?" To find the answer he read the Bible, prayed, and trusted God. He looked for ways to honor God. Whenever he had a chance, Ricardo told his friends about Jesus. Some of them trusted Jesus too. Ricardo also went to church. He sang in the choir. He also helped with an after-school program for the children.

What was God's purpose for Ricardo? To honor God and be a shining light in his neighborhood! That is God's purpose for you as well. God has given you ways to serve him. He has told you about many of them in his Word, the Bible. Ask him to show you each day what you can do to honor him.

And we know that God causes everything to work together for the good of those who love God.
Romans 8:28

YOU CAN PRAY:
Dear God, thank you that I can be a shining light in my neighborhood. Help me to look for ways I can honor you. In Jesus' name. Amen.

WRITE DOWN THREE WAYS THAT YOU CAN HONOR GOD IN YOUR NEIGHBORHOOD.

HOW SHOULD I RESPOND TO HARD TIMES?

October
8

"It's not fair!" "Why do bad things always happen to me?" Have you ever said or thought things like this? We all go through hard times in our lives. Illness or divorce in your family can be hard experiences to go through. Maybe your family has no place to live because your parents don't have a job. Maybe others make fun of you because you're a Christian.

It's tempting to respond to hard times by getting angry with God. You might think, "If God really loved me, he wouldn't let this bad thing happen." That's not true. God always loves and cares for you! He is always working out his plan for your life. God uses hard times to help you trust him more. In this way, others will see Jesus at work in you, and your life will honor God.

When hard times come, remember that God is sovereign—he is in control! He knows about everything that happens to you, and he allows only what is best. Tell God how you feel. Ask him to help you trust him. Ask him to give you quietness on the inside. Then patiently wait for God to work things out for your good.

WRITE WHAT YOU BELIEVE GOD'S PURPOSE IS FOR YOUR LIFE.

And we know that God causes everything to work together for the good of those who love God.
Romans 8:28

YOU CAN PRAY:

Dear God, thank you that you have a purpose for me. Help me to trust you and to wait for you to work out your plan. In Jesus' name. Amen.

October

9

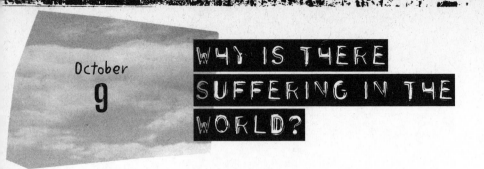

WHY IS THERE SUFFERING IN THE WORLD?

After you have suffered a little while, [God] will restore, support, and strengthen you, and he will place you on a firm foundation.
1 Peter 5:10

YOU CAN PRAY:

Dear God, thank you that you are good and wise. Thank you that you are with me in my suffering. Help me to trust you. In Jesus' name. Amen.

Why can't things just be good all the time? Why does there have to be suffering? God wants you to grow strong to be like him. That means he sometimes allows you to suffer.

Suffering means to hurt in your body or your feelings. Some people suffer from sickness and pain. Other people suffer because of sadness, anger, or hurt feelings. There was no suffering in the world until the first people, Adam and Eve, sinned. Part of the result of that sin is that suffering would be in the world. Now everyone has times of suffering.

Sometimes God allows suffering to help you grow to be more like him. Suffering can help you become more patient as you wait for God to work. Suffering can help you learn to have courage as you trust God to take care of you.

God never lets you suffer alone. He is always there to help you. One day God will take away all suffering from his children. Until then, trust him to be with you. Let him help you to be calm on the inside even while you are suffering. Let God use suffering in your life to help you grow strong.

WRITE SOMETHING THAT MAY BE CAUSING YOU TO SUFFER, THEN TELL GOD ABOUT IT.

HOW CAN I FIND COMFORT IN SUFFERING?

October
10

The Bible tells about a man who suffered more than most people. His name was Job. We learned about him earlier in this book. His children were killed in a storm. He lost his house and all that he owned. He also had a painful sickness. Some people said that God was punishing him, but Job knew that God cared. He told God about his problems and how he felt inside.

You need to do what Job did when you are suffering. You might feel angry. Maybe you think God doesn't care. But God does care. Tell him about your suffering. Ask God to help you be patient and brave.

One way God comforts his children is through his Word. If you have a Bible, read some verses in the book of Psalms. God's Word says that through patience and the comfort of the Bible, we can have hope (Romans 15:4).

As you talk to God and read his Word, he may give you an answer to your problem. However, he may choose to comfort you in a different way. He may just remind you that he loves you and has a plan for your life. Be like Job and trust that God is at work, even in your suffering. Let God comfort you.

After you have suffered a little while, [God] will restore, support, and strengthen you, and he will place you on a firm foundation.
1 Peter 5:10

YOU CAN PRAY:
Dear God, thank you for comforting me when I suffer. Thank you for your Word that gives me hope. Help me to trust your plan for me. In Jesus' name. Amen.

WRITE DOWN TWO WAYS THAT GOD CAN COMFORT YOU WHEN YOU ARE SUFFERING.

October
11

WHAT DOES IT MEAN TO BE PERSECUTED?

After you have suffered a little while, [God] will restore, support, and strengthen you, and he will place you on a firm foundation.
1 Peter 5:10

YOU CAN PRAY:
Dear Lord, thank you that you are with me, even when I am persecuted. Help me to honor you with my words and my attitude. In Jesus' name. Amen.

Did you know that some people suffer because they believe in Jesus? Suffering for what you believe is called persecution. Family members or friends may not understand why you've trusted Jesus Christ as your Savior. They might make fun of you or be mean to you in other ways. Your enemy, Satan, wants you to be discouraged or get angry with God when you are persecuted. He wants to stop you from telling other people about Jesus.

God's Word says, "But it is no shame to suffer for being a Christian. Praise God" (1 Peter 4:16). How can you honor God when you are persecuted? The Bible tells about a man named Stephen. He believed in Jesus as his Savior. He told others about Jesus. Some people hated Stephen and wanted to get rid of him. They threw stones at him until he died. But as Stephen was dying, he had courage and joy. He prayed and knew Jesus was waiting to welcome him to heaven. Stephen honored God, even in his death (Acts 7:57-60).

You may never be persecuted like Stephen. However, if you are persecuted in some way, ask God to give you courage to honor him.

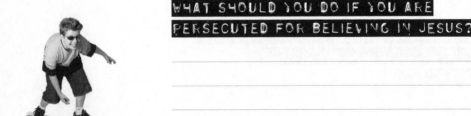

WHAT SHOULD YOU DO IF YOU ARE PERSECUTED FOR BELIEVING IN JESUS?

WHAT SHOULD I DO WHEN I AM PERSECUTED?

October

12

Latisha sat in the school lunchroom staring at her sandwich. She wanted to thank God for her lunch before she ate, but the other kids were watching. Yesterday, she prayed before she ate her lunch. The kids laughed and made fun of her. It made her feel awful. Latisha was being persecuted for being a Christian.

Why does God allow his people to be persecuted? Sometimes it's because persecution helps us learn to trust him more. Also, God may want to use your example to encourage others who are suffering.

What should you do when you are persecuted? First, remember that God is in control of all that happens. He will never allow more than you can handle with his help. Second, think about how Jesus Christ, God's Son, was persecuted for you. He allowed men to beat him and nail him to a cross so that your sins could be forgiven. Third, follow the example of others like Stephen. Pray and think about promises in God's Word. One good promise to remember is the one written at the side of this page. After a little while, God will make you secure and stronger. Trust him and keep doing what's right.

HOW COULD YOU HONOR GOD IF YOU WERE IN LATISHA'S SITUATION?

After you have suffered a little while, [God] will restore, support, and strengthen you, and he will place you on a firm foundation.
1 Peter 5:10

YOU CAN PRAY:

Dear God, help me to honor you, even when I am persecuted. Help me to remember the promises in your Word and do what is right. In Jesus' name. Amen.

October
13

WHAT IF MY FAMILY DOESN'T BELIEVE IN JESUS?

After you have suffered a little while, [God] will restore, support, and strengthen you, and he will place you on a firm foundation.
1 Peter 5:10

YOU CAN PRAY:

Dear Lord, thank you for my family. Help me to be kind and obedient and help me to tell them about you. In Jesus' name. Amen.

You might think that everyone wants to believe in Jesus, but not everyone does. Maybe you're the only one in your family who is a Christian. Perhaps your parents are angry that you've become a Christian. Maybe your brothers and sisters make fun of you. It's hard when your family doesn't understand.

Pray for your family every day. Ask God to help them see that they need to trust Christ too. If you behave in a kind and obedient way, your family will see God's love in you. God can give you strength to be kind even when others are not.

Also, you can ask God to help you tell your family about the Lord Jesus. Let God give you the right words to say at the right time. You can't make your family believe, but God may use your words, spoken in a gentle way, to help them understand. If you go to a church that teaches about Jesus, invite your family to go with you. They may say no, but don't give up. Keep on praying. Keep on being kind. Keep on telling them about Jesus. One day, they might believe. You'll be so glad you didn't give up!

LIST YOUR FAMILY MEMBERS WHO NEED TO BELIEVE IN JESUS.

CAN GOD HELP ME WHEN MY FAMILY HAS TO MOVE?

October
14

Maria watched tearfully as the last pieces of furniture were loaded into a big truck. Her family was moving to a new city. Maria was going to miss her friends. She worried about finding new friends. What would her new school be like?

Maybe your family is moving and you have some of the same questions Maria had. Saying good-bye to friends can be hard. It can be hard getting used to new things and new places, but God can help you! The Bible says, "Give all your worries and cares to God, for he cares about what happens to you" (1 Peter 5:7). You can tell the Lord Jesus about the things that trouble you. You can know that he will take care of you.

Remember that God is in control of all that happens. He has planned every step in your life. He knows about the new place you are going—he's already there! He will be there with you in your new neighborhood and your new school. Ask God to help you to trust him to take care of things. Ask him to lead you to new friends. Thank him that he is with you wherever you go.

Give all your worries and cares to God, for he cares about what happens to you. 1 Peter 5:7

YOU CAN PRAY:
Dear Lord, thank you that you are with me and will take care of me wherever I go. In Jesus' name. Amen.

HOW CAN GOD HELP YOU WHEN YOU HAVE TO MOVE TO A NEW PLACE?

October
15

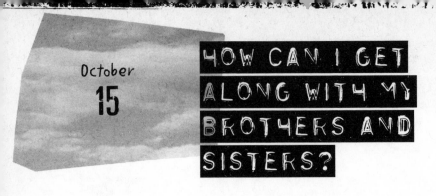

HOW CAN I GET ALONG WITH MY BROTHERS AND SISTERS?

Give all your worries and cares to God, for he cares about what happens to you.
1 Peter 5:7

YOU CAN PRAY:
Dear Lord, thank you for my brothers and sisters. Help me to appreciate my family and to get along with each one. In Jesus' name. Amen.

Sometimes the people you live with are the hardest ones to love! Maybe your brother or sister is different from you. Perhaps you are neat and he or she is messy. Maybe you get better grades or your sister is better at sports. Perhaps your brother gets to do things you're not allowed to do. It's easy to get angry and fight, especially if you share a bedroom! It's often hard to get along with people who are different from you. You need to give that trouble to Jesus!

You didn't choose your brothers and sisters—but God did! He planned each member of your family. He knows what each of you is like. Try to think of good things about your brother or sister. What talents or abilities does each have? What talents or abilities do you have? How can you help each other? Maybe you can help your brother with a subject in school that is hard for him. Perhaps your sister can help you learn to do something well. Thank God for the family he's given you. Ask him to help you appreciate your brothers and sisters instead of fighting with them.

WRITE THREE THINGS YOU APPRECIATE ABOUT YOUR BROTHERS OR SISTERS.

WILL GOD BE WITH ME EVEN IN THE HOSPITAL?

October
16

When your body doesn't feel good, trusting God can be hard. If you are very sick, you may need to go to the hospital. You might feel afraid, but remember that God always knows where you are. He is right there with you. God is the one who made your body. He knows more about it than even the best doctor. He will allow only what is best for you. He can give the doctor wisdom to find out what is wrong and how to help.

When you must go to the hospital, give that trouble to Jesus. Pray for your doctor—that God will help him to know what to do for you. Ask God to help you be brave. You can say along with one of the Bible writers, "When I am afraid, I put my trust in you [God]" (Psalm 56:3).

Maybe you'll get to share with your doctor or nurse how God is helping you to be brave. You may even be able to encourage someone else who is scared. Whether you're in the hospital for just a few days or for a long time, God will be there. You can trust him to help and care for you!

Give all your worries and cares to God, for he cares about what happens to you. 1 Peter 5:7

YOU CAN PRAY:
Dear Lord, thank you that you know all about my body. Help me to be brave even if I have to go into the hospital. In Jesus' name. Amen.

WHY CAN YOU TRUST GOD EVEN IN THE HOSPITAL?

October

17

IS IT OKAY TO MISS SOMEONE WHO DIES?

Jeremy's grandpa died. Jeremy would miss Grandpa so much. Tears came to his eyes as he thought about all the fun times he'd had with Grandpa.

When someone you love dies, it's normal to feel sad. It's okay to cry. God knows how you feel. You will miss that person, and you may wonder why he had to die. God has planned all of our days. He knew when we would be born. He knows when each person will die.

The Bible says, "The Lord's loved ones are precious to him; it grieves him when they die" (Psalm 116:15). A saint is a person who knows Jesus as his Savior. When that person dies, he goes to be with the Lord Jesus. If you know Jesus as your Savior, you'll see that person again in heaven someday. You can know he is happy and peaceful in heaven. Maybe you're not sure if the person who died knew Jesus. You'll have to trust that God knows. God always does what is fair and right. Talk to God about how you feel. God is your heavenly Father. He can comfort you when you are sad. Isn't it good to know you can give this trouble to Jesus?

Give all your worries and cares to God, for he cares about what happens to you. 1 Peter 5:7

YOU CAN PRAY:

Dear Lord, I'm glad you know how I feel when someone I love has died. Help me to remember the good things about that person. In Jesus' name. Amen.

WRITE SOMETHING GOOD YOU REMEMBER ABOUT SOMEONE WHO HAS DIED.

WHY DO MY MOM AND DAD ALWAYS YELL AT ME?

October

18

Jenna's mom had a bad temper and yelled a lot. Jenna knew her mom worked hard and worried about having enough money to pay their bills. Jenna knew it wasn't her fault when her mom yelled, but it made her feel bad. Sometimes it made her angry.

Maybe you have a mom or dad who yells at you a lot. Perhaps your parent even uses bad language. It's not your fault. It's normal for you to feel bad and maybe even angry. But God can help you love your parents even when they yell.

Choose a time when things are calm and talk to your parents about the problem. Tell them how their yelling makes you feel. They might not realize that they are hurting you this way. Be sure that you are obeying your parents when they give you a chore to do. You might want to ask if there's something else you can do that will make it easier for them.

Most of all, pray for your parents. Perhaps they need to trust Jesus as their Savior so that he can change them on the inside. Remember that God knows about your family. Give your family troubles to the Lord Jesus. You can trust him to help you.

HOW COULD YOU SHOW YOUR PARENTS YOU LOVE THEM?

Give all your worries and cares to God, for he cares about what happens to you.
1 Peter 5:7

YOU CAN PRAY:

Dear God, thank you for my parents. Help me to be patient with them. Help me to show them love and kindness. In Jesus' name. Amen.

October

19

WILL GOD BE WITH ME IF MY PARENTS GET DIVORCED?

Give all your worries and cares to God, for he cares about what happens to you. 1 Peter 5:7

YOU CAN PRAY:

Dear God, thank you for always taking care of me. Help me to love my parents, no matter what. In Jesus' name. Amen.

Having divorced parents is a big difficulty for many children! It's scary to think that your family won't be together. It's sad when one of your parents goes to live somewhere else. But God knows all about it. He can help you through any situation—even divorce. You can give this big hurt to the Lord Jesus.

One thing you need to know is that it's not your fault if your parents get divorced. There are many reasons why some parents decide they can't be married anymore. Divorce is an adult decision. You don't need to feel guilty.

If your parents divorce, ask God to help you have a right attitude. You need to be loving and kind to both parents. They will need your love in a special way during this painful time. Pray for your parents. If they don't know Jesus as their Savior, ask God to help them realize that they need him. Ask God to bring healing to your family. Also, ask God to help you trust him. God is with you no matter where you live. He knows what is happening in your family. He is your heavenly Father and he will always take care of you.

HOW COULD YOU HELP YOUR PARENTS WHEN THEY ARE GETTING DIVORCED?

CAN GOD HELP ME GET ALONG WITH MY STEPMOM AND HER KIDS?

October
20

Juan was so sad when his parents divorced. Juan and his sisters lived with their father. Two years later, Juan's father married a lady who had two children. Now Juan had a stepmother and two stepbrothers. Juan didn't like it when his stepmother gave him a job to do. He wanted to yell, "You're not my mother!" Juan worried that maybe his dad liked his new sons more than he liked Juan.

Do you live with a stepfamily? Maybe you sometimes feel like Juan. It's normal to feel angry that someone is taking the place of your parent. It's hard to get used to having new brothers and sisters.

Remember that God is in control, and he knows everything. He knows all about your new family. He has allowed your stepparent to be in charge of you. Ask God to help you to grow in love and respect for your stepparent. Ask him to help you get along with stepbrothers or stepsisters. God has allowed them in your family. Find out what they like to do. Maybe you would enjoy doing those things together. Give this situation to the Lord Jesus. He can help you learn to love your stepfamily.

WRITE SOMETHING YOU LIKE ABOUT YOUR STEPPARENT OR STEPBROTHERS OR STEPSISTERS.

Give all your worries and cares to God, for he cares about what happens to you.
1 Peter 5:7

YOU CAN PRAY:
Dear God, put your love in my heart for my new family. Help me to obey my stepparent and to get along with stepbrothers and stepsisters. In Jesus' name. Amen.

October

21

SHOULD I TELL IF SOMEONE TOUCHES ME IN WRONG WAYS?

God made your body in a wonderful way. He made you to enjoy certain kinds of touch. Maybe you enjoy holding your dad's hand when you walk or hugging your mom before you go to bed.

Some parts of your body are to be kept private. God made them to bring you special joy when you are married. Until then, God wants you to be careful not to allow anyone to touch the private parts of your body in a wrong way.

If someone touches you this way, you need to tell an adult. You may feel ashamed, but it's not your fault. The person touching you is the one who is wrong. The person touching you may say it's a secret, but you need to tell. Tell God about this situation. Ask him to give you courage to talk to an adult. Perhaps you can tell your parent, your teacher, the pastor of your church, or some other adult you trust.

If you've trusted Jesus as your Savior, God says your body is a temple—the place where his Spirit lives (1 Corinthians 6:19-20). He wants you to honor him with your body. He also wants other people to treat your body with respect. Don't let anyone treat it in a wrong way.

Give all your worries and cares to God, for he cares about what happens to you. 1 Peter 5:7

YOU CAN PRAY:

Dear God, thank you for making my body special. Give me courage to tell if someone touches me in a wrong way. In Jesus' name. Amen.

WHAT SHOULD YOU DO IF SOMEONE TOUCHES YOU IN WRONG WAYS?

DOES GOD CARE WHEN THERE'S VIOLENCE IN MY FAMILY?

October
22

Elisa's dad drank a lot and became angry. He hit her mom, and sometimes he hit her. Elisa didn't want anyone to know. She wore blouses with long sleeves to cover her bruises. Elisa thought about telling someone. However, she was afraid of making her dad angrier.

Elisa had believed in the Lord Jesus Christ as her Savior. She began to cast (put) her troubles on Jesus. She told him about her father. She knew Jesus cared for her. God gave Elisa courage to tell her teacher about her father. The teacher told Elisa that it wasn't her fault that her father hurt her. The teacher found help for Elisa's family.

If you live in a family like Elisa's, you might think that nobody cares about you, but God cares. Remember what you learned from Joseph's story (October 4)? Even though people do evil things to you, God can turn them to good (Romans 8:28). He wants you to cast your troubles on him. He can give you courage to tell an adult about what is happening to you. If you live in this kind of home, don't try to keep it to yourself. Tell someone and let that person help you.

WRITE WHAT YOU CAN DO IF SOMEONE IN YOUR HOME IS HURTING YOU.

Give all your worries and cares to God, for he cares about what happens to you. 1 Peter 5:7

YOU CAN PRAY:
Dear God, thank you for caring about me. Please give me courage to tell someone if I am being hurt in my home. In Jesus' name. Amen.

October

23

WILL GOD TAKE CARE OF ME IF MY FAMILY DOESN'T HAVE A HOME?

Give all your worries and cares to God, for he cares about what happens to you. 1 Peter 5:7

YOU CAN PRAY:

Dear God, I'm glad you know all about me and my family. Thank you for caring for us every day. In Jesus' name. Amen.

Have you ever watched a bird build a nest? She uses twigs, grass, or other things to make her nest safe and secure. God made you with that same need for a place of safety. However, there are children whose families don't have a house in which to live. Sometimes they live in shelters with other homeless families. Some live in their cars or even on the street. Does God know and care about where you live? Yes, he does!

Things don't always go well, even for Christian families. A parent may lose his job or get sick. There might not be enough money to pay for a home. God knows about everything that happens to his children. He is never surprised. He is always working out his perfect plan for you. This is another situation you can talk about with the Lord Jesus. He wants you to bring your needs to him and trust him.

If your family is homeless, you are still a family. Talk to your heavenly Father. Tell him about your needs and trust him to help you. He may provide a job. He may send someone to help your family. Whatever he chooses to do will be right and good.

WRITE A PRAYER TO GOD, THANKING HIM FOR CARING FOR YOU AND YOUR FAMILY.

October
24

WHAT IS FAITH?

Are you sitting down? Did you examine the chair first to see if it would hold you? No! You probably didn't even think about it. Now lift your feet off the floor. With all of your weight on the chair, you are now trusting the chair alone to hold you. You have faith in the chair.

The Bible says, "It is impossible to please God without faith" (Hebrews 11:6). Faith in God means believing without questioning what God says and acting on it. It means trusting him completely. You put your faith in the Lord Jesus Christ when you believed in him as your Savior. Now that you are a Christian, God wants you to continue to have faith in him.

You need faith to handle the hard things that come into your life. You need faith to say "no" to sin. You need faith to trust God's plan for you. In Hebrews, chapter 11, the Bible lists a whole group of people who were heroes because of their faith in God. They were just like you and me. God tells us about them to encourage us to have faith. God is faithful to you—you can have faith in him!

FINISH THIS SENTENCE: TO ME, FAITH IN GOD MEANS . . .

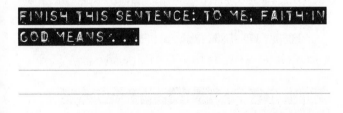

"For I know the plans I have for you," says the Lord. "They are plans for good and not for disaster, to give you a future and a hope."
Jeremiah 29:11

YOU CAN PRAY:

Dear God, thank you that you are faithful to me. Help me to have faith in you for everything in my life. In Jesus' name. Amen.

October

25

AM I A DOUBTER?

Have you heard the words "Seeing is believing"? Many people are doubters—they refuse to believe something until it is proven. Even Christians can be doubters. They have trouble trusting God and his Word.

In John 20:24–29, the Bible tells about a doubter named Thomas. He was a friend and follower of the Lord Jesus. Jesus had told his followers that he would die. He had also told them he would come back to life again. After Jesus died, his followers were sad and afraid. Then, Jesus appeared to them—but Thomas wasn't there. When the others told him that Jesus was alive, Thomas doubted. He told them that unless he could see Jesus and touch the nail scars in his hands, he would not believe (John 20:25).

Later, Jesus appeared again. This time, Thomas was there. The Lord Jesus invited Thomas to touch his hands so he would no longer doubt. Thomas now believed. He fell to his knees and worshiped Jesus as his Lord. Jesus said, "You believe because you have seen me. Blessed are those who haven't seen me and believe anyway" (John 20:29).

Someday you'll see Jesus in heaven. Until then, don't be a doubter. Have faith in God—believe his Word.

"For I know the plans I have for you," says the Lord. "They are plans for good and not for disaster, to give you a future and a hope."
Jeremiah 29:11

YOU CAN PRAY:
Dear God, thank you that I can have faith in you and in your Word. Help me not to doubt but to believe you. In Jesus' name. Amen.

WHY IS IT WRONG TO BE A DOUBTER ABOUT GOD?

WHY SHOULD I TRUST GOD?

October
26

Have you ever looked at an American dollar bill? These important words are printed on it: “In God we trust.” The men and women who founded America knew that God is trustworthy. He deserves our trust—our faith. There aren’t too many things in our world that are trustworthy. Things that you buy will eventually break or wear out. Even people that you love are not always deserving of your trust.

But God is always trustworthy. That’s because God cannot lie—he always keeps his promises. And God also has power to do what he says he will do. When God tells you to cast your care on him because he cares for you, you can trust him. When God says, “I know the plans I have for you. . . . They are plans for good and not for disaster, to give you a future and a hope,” you can trust him.

God has always been faithful to do what he says. The Bible says, “God can be trusted to keep his promise” (Hebrews 10:23). No matter what happens, you can trust God. He knows all about your life and he is working out his plan. Don’t worry. Don’t doubt. Trust God, who is trustworthy!

WRITE TWO REASONS THAT YOU CAN TRUST GOD.

“For I know the plans I have for you,” says the Lord. “They are plans for good and not for disaster, to give you a future and a hope.”
Jeremiah 29:11

YOU CAN PRAY:
Dear God, thank you that you are trustworthy. Help me to trust you more each day. In Jesus’ name. Amen.

October

27

HOW CAN I TRUST GOD?

When David was young, he had a GIANT problem! The Bible tells about a giant named Goliath, who shouted threats at the army of Israel. He made fun of the true and living God. The Israelites were all afraid—even the king!

David was angry when he heard Goliath's evil words. He went to King Saul and said he would fight the giant. But David was young. He was not a mighty soldier. How could he fight this huge enemy?

David knew he couldn't beat Goliath—but God could. David told the king that when he took care of his father's sheep, a lion and then a bear came to attack them. God helped David kill them. Then David said, "The Lord who saved me from the claws of the lion and the bear will save me from this Philistine!" (1 Samuel 17:37).

When you have a problem, you can do what David did. Think about problems God has helped you with before. Think about how faithful and trustworthy God is. Then trust God to help you again. He did it for David! With God's help, David killed the giant. God will help you, too, if you'll trust him.

"For I know the plans I have for you," says the Lord. "They are plans for good and not for disaster, to give you a future and a hope."
Jeremiah 29:11

YOU CAN PRAY:
Dear God, thank you for the ways you've helped me before. Thank you that I can trust you with all kinds of problems, even giant ones. In Jesus' name. Amen.

WRITE ONE WAY GOD HELPED YOU WITH A BIG PROBLEM.

IF I PRAY, WILL GOD MAKE PROBLEMS STOP?

October
28

Often when people pray, God makes problems stop, but not always. A man in the Bible named Paul had a big problem. It might have been a painful physical problem. Whatever it was, Paul wanted to get rid of it. So he prayed—not once or twice, but three times! Each time, Paul asked God to take the problem away (2 Corinthians 12:7-8).

God answered Paul's prayer, but not in the way you might think. God said to Paul, "My gracious favor is all you need. My power works best in your weakness" (2 Corinthians 12:9). Because God's strength shows up best in our weak areas, his answer to Paul was "no." He allowed Paul's problem to continue. God wanted to show his grace in Paul's life by giving him the strength to go through the problem.

God may take away your problem when you pray, but sometimes God wants to give you grace to go through it. He wants your life to bring honor and praise to him. At times, that may be done best through suffering. As others see how God gives you strength to trust him, they will praise him. Maybe they will be encouraged to trust him too.

WHY DOESN'T GOD ALWAYS TAKE AWAY YOUR PROBLEMS?

"For I know the plans I have for you," says the Lord. "They are plans for good and not for disaster, to give you a future and a hope."
Jeremiah 29:11

YOU CAN PRAY:
Dear God, thank you that I can have your strength to go through problems. Help me to trust you even through my suffering. In Jesus' name. Amen.

October
29

HOW CAN I THANK GOD IN HARD TIMES?

There has probably never been anyone who suffered as a Christian more than a follower of Jesus named Paul. In 2 Corinthians 11:23-33, Paul tells about many of his hard times. Often he was put in prison for telling people about Jesus. He was beaten many times. He suffered in shipwrecks and was stranded on the open sea. He was attacked by bandits. He was falsely accused of wrongdoing. His life was constantly in danger. Toward the end of his life, Paul was chained in a cold, damp prison dungeon. Eventually, he would be put to death for being a Christian.

Did Paul complain or feel sorry for himself? No, he thanked God! In his dark prison cell, Paul wrote, "Always be full of joy in the Lord" (Philippians 4:4). How could Paul rejoice? He knew that God was in control. He trusted in God no matter what.

What about you? Are you thankful, even in hard times? Don't give in to grumbling and complaining or feeling sorry for yourself. Instead, be thankful. How? Remember all God has done for you. Thank him that he is in control and that he's there to help you.

"For I know the plans I have for you," says the Lord. "They are plans for good and not for disaster, to give you a future and a hope."
Jeremiah 29:11

YOU CAN PRAY:
Dear God, thank you that you're always with me to help me, even in hard times. In Jesus' name. Amen.

WRITE A SHORT POEM, THANKING GOD FOR HELPING YOU EVEN IN HARD TIMES.

WHAT SHOULD I DO ABOUT PEOPLE WHO HURT ME?

October
30

Have you ever wanted to get even with someone who hurt you? That is a normal response. But angry feelings kept inside will grow into bitterness and hate. They may even cause you to become physically ill.

Instead of being angry and hateful, God wants you to forgive. Forgiveness means letting go of your anger and your desire to get even. The Bible says you should forgive others "just as God through Christ has forgiven you" (Ephesians 4:32). Think of all God has forgiven in your life. Your sin against God is worse than anything anyone could do to you. If you're his child, he has forgiven you for all of your bad thoughts, words, and actions. God forgives you because Jesus Christ, his perfect Son, took the punishment you deserved!

Forgiving others can be hard, but the Lord Jesus said that God will forgive you only as you are willing to forgive others (Matthew 6:14-15). You may not be able to forget the hurt, but you can choose to forgive the one who has hurt you. Are you keeping angry feelings inside toward someone? Confess them to God and ask him to help you forgive.

WHY IS IT IMPORTANT FOR YOU TO FORGIVE?

"For I know the plans I have for you," says the Lord. "They are plans for good and not for disaster, to give you a future and a hope."
Jeremiah 29:11

YOU CAN PRAY:

Dear God, thank you for forgiving me for all my sin. Help me to be willing to forgive others who have hurt me. In Jesus' name. Amen.

October
31

WHAT DOES IT MEAN TO PERSEVERE?

Are you a quitter? A quitter gives up when things are hard or uncomfortable. A quitter gets discouraged, thinking a job will never be finished. Instead of quitting, God wants you to persevere.

Persevering means continuing through a hard time without giving up. The Bible tells about a man named Nehemiah. God gave him a big job to do. The wall around the city of Jerusalem had been broken down by enemies. Nehemiah was in charge of getting the huge wall rebuilt. As Nehemiah began the work, many problems came along. Nehemiah faced fear and discouragement, but Nehemiah persevered until the wall was finished!

There will be hard times in your life when you'll be tempted to quit. You might feel sorry for yourself and think it's just too hard to be a Christian, but God can give you perseverance. God has wonderful plans for you. He just wants you to trust him as he works them out in your life. Don't get discouraged. Don't be a quitter. Keep on keeping on! The Bible says, "So don't get tired of doing what is good. Don't get discouraged and give up, for we will reap a harvest of blessing at the appropriate time" (Galatians 6:9).

"For I know the plans I have for you," says the Lord. "They are plans for good and not for disaster, to give you a future and a hope."
Jeremiah 29:11

YOU CAN PRAY:
Dear God, please help me to persevere, even through the hard times when I feel like quitting. In Jesus' name. Amen.

FINISH THIS SENTENCE: THIS WEEK I WILL PERSEVERE BY . . .

THE MEMORY ZONE

Here are some great Bible verses about what you've learned so far. Put a check mark in the box as you memorize each one!

- ❑ **Hebrews 11:6** "So, you see, it is impossible to please God without faith. Anyone who wants to come to him must believe that there is a God and that he rewards those who sincerely seek him."

- ❑ **Joshua 1:9** "Be strong and courageous! Do not be afraid or discouraged. For the Lord your God is with you wherever you go."

- ❑ **I Peter 4:16, 19** "But it is no shame to suffer for being a Christian. Praise God for the privilege of being called by his wonderful name! . . . So if you are suffering according to God's will, keep on doing what is right, and trust yourself to the God who made you, for he will never fail you."

- ❑ **Philippians 4:4-5** "Always be full of joy in the Lord. I say it again—rejoice! Let everyone see that you are considerate in all you do. Remember, the Lord is coming soon."

- ❑ **I Corinthians 6:19-20** "Don't you know that your body is the temple of the Holy Spirit, who lives in you and was given to you by God? You do not belong to yourself, for God bought you with a high price. So you must honor God with your body."

- ❑ **Psalm 27:1** "The Lord is my light and my salvation—so why should I be afraid? The Lord protects me from danger—so why should I tremble?"

- ❑ **Galatians 6:9** "So don't get tired of doing what is good. Don't get discouraged and give up, for we will reap a harvest of blessing at the appropriate time."

- ❑ **I Corinthians 15:58** "Be strong and steady, always enthusiastic about the Lord's work, for you know that nothing you do for the Lord is ever useless."

Activity 10: Trusting God

I CAN TRUST GOD

Unscramble the letters and write the mystery word in the blanks below. Then complete the sentence.

G O F

Y I L R

I will ___ ___ ___ ___ ___ ___ ___ God in my life by . . .

____

____

THINKING IT OVER!

Trusting God

Write the answers to these questions from your devotionals in the blanks.

1. What does God control in your life?

____

2. What can you remember to help you during hard times?

____

3. What should you do if your family doesn't believe in Jesus?

____

4. What can you do when you are worried about your family?

____

5. What is faith in God?

____

6. What does it mean to persevere during a hard time?

____

If you need help, you can look back in this month's devotionals. The number in ( ) tells you which devotional to check for each question. 1. (1) 2. (8) 3. (13) 4. (18) 5. (24) 6. (31)

NOVEMBER

Taking a Stand

November

1

ARE SOME THINGS ABSOLUTELY RIGHT OR WRONG?

"I'm going to tell!" yelled Justin. Ricky knew he'd be in trouble if anyone found out what he had done.

"Wait, Justin. If you don't tell, I'll give you my lunch money."

If Justin took the money, he could buy a treat after school. He thought that maybe what Ricky did wasn't that bad.

Have you ever had to make a choice like the one Justin had to make? Maybe you told a lie because you thought it was just a "little" one. Or maybe you copied an answer from a friend's paper because you wanted to get a good grade. You might try to fool yourself into thinking your sin isn't so bad, or that you have a good reason to do wrong. The Bible tells us that some things, like showing God's love to others, are always right. Other things, like lying and stealing, are always wrong. God warns you to stay away from these wrong things because he knows they will hurt you. God loves you and wants the best for you. In his Word he says, "Do what is right and good in the Lord's sight, so all will go well with you" (Deuteronomy 6:18).

So be careful how you live, not as fools but as those who are wise. Make the most of every opportunity for doing good in these evil days.
Ephesians 5:15-16

YOU CAN PRAY:
Dear God, thank you that you love me. Help me to say no to what is wrong and to do what you have said is right. In Jesus' name. Amen.

WRITE ONE THING YOU KNOW IS RIGHT AND ONE THING YOU KNOW IS WRONG.

DOES GOD ACCEPT PEOPLE NO MATTER HOW THEY LIVE?

November
2

The Bible tells about two cities that you won't find on a map—Sodom and Gomorrah. The people who lived in these places did terrible things. God loved them, but he hated the wrong things they were doing. The people didn't care about God. They liked living in sin. They didn't want to change. God could not let them live in this sinful way anymore. The things they did were so bad that God had to destroy them. Even the cities were completely destroyed. That's why you won't find them on any map!

Did you know that God cares about the way you live? If you have never trusted Jesus as your Savior, you need to know that God loves you, but your sin is serious to him. He may not destroy you because of your sin, but you will be separated from him forever if your sin is not forgiven.

If you are a Christian, you should want to live God's way. When you choose to obey the Lord and say "no" to sin, you please God. The Bible calls this living as a wise person. Do you know people whose lives don't please the Lord? Pray for them and be an example by the wise way you live.

So be careful how you live, not as fools but as those who are wise. Make the most of every opportunity for doing good in these evil days.
Ephesians 5:15-16

YOU CAN PRAY:
Dear God, thank you for helping me live a life that will please you. Please help me to be wise and obey your Word. In Jesus' name. Amen.

WHY DOES GOD CARE ABOUT THE WAY YOU LIVE?

November
3

HOW CAN I MAKE CHOICES THAT HONOR GOD?

The Bible tells about King Rehoboam, the king of Israel, who made a BIG mistake! His friends had told him to do some awful things—and he did them! Now the people of Israel were angry. Things would never be the same again. If only he had listened to the godly men who had tried to tell him what was right, but now it was too late. He had made a bad choice.

Have you ever let someone talk you into doing something wrong? Afterwards, were you glad you had listened to them, or did you wish you had done the right thing instead? Many times you know right away what is right and what is wrong, but sometimes the choice is not so easy.

How can you make choices that honor God? First, pray and ask God to help you know what is right. Second, read your Bible. Look for things that will help you understand the right thing to do. Third, ask people who love God what they would do if they had to make your choice. Fourth, when you know the right thing to do, DO IT!

So be careful how you live, not as fools but as those who are wise. Make the most of every opportunity for doing good in these evil days.
Ephesians 5:15-16

YOU CAN PRAY:
Dear God, thank you for giving me all I need to make wise choices. When I know what is right, help me to do it. In Jesus' name. Amen.

WRITE THE NAMES OF THREE PEOPLE WHO CAN HELP YOU MAKE WISE CHOICES.

____

____

____

____

DO MY REACTIONS TO OTHERS MATTER TO GOD?

November

4

What food do you like best? What games do you like to play? Usually, the things we like best are the things we are used to. It can be hard to get used to things that are different. Sometimes people are mean to each other just because they are different. They may have a different skin color, speak a different language, or have a different personality than you. Perhaps they just don't enjoy the things you enjoy.

God says being mean to others is sin. He loves everyone. Every person is important to God. It does not matter what they're like, where they live, or how they look. God says you should not make up your mind about what people are like just by looking at them. The Bible says, "People judge by outward appearance, but the Lord looks at a person's thoughts and intentions" (I Samuel 16:7).

Do you know people who are different than you are? As a Christian it is your job to show them God's love. Get to know them. Soon you will find out that you have more in common than you thought. You will begin to forget that they are different at all.

So be careful how you live, not as fools but as those who are wise. Make the most of every opportunity for doing good in these evil days.
Ephesians 5:15-16

YOU CAN PRAY:
Dear God, thank you that you love everyone. Help me to show your love to people who are different. In Jesus' name. Amen.

HOW CAN YOU SHOW KINDNESS TO SOMEONE WHO IS DIFFERENT THAN YOU ARE?

November

5

HOW CAN I BE RESPECTFUL, YET STILL STAND TRUE TO GOD?

So be careful how you live, not as fools but as those who are wise. Make the most of every opportunity for doing good in these evil days.
Ephesians 5:15-16

YOU CAN PRAY:
Dear God, thank you for the people you put in charge of me. Help me to be respectful to them as I obey you. In Jesus' name. Amen.

The Bible tells about a man named Daniel who loved God. He obeyed the people in charge and they trusted him. There were some men who wanted to get rid of Daniel. These men talked the king into writing a new law saying that people could only pray to the king. Anyone breaking the law would be thrown to the lions to be eaten alive.

Daniel heard about the law, but he did not argue or complain. He just did what he knew was right. He prayed to the one true God. The king's men found out that Daniel was still praying to God, and they told the king. When the king heard about Daniel, he wished he had never made the law. But the law couldn't be changed. The king told Daniel that he hoped God would keep him safe. Then the king's men had Daniel thrown to the lions. The next day, the king came to see if Daniel had been eaten, but he was alive! God had shut the mouths of the lions, and Daniel was safe.

You please God by obeying the people in charge of you. But if you are told to do something that would cause you to disobey God, ask him for the courage to do what's right. Like Daniel, you can be respectful yet still take a stand for God!

WHAT SHOULD YOU DO WHEN SOMEONE IN CHARGE TELLS YOU TO DO SOMETHING WRONG?

WHY SHOULD I OBEY GOD WHEN OTHERS DON'T?

November
6

Why should you bother doing what's right when other people seem to get away with doing wrong? A long time ago a man named Asaph was unhappy. Many people were getting away with the wrong things they were doing. Asaph told God how angry he was. He asked God to help him understand.

God helped Asaph, and he began to see things God's way. He learned that God wanted him to do right even when others were getting away with doing wrong. He knew that God wanted him to be different.

You should be different than the people who don't belong to God. His Holy Spirit will help you have the power to obey even when it is hard. God has promised you good things in your life when you do right. He has also promised you a reward in heaven.

Keep doing what you know is right even though other people might be doing wrong. It may seem like some people are getting away with doing wrong, but someday God will make everything right. Ask God to help you see things his way. The Bible says, "So don't get tired of doing what is good" (Galatians 6:9).

WHY IS IT IMPORTANT FOR YOU TO DO RIGHT, EVEN IF OTHERS ARE DOING WRONG?

So be careful how you live, not as fools but as those who are wise. Make the most of every opportunity for doing good in these evil days.
Ephesians 5:15-16

YOU CAN PRAY:
Dear God, thank you for giving me the power to obey. Please help me to do right no matter what other people do. In Jesus' name. Amen.

November

7

HOW CAN I OBEY GOD AND NOT JUDGE OTHERS?

Have you ever tried to learn a new game that had a lot of rules? Forgetting a rule might make you lose the game. Some people think that being a Christian is like that. They think that to make God happy, they have to learn a lot of rules.

In Bible times people called Pharisees, the religious leaders, did just that. They made up a lot of rules and said that the only way to make God happy was to obey all the rules on their list. Many of the Pharisees were busy judging others. They were forgetting God's most important rule—to show his love to others.

In the Bible, God has given you rules or commands to obey. You are responsible for your own behavior in obeying God by keeping his rules. You may not agree with someone else's choices, but you are not responsible for what other people do. Let God judge (decide) if that person's actions are right or wrong. Your job is to show him God's love and help him do what is right. Be wise. Don't be like the Pharisees who loved finding fault in others and judging them.

So be careful how you live, not as fools but as those who are wise. Make the most of every opportunity for doing good in these evil days.
Ephesians 5:15-16

YOU CAN PRAY:
Dear God, thank you for loving me. Help me not to judge others even when I think they are doing wrong. Help me to love them instead. In Jesus' name. Amen.

HOW SHOULD YOU RESPOND WHEN YOU THINK OTHERS ARE DOING WRONG?

DID GOD REALLY MEAN TO MAKE EVERYONE DIFFERENT?

November
8

What would happen if God made everyone the same? It would be confusing and boring! God has made each person unique. Even twins who look exactly alike have things about them that are different. God made people different so we could each do an important job that is just right for us. The Bible says he gave each person his or her own special gifts. "God has given each of us the ability to do certain things well" (Romans 12:6).

God compares our differences to the different parts of the body. If the eye wanted to do the same job as the ear, we would not be able to see. If the foot wanted to do the same job as the heart, we would not be able to walk. Each part of the body is important.

You are special and important too. God has given you gifts and abilities that he can use in a special way. He did that on purpose. He wants you to be able to do the work he has for you. He has given you just the right body, talents, and family to be able to serve him. Thank him for the way he has made you.

WRITE THREE GIFTS OR ABILITIES THAT GOD HAS GIVEN YOU.

____

____

So be careful how you live, not as fools but as those who are wise. Make the most of every opportunity for doing good in these evil days.
Ephesians 5:15-16

YOU CAN PRAY:
Dear God, thank you for making me special. Help me to appreciate the way you have made each person different. In Jesus' name. Amen.

November
9

HOW CAN I LOVE PEOPLE I DON'T AGREE WITH?

So be careful how you live, not as fools but as those who are wise. Make the most of every opportunity for doing good in these evil days.
Ephesians 5:15-16

YOU CAN PRAY:
Dear God, thank you that Jesus loves me even though I have done wrong things. Help me to show your love to others. In Jesus' name. Amen.

When Jesus lived on earth, many of the religious leaders didn't like the men and women he spent time with. Jesus went to dinner with people who had stolen and lied. He was friendly with people who broke God's rules.

Did Jesus know that they had done so many wrong things? Yes! Jesus was God the Son. He knew all about the wrong things these people had done. He never said that their sinful ways were right. He explained that anyone who sins is someone who needs God. He showed them his love so they would know the way to have their sins forgiven.

Do you know people who do things or believe things you know are wrong? Do not join them in doing wrong. Tell them that God loves them. Show them kindness. Let them see Jesus living in you.

When Jesus was on earth, he saw the sins of the world. He did not agree with the wrong things people were doing, but he still showed them God's love when he died and rose again. He can give you the power to show his love to others, no matter what they choose to do. "Love is patient and kind" (1 Corinthians 13:4).

FINISH THIS SENTENCE: I SHOULD LOVE OTHERS I DON'T AGREE WITH BECAUSE . . .

HOW DOES SATAN LIE ABOUT GOD?

November

10

Did you know the very first lie was told to the first people God ever created? It happened when Satan, God's enemy, tricked Adam and Eve into disobeying God. He made them believe a lie.

Did you know that Satan, the devil, will try to trick you, too? He will make you doubt that God is in control. He wants you to think that God doesn't care because he allows things like sickness, hurt, and war. The truth is that all sickness, hurt, and war started because of sin and Satan. God is a good and loving God. The Bible says, "He is good! His faithful love endures forever" (Psalm 106:1).

Satan might try to make you believe that he is stronger than God. The truth is that God has already won the battle with Satan. When Jesus came alive again after dying on the cross for our sins, he showed that Satan did not have any power over him. If you have trusted Jesus as your Savior, Satan has no power over you, either. The Bible says, "The Spirit who lives in you is greater than the spirit who lives in the world" (1 John 4:4).

Satan is called the father of lies. When you are afraid or worried, don't listen to Satan's lies. Instead, talk to God. Ask him to help you see the truth.

[The devil] is a liar and the father of lies.
John 8:44

YOU CAN PRAY:

Dear God, I know you are stronger than Satan. I know you never lie. Help me to trust your Word and not to believe Satan's lies. In Jesus' name. Amen.

WHY SHOULDN'T YOU FEAR SATAN OR HIS LIES?

November
11

HOW DOES SATAN LIE ABOUT JESUS?

Many people believe that Jesus Christ was a good man and a great teacher, but they don't believe that he is God's Son and their Savior. They've believed one of Satan's lies. Satan wants you to believe that the Lord Jesus was just a man. He does not want you to trust Jesus as your Savior.

But Jesus was more than just a man; he was God in a human body. "The Word became human and lived here on earth among us" (John 1:14). Jesus never did anything wrong. He was perfect. "God made Christ, who never sinned, to be the offering for our sin" (2 Corinthians 5:21). No other man has ever been perfect, no matter how great he may have been.

Because Jesus Christ was perfect, he could die to pay the price for your sins. Because he was God, he could come back to life. "God raised [Jesus] from the dead" (Acts 2:32). No other great man has ever raised himself from the dead.

Remember, Satan is a liar. Listen to God's truth. "Jesus told him, 'I am the way, the truth, and the life. No one can come to the Father except through me' " (John 14:6).

[The devil] is a liar and the father of lies.
John 8:44

YOU CAN PRAY:
Dear God, thank you for sending your Son to die for me. Thank you for raising him to life. In Jesus' name. Amen.

NAME TWO WAYS THAT JESUS IS DIFFERENT FROM ANY OTHER PERSON THAT EVER LIVED.

HOW DOES SATAN LIE ABOUT OUR RELATIONSHIP TO GOD?

November
12

God created people to have a close, loving relationship with him. God gave Adam and Eve, the first man and woman, a beautiful home with plenty of food and lots to do (Genesis 2:15). Every day God came to their garden home to spend a special time with them (Genesis 3:8).

But there was someone who wanted to spoil this special relationship. That was Satan. Satan lied to Eve and convinced her to disobey God. He made her believe that God might not know what was best and that it wouldn't hurt to disobey. Then Adam disobeyed God too. When Adam and Eve disobeyed God they were filled with fear and shame. God couldn't let them stay in their beautiful home anymore. The special times they had with God were ruined (Genesis 3:1-8, 23).

Satan wants to spoil your relationship with God too. He wants to convince you that your loving heavenly Father doesn't really care about you. He doesn't want you to trust that God is in control. He wants you to disobey God. Don't listen to Satan's lies. Spend time with God each day. Trust him and obey his commands. Ask him to make you wise and strong so you can say no to Satan's tricks.

WHAT CAN YOU DO TO BUILD YOUR RELATIONSHIP WITH GOD?

[The devil] is a liar and the father of lies.
John 8:44

YOU CAN PRAY:
Dear God, thank you that you want to spend time with me. Please help me to get to know you better. In Jesus' name. Amen.

November

13

WHAT IS NEW AGE TEACHING?

Have you ever heard the words New Age? You may have heard these words in school or on television, or you may have read about them in a book. New Age is a way of thinking and believing that goes against what the Bible teaches. It's not really new—it's full of Satan's old lies.

One New Age belief is that people are good and not sinners. God's Word says, "For all have sinned" (Romans 3:23). Another New Age belief is reincarnation. People who believe in reincarnation believe that people die and come back to earth many times in different forms. But the Bible says, "It is destined that each person dies only once and after that comes judgment" (Hebrews 9:27). New Age also teaches that you are god. New Age believers say, "You can do anything—you are your greatest power." However, in the Bible God tells us he is the one true and living God. Jesus Christ, God the Son, says, "Apart from me you can do nothing" (John 15:5).

There are many other false New Age ideas. Satan often makes them sound like truth. Always check to see if an idea agrees with what the Bible says. If it disagrees, it is wrong. Don't be fooled!

[The devil] is a liar and the father of lies.
John 8:44

YOU CAN PRAY:
Dear God, thank you for telling me the truth in your Word. Help me to recognize Satan's lies and not to be fooled. In Jesus' name. Amen.

WHY DO YOU THINK SATAN WANTS PEOPLE TO BELIEVE NEW AGE TEACHING?

CAN I BE GOOD WITHOUT GOD?

November
14

[The devil] is a liar and the father of lies.
John 8:44

"Why did I do that?" "I can't believe I did something so terrible!" Have you ever said words like these after doing something wrong? Sometimes, even when we want to be good, we aren't.

God's faithful servant Paul asked himself the same kind of questions. In Romans chapter 7 he wrote, "I know I am rotten through and through. . . . No matter which way I turn, I can't make myself do right. I want to, but I can't" (Romans 7:18). Paul said that many times he *didn't* do what he knew was right, and all too often he *did* do what he knew was wrong. He knew that he could not be good in his own strength.

Just like Paul, you cannot be good without God. But there's good news. If you're a child of God, you have his Holy Spirit living inside of you. He can give you the power to do what's right and to stay away from what's wrong. Tell God that you know you need his power to be good. Ask him to help you know what's right through his Holy Spirit. Obey his Spirit when it's time to make a choice between right and wrong.

YOU CAN PRAY:
Dear God, I know I need your help to obey. Please give me the strength to do what is right. In Jesus' name. Amen.

WRITE SOMETHING YOU NEED GOD'S HELP TO STOP DOING.

November
15

WHY CAN'T I SAVE MYSELF?

One night a young man came to talk to the Lord Jesus. He wanted to know how to be saved. Perhaps he expected Jesus to tell him that he was already doing all of the right things. He knew the Scriptures, spent a lot of time in prayer, and did his best to be a good person. Jesus' answer surprised him. Jesus let the young man know that all of these things were good, but none of them would save him. The disciples were surprised too. The Bible says, "The disciples were astounded. 'Then who in the world can be saved?' they asked" (Matthew 19:25).

God tells us in his Word that no one can save himself. You were born with a sinful nature already inside of you. Only Jesus can give you the gift of salvation because he never sinned. "God made Christ, who never sinned, to be the offering for our sin" (2 Corinthians 5:21). Because Jesus took the punishment for your sins, you can be saved. The gift of salvation is possible only because of God's love and grace. "God saved you by his special favor when you believed. And you can't take credit for this; it is a gift from God" (Ephesians 2:8).

[The devil] is a liar and the father of lies.
John 8:44

YOU CAN PRAY:
Dear God, thank you for doing what I couldn't do. Thank you for saving me from my sins. In Jesus' name. Amen.

HOW CAN YOU BE SAVED FROM YOUR SINS?

ARE GOD'S PROMISES REALLY FOR ME?

November
16

Has anyone ever made you a promise and then let you down? There's one person who will never break his promises to you—God. The Bible says, "He has given us all of his rich and wonderful promises" (2 Peter 1:4). For example, God has promised to give eternal life to all who will believe in his Son, Jesus Christ. He has promised to care for his children. He has promised to always hear and answer prayers. He has promised to be with you always if you are his child.

Satan, the father of lies, will try to make you believe that God has not kept his promises. He might even try to trick you into believing that God's promises aren't really for you. He wants you to think that God has forgotten about you. Don't believe Satan's lies. God's Word says, "God can be trusted to keep his promise" (Hebrews 10:23).

Sometimes God may answer your prayers in a different way or at a different time than you expected. These are times when Satan might try to fool you. Remember God loves you. He wants the best for you. He will keep his promises at just the right time.

LIST THREE OF GOD'S PROMISES TO YOU.

[The devil] is a liar and the father of lies.
John 8:44

YOU CAN PRAY:

Dear God, thank you for keeping your promises. Please help me to keep mine, too. In Jesus' name. Amen.

November
17

HOW DOES SATAN LIE ABOUT THE BIBLE?

Satan does not want you to read your Bible. He knows it will build your faith and help you stay away from sin. The Bible says, "I have hidden your word in my heart, that I might not sin against you" (Psalm 119:11).

To keep you from reading your Bible, Satan will lie to you. He might try to make you believe that God's Word is full of mistakes. God is perfect. He cannot make mistakes. His Holy Spirit spoke to men who wrote exactly what God wanted written. The Bible says, "It was the Holy Spirit who moved the prophets to speak from God" (2 Peter 1:21).

Satan might try to make you think the Bible is just a good book. The Bible says, "All Scripture is inspired by God" (2 Timothy 3:16). Every Word God has written is true because God cannot lie.

Also, Satan may try to make you believe that reading your Bible is not important. Don't let him trick you. Take time to read your Bible every day. God says to study his Word carefully so that you'll know what it says and means. When you do this, you'll be able to stand against Satan's lies about the Bible.

Instead of believing what they knew was the truth about God, they deliberately chose to believe lies. So they worshiped the things God made but not the Creator himself.
Romans 1:25

YOU CAN PRAY:
Dear God, thank you for the Bible. Help me to read it every day. In Jesus' name. Amen.

HOW DO WE KNOW THE BIBLE IS GOD'S WORD?

WHAT DOES SATAN WANT ME TO BELIEVE ABOUT CREATION?

November
18

Pretend that your family is building a house. Instead of carefully planning what your house will look like, you take all of the boards, nails, and paint and throw them up in the air. Will the pieces fall together to make a beautiful home? Of course not! There has to be a plan. There also has to be someone to carry out the plan.

A house can't be built without a builder. The earth was not created without a Creator. "In the beginning God created the heavens and the earth" (Genesis 1:1). Satan has tried to make people believe that the earth was created by accident after a big explosion.

Satan also lies and says that God didn't create people. He says that, over a long time, people evolved (changed) from animals. God says that's not true. "The Lord God formed a man's body from the dust of the ground and breathed into it the breath of life. And the man became a living person" (Genesis 2:7).

Why does Satan want you to believe you're an accident? He doesn't want you to know that you're special and that you have a loving heavenly Father who made you in his image.

DO YOU BELIEVE GOD CREATED THE WORLD? WHY?

Instead of believing what they knew was the truth about God, they deliberately chose to believe lies. So they worshiped the things God made but not the Creator himself.
Romans 1:25

YOU CAN PRAY:

Dear God, thank you for all the things you have created. Thank you for making me just the way you wanted me to be. In Jesus' name. Amen.

November

19

WHAT IS THE OCCULT?

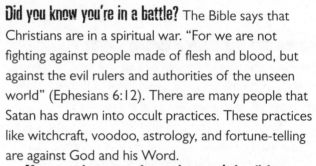

Did you know you're in a battle? The Bible says that Christians are in a spiritual war. "For we are not fighting against people made of flesh and blood, but against the evil rulers and authorities of the unseen world" (Ephesians 6:12). There are many people that Satan has drawn into occult practices. These practices like witchcraft, voodoo, astrology, and fortune-telling are against God and his Word.

Many people use occult practices as their religion. They worship the earth, the sun and moon, or even Satan himself. The Bible says, "Instead of believing what they knew was the truth about God, they deliberately chose to believe lies. So they worshiped the things God made but not the Creator himself" (Romans 1:25). Others get involved because they think it's fun. They read their horoscope or go to fortune-tellers. They hope to find supernatural knowledge and power, but this knowledge and power doesn't come from God. It comes from Satan, who wants to trick people into serving and worshiping him. These things may look like fun, but they will lead you away from God.

Satan does not want good things for you. He doesn't want you to believe God's truth. God says to stay away from occult practices. Trust him to help you win your spiritual battles.

Instead of believing what they knew was the truth about God, they deliberately chose to believe lies. So they worshiped the things God made but not the Creator himself.
Romans 1:25

YOU CAN PRAY:
Dear God, thank you that you are stronger than Satan. Help me to stay away from occult practices. In Jesus' name. Amen.

WHY SHOULD YOU STAY AWAY FROM OCCULT PRACTICES?

CAN PEOPLE REALLY SEE INTO THE FUTURE?

November
20

What's going to happen in the future? To find out, some people ask a fortune-teller, sometimes called a psychic. Psychics claim to know the future. Most of them just make guesses. Sometimes their guesses are right and sometimes they are not.

Some psychics are not just good guessers, though. There are some who are listening to Satan and his demons. God's Word tells about a time when a man named Paul met a fortune-teller. She was a slave and was making a lot of money for her masters by telling fortunes. She wasn't just making guesses. She was controlled by a demon. The Bible says Paul, who was preaching God's Word, commanded the demon to leave her. When it left, the girl could no longer see into the future. Satan's power over her was broken (Acts 16:16-18).

If you have ever listened to a psychic, you "deliberately chose to believe lies." Satan wants to keep you from trusting God for your future. You may think psychics are just for fun, but listening to them and taking their advice can be very dangerous. Don't be fooled by Satan's lies! Trust God and his Word for your future.

WHY SHOULD YOU NOT LISTEN TO A PSYCHIC?

Instead of believing what they knew was the truth about God, they deliberately chose to believe lies. So they worshiped the things God made but not the Creator himself.
Romans 1:25

YOU CAN PRAY:

Dear God, thank you that you know the future. Help me to trust you alone and not be fooled by Satan's tricks. In Jesus' name. Amen.

November 21

WHY DO SOME PEOPLE BELIEVE IN ASTROLOGY?

Instead of believing what they knew was the truth about God, they deliberately chose to believe lies. So they worshiped the things God made but not the Creator himself.
Romans 1:25

YOU CAN PRAY:
Dear God, thank you for your beautiful Creation. Help me to remember to trust you for my future. In Jesus' name. Amen.

Have you ever heard of the zodiac? It is a chart divided into sections or signs. Each sign shows the positions of the stars and planets for particular years. Astrologists (people who study the zodiac) use these signs to write horoscopes. Horoscopes tell people what they should and shouldn't do according to their signs, and they make predictions of what will happen to people. Many individuals read their horoscopes each day. They believe the stars and planets cause them to act a certain way. They depend on astrology to show them the future.

Your enemy, Satan, would love for you to depend on your horoscope instead of God. He wants you to think that astrology can answer your questions about the future. However, God didn't make the stars and planets to answer your questions about life and the future. The answers to those questions can be found in the Bible. God gave you his Holy Spirit to help you understand his Word. He helps you grow in wisdom as you learn about him and trust him with your future.

Learn about God's Creation. Praise him for the wonderful things he has made. Be sure to worship the Creator, and not his Creation.

WHERE CAN YOU FIND ANSWERS TO YOUR QUESTIONS ABOUT LIFE?

WHAT'S WRONG WITH PLAYING OCCULT GAMES?

November

22

Have you ever had someone tease you and then seem surprised when your feelings were hurt? Maybe they said, "I was just kidding around." They thought what they were doing was fun, but it really turned out to be hurtful. There are some things like that—things like horoscopes and Ouija boards. They look like fun, but they could really be hurtful. Satan can use these games to take control of you and cause you to think and do things that are against God.

Some people think games that ask you to pretend you have supernatural powers, cast spells, or look into the future are harmless fun. That's just what Satan wants them to think. Satan can make things look good when they are really harmful. God's Word says to stay away from occult practices—things that involve demons, witchcraft, and fortune-telling.

God loves you and wants the best for you. Satan only wants to hurt and destroy. Obey God's Word. Refuse to play games that could be tricks from the devil. Don't let Satan fool you into disobeying God. "Be strong with the Lord's mighty power. . . . Stand firm against all strategies and tricks of the Devil" (Ephesians 6:10-11).

WHY SHOULD YOU STAY AWAY FROM OCCULT GAMES?

Instead of believing what they knew was the truth about God, they deliberately chose to believe lies. So they worshiped the things God made but not the Creator himself.
Romans 1:25

YOU CAN PRAY:

Dear God, thank you for loving me and showing me the truth in your Word. Help me not to be fooled by Satan's tricks. In Jesus' name. Amen.

November
23

WHERE DOES TRUE POWER COME FROM?

Instead of believing what they knew was the truth about God, they deliberately chose to believe lies. So they worshiped the things God made but not the Creator himself.
Romans 1:25

YOU CAN PRAY:
Dear God, thank you for sending your Holy Spirit to live in me. Help me to depend on your power to win against sin and Satan. In Jesus' name. Amen.

You've probably seen characters in cartoons or comic books that have supernatural power. They can do amazing things and no one can stop them! Have you ever wished you had power like that? Some people believe you can have power by building up your body or taking special vitamins. Others think that you already have supernatural power within you—you just need to bring it out! What is the truth? Where does true power come from?

True power comes from God. When you became a Christian, God's Holy Spirit came to live in you. Only God can give you real power. Having God's power doesn't mean having a superstrong body. God's power is inner strength that makes you able to stand up for him and live your life in a way that's pleasing to him.

God gives you the power of his Holy Spirit to help you win over sin and Satan. You can grow strong in God's power by reading God's Word and praying every day. Ask his Holy Spirit to give you the power you need to stand for him. Choose to obey God and do what's right. Thank God for the victory his power gives you.

WHAT CAN YOU DO TO GROW STRONG IN GOD'S POWER?

HOW CAN I BECOME WISE?

November
24

If you could have any one thing in the world that you wanted, what would it be? Money? Friends? God told a king named Solomon that he would give him anything he asked for. Solomon asked God for wisdom. King Solomon knew that wisdom came from God and was very valuable (1 Kings 3:5, 7-12).

Wisdom is knowing what is right in God's eyes and then doing it. Did you know that God promises to give you wisdom if you ask for it? "If you need wisdom—if you want to know what God wants you to do—ask him, and he will gladly tell you" (James 1:5).

Maybe you don't feel very wise. Sometimes you might make mistakes even though you try very hard. The good news is that you don't have to become wise in your own strength. God says that his power will give you the strength you need. "My gracious favor is all you need. My power works best in your weakness" (2 Corinthians 12:9). If you really want God's help to be wise, ask him to give you wisdom. Read his Word and obey it. Ask him to help you make wise choices. God will keep his promise.

HOW CAN YOU BE WISE?

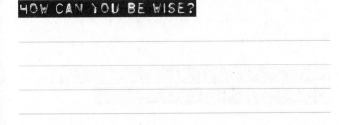

My gracious favor is all you need. My power works best in your weakness.
2 Corinthians 12:9

YOU CAN PRAY:

Dear God, please give me wisdom. Help me to please you in all I do. In Jesus' name. Amen.

November
25

WHERE CAN I FIND ANSWERS TO THINGS I DON'T UNDERSTAND?

King David lived a very unusual life. Sometimes he must have wondered why God chose to give him so many adventures. There must have been many things David didn't understand. Some of David's questions were probably never answered while he lived.

Are there things you don't understand? You can find many answers in the Bible. God can give you understanding when you pray, too. God also may have given you wise, godly adults to help you when you don't understand something. However, sometimes you will have questions that will not be answered until the day you are with God in heaven.

When there is something you don't understand, search God's Word and ask him to help you. If you still don't understand why things are a certain way, decide to trust him anyway. Don't rely only on what you understand, but admit that God's mind is greater than yours. Remember that he loves you. He has promised that when you trust him, he will guide your paths. The Bible says, "Trust in the Lord with all your heart; do not depend on your own understanding. Seek his will in all you do, and he will direct your paths" (Proverbs 3:5-6).

My gracious favor is all you need. My power works best in your weakness.
2 Corinthians 12:9

YOU CAN PRAY:
Dear God, help me to trust you when I don't understand why things happen. In Jesus' name. Amen.

WRITE SOMETHING ABOUT YOUR LIFE THAT YOU DON'T UNDERSTAND.

DOES GOD TALK TO ME?

November
26

How do you know if someone is talking to you? Normally you can see that person looking at you and hear his or her voice. When God talks to you, you can't see his face, and you won't hear his voice, but he does talk to you.

God can talk to you through his Word. When you read your Bible, you are seeing God's words written down. God wants you to pay attention to his written Word just as well as you would if he spoke to you aloud.

God can talk to you through his Holy Spirit. When you pray and think about God's Word, his Holy Spirit can bring Scripture and godly thoughts into your mind. When you wonder if something is right or wrong, his Spirit can give you an understanding to know the truth.

God can also talk to you through other Christians. Sometimes God uses people to help you understand what he has to say to you. Listen to godly people and ask God to help you see if what they are saying agrees with the truth in God's Word. God does talk to you. Do you listen?

My gracious favor is all you need. My power works best in your weakness.
2 Corinthians 12:9

YOU CAN PRAY:

Dear God, please help me to listen and obey when you talk to me. In Jesus' name. Amen.

WRITE THREE WAYS GOD CAN TALK TO YOU.

November

27

DOES GOD HAVE GRACE FOR EVERYONE?

It was terrible. He was sure no one had ever done anything as awful as he had done. Surely, God would never forgive him. He was so ashamed.

This must be how Peter, one of Jesus' followers, felt. On the night that the Lord Jesus was arrested, Peter told three different people that he didn't even know Jesus. Peter was so afraid! Did he deserve to be forgiven? No, but he was! Jesus Christ died on the cross to take the punishment for Peter's sins and the sins of the whole world. This was God's grace—his undeserved kindness toward sinful people.

God's grace is for you, too. There is nothing you can do to earn God's forgiveness. God promises to forgive you when you trust in Jesus as your Savior. But God's grace doesn't end there. God's grace continues throughout your life. It is by God's grace that you have health and life. It is by his grace that you can pray and witness for him. God also forgives you by his grace when you confess your sins each day to him. Aren't you glad for God's wonderful grace in your life? Have you thanked God for his grace today?

My gracious favor is all you need. My power works best in your weakness.
2 Corinthians 12:9

YOU CAN PRAY:

Dear God, thank you for your grace. Thank you that you forgave me even though I didn't deserve it. In Jesus' name. Amen.

WHAT IS GRACE?

WHEN DOES GOD'S GRACE END?

November
28

The Lord Jesus told the story of a young man who asked his father to give him the money that would be his when his father died. Even though it made the father sad, he gave his son what he asked for.

The young man moved to a big city and spent his money on everything he wanted. Soon he ran out of money. He had nowhere to live and nothing to eat. He finally realized how wrong he had been. He hoped that if he begged, his father might give him a job as a servant. He decided to go home.

Before he even reached his house, his father ran to hug him. He was so glad his son had come home. He had never stopped loving him. The father was eager to show his love and kindness to his son, who didn't deserve it. He welcomed his son back into the family and had a big party to celebrate his return (Luke 15:11-32).

This story is a wonderful picture of God's grace for you. God will never stop loving you no matter what you do. He will always forgive you when you confess your sins to him. His grace never ends!

WRITE A SHORT PRAYER, THANKING GOD FOR HIS GRACE.

My gracious favor is all you need. My power works best in your weakness.
2 Corinthians 12:9

YOU CAN PRAY:

Dear God, thank you that you always forgive. Help me to show you my love by obeying you. In Jesus' name. Amen.

November

29

HOW CAN I EXPERIENCE GOD'S GRACE?

My gracious favor is all you need. My power works best in your weakness.
2 Corinthians 12:9

YOU CAN PRAY:

Dear God, thank you for loving me and for showing your grace through the Lord Jesus Christ. In Jesus' name. Amen.

One day a man named Saul traveled toward a city to arrest Christians. He hated them and wanted to stop them from telling others about Jesus. As he traveled, a bright light suddenly flashed around him, causing him to fall to the ground. Then he heard a voice saying, "Saul, Saul, why do you persecute me?" (Acts 9:1-6). It was the Lord Jesus speaking to him! Saul was never the same again. He realized that Jesus truly is God the Son. He learned that he could be forgiven because of God's grace—his undeserved kindness.

Have you ever experienced God's grace? God loves you even though you don't deserve his love. God's Word says, "But God showed his great love for us by sending Christ to die for us while we were still sinners" (Romans 5:8). God wants to forgive your sin and make you part of his family, not because you deserve it but because of his grace. "God saved you by his special favor when you believed. And you can't take credit for this; it is a gift from God" (Ephesians 2:8). You experience God's grace by trusting in God's Son, the Lord Jesus, to save you from your sin. Have you experienced God's grace?

HOW CAN YOU EXPERIENCE GOD'S GRACE?

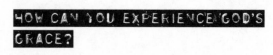

HOW CAN I LIVE BY GOD'S GRACE?

You have learned how God shows his grace to you by forgiving your sins and how you can experience his grace in your life. But how can you live each day by God's grace?

First, you can be thankful for God's grace which saved you from the punishment for your sins. When was the last time you said "thank you" to God for the Lord Jesus, who died for your sins and rose again?

Second, you can depend on God to give you grace to live for him each day. Everything that you do is by God's grace. Can others tell by what you do and say that you are depending on God?

Third, you can be kind to others and forgive them when they hurt you. The Bible says, "Be kind to each other, tenderhearted, forgiving one another, just as God through Christ has forgiven you" (Ephesians 4:32). Because God has shown his grace to you by forgiving you for your sins, you should show his grace to others by forgiving them when they do something against you.

Ask God to help you be thankful for his grace, depend on his grace, and show his grace to others today!

My gracious favor is all you need. My power works best in your weakness.
2 Corinthians 12:9

YOU CAN PRAY:

Dear God, thank you for the grace you have given to me. Help me to live by your grace each day. In Jesus' name. Amen.

HOW CAN YOU LIVE BY GOD'S GRACE?

Activity 11: Taking a Stand

I CAN MAKE RIGHT CHOICES

Use the words in the box below to fill in the spaces.

I ask God through ______________________________.

I ______________________ and obey the ______________________.

I ask other ______________________ who love ______________________.

When I know what's ______________________, I ______________________ it.

people	Bible	God	do
prayer	right	ask	read

This month God helped me make a right choice when . . .

____

THINKING IT OVER!

Taking a Stand

Write the answers to these questions from your devotionals in the blanks.

1. Where can you find out what is right or wrong?

____

2. How should you treat people who are different from you?

____

3. What is one thing Satan lies about?

____

4. Why can't you save yourself?

____

5. What does Satan want to do to you?

____

6. What is one way God can talk to you?

____

If you need help, you can look back in this month's devotionals. The number in ( ) tells you which devotional to check for each question. 1. (1) 2. (4) 3. (10) 4. (18) 5. (22) 6. (26)

DECEMBER

What I Believe

GOD IS THREE IN ONE!

Sometimes you may think no one understands you, how you feel, why you do what you do. Guess what! God knows all about you—even better than you know yourself! It doesn't work the other way, though. Nobody even comes close to understanding God! God said, "Just as the heavens are higher than the earth, so are my ways higher than your ways" (Isaiah 55:9).

One of the hardest things to understand is the Trinity. *Trinity* means "three in one." God is three persons—God the Father, God the Son, and God the Holy Spirit. All three of these persons make one God—not three gods. We can't fully understand it now, but one day we will when we are face-to-face with God in heaven.

Think how small God would have to be for us to know all about him! Be glad there's more about him than you can understand. The Bible says, "Great is the Lord, and how much we should praise him" (Psalm 48:1). No one really understands all about God now, but when we get to heaven, we'll understand him more.

How great is the Lord, and how much we should praise him.
Psalm 48:1

YOU CAN PRAY:
Dear God, thank you that you understand all about me! In Jesus' name. Amen.

WHAT WOULD YOU LIKE GOD TO EXPLAIN TO YOU ABOUT HIMSELF?

December

2

GOD IS HOLY!

Do you know someone who never makes mistakes? Can you picture anyone who is always good? Have you ever met anyone who never tells lies? Imagine someone who cannot even think of doing or saying anything wrong. A person like this would be holy. To be holy means to be perfect, to never sin. Nobody on earth is holy. The only one like that is God.

God, our heavenly Father, is holy. God said, "You must be holy because I am holy" (1 Peter 1:16). He wants his children to be holy too! How can you be holy when you know you sometimes sin? Does God really think you can be perfect? No, but he wants you to do your best to be like him. God lives in you to give you the power to live a clean, holy life and not to sin. He will help you to say "no" to sin. He will help you to obey his Word and do what is right.

Isn't it wonderful to know our heavenly Father is a perfect example for us to follow? Our God is so great and worthy of our praise! Ask God to help you be more like him today.

WHAT DOES IT MEAN TO BE HOLY?

How great is the Lord, and how much we should praise him.
Psalm 48:1

YOU CAN PRAY:

Dear God, I'm glad you are perfect. I want to be more like you every day. In Jesus' name. Amen.

December
3

GOD'S WORD IS TRUE!

Many people try to find something wrong in the Bible, so they read it carefully. What happens? They end up finding out that the Bible really is true! God never makes mistakes or tells lies. He could never give us a book about himself that is wrong in any way. God used many men to write down the ideas and stories he wanted everyone to know. Someone may say, "Even though it's God's book, these men might have made mistakes. Maybe some things got in that weren't right."

That's not true! God told the writers just what to say though he let them tell the stories in their own way. The writers did not put anything in the Bible that was wrong. There are absolutely no mistakes in God's Word.

Some people don't agree with what the Bible says. Here's an example: God's Word says, "Do not lie" (Leviticus 19:11). That means telling lies is wrong. Some people say it's okay to tell a lie if you have a good reason, but they are wrong. You know that the Bible is always right. That's because it's from God, and he is never wrong!

How great is the Lord, and how much we should praise him.
Psalm 48:1

YOU CAN PRAY:
Dear God, thank you that I can believe everything in the Bible and not wonder if it's true. In Jesus' name. Amen.

WHY IS IT NEVER OKAY TO LIE?

GOD CAN DO ANYTHING!

December

4

What can God do? Anything he chooses! He created the world. "When he spoke, the world began!" (Psalm 33:9). We don't know how he could do that, but he did! The Bible tells us that he keeps everything going "by the mighty power of his command" (Hebrews 1:3).

The Bible says, "O Lord, . . . you are powerful and mighty; no one can stand against you!" (2 Chronicles 20:6). God can do anything he chooses, and no one can stop him! Remember, though, that God is also perfectly good. He never uses his power to hurt you.

God can give you his power to use when you need it! God's Word says, "He offers strength to the weak" (Isaiah 40:29). You can't give your strength to anyone else, but God can give you strength when you need it without losing any of his own power. How do you get some of God's strength when you need it? Just ask him for it! God will always give you the strength you ask for if what you are doing is right.

HOW HAS GOD GIVEN YOU STRENGTH TO DO SOMETHING FOR HIM?

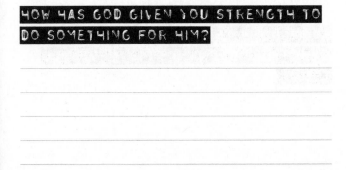

How great is the Lord, and how much we should praise him.
Psalm 48:1

YOU CAN PRAY:

Dear God, thank you for giving me strength when I need it. Help me to use your strength to help others. In Jesus' name. Amen.

December

5

GOD HAS A PLAN FOR ME!

Grown-ups often ask children, "What do you want to be when you grow up?" It's fun to think about that. Keep in mind that God has a plan for you. Since he is so great, God's plans for you are great too.

Long ago, God told his people, "I know the plans I have for you" (Jeremiah 29:11). Following God's plan means you always obey him in every step of your life. You need to learn all you can about God. You can do this by reading the Bible and listening to people who can teach you about him.

God always does what's right, so he plans for you to do good things (Ephesians 2:10). If you talk to God and read his Word, you'll know what he wants you to do each day. For instance, he'll want you to obey the grown-ups in charge of you and to be kind to other people. When you try to do what you know God wants, he'll help you know what to do next. Then, when you grow up to be a doctor, homemaker, or store clerk—no matter what you do—you'll be following God's plan.

How great is the Lord, and how much we should praise him.
Psalm 48:1

YOU CAN PRAY:
Dear God, please show me your plan for me as I try to obey you every day. In Jesus' name. Amen.

WRITE DOWN THREE WAYS THAT YOU HAVE FOLLOWED GOD'S PLAN FOR YOU TODAY.

I KNOW GOD LOVES ME!

December

6

How can you tell if someone loves you? That person says nice things to you. God says nice things to you in the Bible. He said, "I have loved you, my people, with an everlasting love" (Jeremiah 31:3).

The person who loves you listens when you talk to him or her. God listens when you talk to him, and he gives answers! He says, "Ask me and I will tell you some remarkable secrets" (Jeremiah 33:3).

The person who loves you gives you things he or she knows you like. God has given us "all we need for our enjoyment" (1 Timothy 6:17). Thank him today for something good he's given you!

The person who loves you helps you when you need it. God said, "Trust me in your times of trouble, and I will rescue you" (Psalm 50:15).

The person who loves you keeps his or her promises. So does God. He is "faithful in all he says" (Psalm 145:13). He always does what the Bible promises he will do.

Besides all these things, "God showed how much he loved us by sending his only Son into the world so that we might have eternal life through him" (1 John 4:9). No one else who loves you has ever done that much for you!

How great is the Lord, and how much we should praise him.
Psalm 48:1

YOU CAN PRAY:
Dear God, thank you for all the ways you show me that you love me. In Jesus' name. Amen.

IN WHAT SPECIAL WAY HAS GOD SHOWN YOU THAT HE LOVES YOU?

December

7

I CAN SHOW GOD'S LOVE TO OTHERS!

How great is the Lord, and how much we should praise him.
Psalm 48:1

YOU CAN PRAY:

Dear God, thank you for always loving me even when I'm hard to love! Help me to show your love to others. In Jesus' name. Amen.

Showing God's love to others sounds easy, but it means more than just being nice to people and not hurting them. Showing God's love means you wait for your turn without getting upset. You don't feel jealous of a friend's new clothes. You let someone else have the biggest—or last—dessert. You don't call anyone bad names to get even for something they did. When others say bad things about a person, you think of good things to say. You don't tell someone a bad thing another person said about them. You say things that help others do their best. You don't laugh at someone who is having trouble with something, like soccer. You try hard to keep your promises.

You may be thinking, "I'm like that part of the time but not all of the time." Only God loves perfectly all the time. Ask him to help you work on one way you can show his love to other people this week. Some people are easy to love and some aren't! Ask God to help you love the ones who are hard to love. He is great at helping you do what is right, and your life will show others how loving he is.

HOW CAN YOU SHOW GOD'S LOVE TO SOMEONE IN A SPECIAL WAY TODAY?

GOD WANTS ME TO TELL OTHERS ABOUT HIM!

December
8

Imagine that someone gave you money and said, "Tell your friends to come to me, and I'll give them money, too." What would you do? You'd tell everyone how he or she could get this gift!

God has given you an even better gift! If you have received Jesus as your Savior from sin, God has given you eternal life. That means you have God's life in you now. Then someday you'll live with him in heaven. All the money in the world couldn't buy eternal life, but God gives it to anyone who receives Jesus. Somebody told you how to get this gift, and God wants you to tell somebody else.

Imagine that you told a friend how to get that gift of money. You said he could get some too. Then, the friend just laughed at you and walked away. That would make you feel bad, but you would know you did the right thing by telling him about the money.

What if you tell someone how to receive eternal life and the person laughs at you? It's still the right thing to do. Are you going to tell someone about God's gift, or are you going to keep it a secret? Do you know how to tell someone about receiving Jesus? The devotions in this book for June 17 through June 22 can help you.

WHAT WOULD YOU TELL SOMEONE ABOUT JESUS?

How great is the Lord, and how much we should praise him.
Psalm 48:1

YOU CAN PRAY:
Dear God, help me to tell someone this week how he or she can receive the gift of eternal life. In Jesus' name. Amen.

December 9

GOD MADE ME SPECIAL!

To "create" something, like a picture, means you try hard to make it special. You do the best work you can on it. The Bible says, "God created people. . . . Male and female he created them" (Genesis 1:27). God created the body of every girl and boy to be special. The Bible also says he "made all the delicate, inner parts of my body" (Psalm 139:13). That means God made you special on the inside, too. He made your body exactly the way he wanted it to look and work. He made your mind to think the way it does.

A person who paints special pictures is called an artist. He works hard on each one. His pictures are called works of art. No two pictures are just alike. People give lots of money to buy them.

The Bible says you are God's "masterpiece" (Ephesians 2:10). That word means "work of art." God didn't make any two people just the same on the outside or on the inside. You're worth a lot to God. He created a beautiful home for you to live in with him someday. To remember how special you are to God, read Psalm 139 in the Bible. If you don't have a Bible, read this page again!

We are already God's children. . . . When he comes we will be like him.
1 John 3:2

YOU CAN PRAY:
Dear God, thank you that there is no one just like me and I'm special to you! In Jesus' name. Amen.

WRITE DOWN THREE WAYS YOU ARE SPECIAL TO GOD.

I CAN BELONG TO GOD'S FAMILY!

December
10

You'd have to love someone a lot to wish he or she could be part of your family. God loves you that much! When you're in God's family, you can always feel close to him. You can talk to him anytime. Best of all, someday you'll live with him and his other children in heaven.

How do you join God's family? By receiving Jesus. The Bible says, "To all who believed him and accepted him, he gave the right to become children of God" (John 1:12).

To "receive Jesus" means you tell God that you've sinned and you're sorry. Tell God that you believe Jesus is his Son. You believe Jesus died to take the punishment for your sin so you wouldn't have to. Tell God that you believe Jesus came back to life and he's in heaven right now. Then, tell God you want to be his child. If you have received Jesus, you belong to God's family!

How can people tell what family you're in? One way is that you obey the grown-ups in that home. Jesus said anyone who obeys God "is my brother and sister" (Mark 3:35). The children in God's family obey him! Can people tell you're in God's family?

HOW CAN OTHERS TELL IF YOU'RE IN GOD'S FAMILY?

We are already God's children. . . . When he comes we will be like him. 1 John 3:2

YOU CAN PRAY:

Thank you, heavenly Father, that I can be in your family. In Jesus' name. Amen.

December

11

I NEED TO CONFESS MY SINS TO GOD!

Isn't it great that God gives his children the strength to say "no" to sin? You don't have to give in when Satan tempts you to do wrong. The Bible says, "The Lord is my helper" (Hebrews 13:6). What happens if you do sin? If you're God's child, the Lord Jesus will never leave you. But sin spoils your fellowship (friendship) with God. It makes him sad because he hates sin.

The Holy Spirit convicts you about your sins. He lets you know that things are no longer right between you and God. Sinning makes you feel far away from God. Only by confessing your sins to God can you be forgiven.

To confess your sins to God means to agree with him that you did wrong. Don't say, "I made a mistake" or "I made a bad choice." Tell him you have sinned and that you're sorry. The Bible says when we confess our sins, God will "forgive us and . . . cleanse us from every wrong" (1 John 1:9). When you confess your sins, your friendship with God will be made right. He will hear and answer your prayers. Thank God for his forgiveness and ask him to help you not to sin again.

We are already God's children. . . . When he comes we will be like him.
1 John 3:2

YOU CAN PRAY:
Dear God, thank you for always forgiving me when I confess my sins to you. In Jesus' name. Amen.

WHY DO YOU NEED TO CONFESS YOUR SINS TO GOD?

GOD CAN GIVE ME VICTORY OVER SIN!

December
12

If you are God's child, you have an enemy—Satan! Satan probably thought he had won the battle when Jesus died on the cross. That was the most important battle of all time! Jesus Christ died to take the punishment for your sins. Jesus won when God the Father brought him back to life! His victory over Satan is your victory too. Now you can have victory over sin as you trust God to help you.

But Satan doesn't want you to have victory over sin. He tries to keep you from obeying God. He doesn't want you to please God. Fighting Satan by yourself is hard because Satan is stronger than you are! But remember the Holy Spirit inside you is "greater than the spirit who lives in the world" (1 John 4:4). The Holy Spirit helps you to do what's right when Satan tries to get you to sin.

You need to ask God for help every day. Learn as much as you can from the Bible. It will help you not to sin. God's Word and prayer are your weapons against Satan. Trust God to give you victory every day.

We are already God's children. . . . When he comes we will be like him. 1 John 3:2

YOU CAN PRAY:

Dear God, thank you that I can have victory over sin. Help me to trust you for victory every day. In Jesus' name. Amen.

HOW CAN GOD GIVE YOU VICTORY OVER SIN?

December

13

I CAN USE GOD'S ARMOR!

Long ago, soldiers wore armor to protect themselves in battle. God gives Christians special armor in their battle against Satan. You have read about God's armor earlier in this devotional book. You can also read about it in Ephesians 6:14-18 in the Bible. Can you remember what each piece of the armor is and what it's for? (If you have trouble, go back to the devotional for April 12 for help!)

See if you can fill in these blanks: One piece is called the belt of ____________. This piece helps you to know what is true and not to be fooled by Satan's lies. Another piece is the body armor of __________. It protects your heart and helps you to do what's right. The shoes of the ________________ help you to share God's peace with others. The shield of ___________ helps you to believe God's promises. It will protect you against Satan's attacks. The helmet of __________ protects your mind. It gives you confidence that you are God's child so you can say no to Satan's attacks. The ____________ of the Spirit is the Word of God. It will help you to fight Satan's attacks. Ask God to help you use his armor so you can stay close to him and not sin.

We are already God's children. . . . When he comes we will be like him. 1 John 3:2

YOU CAN PRAY:
Dear God, help me to remember to use every piece of the armor every day. In Jesus' name. Amen.

HOW DID YOU USE THE ARMOR THIS WEEK IN YOUR BATTLE AGAINST SATAN?

GOD CAN GIVE ME SELF-CONTROL!

December
14

Maybe you know someone who gets angry and hits people or says mean things to hurt them. Maybe you know someone who can't quit playing a game or reading a book when it's time for bed. These people are letting their feelings control what they do. They do not have self-control.

Self-control is a part of the fruit of the Spirit (Galatians 5:22-23). It's something God the Holy Spirit wants to bring out in your life. You read about it earlier in this devotional book. Self-control means that you take charge of your thoughts, feelings, and actions instead of letting them control you. You handle anger without hurting anyone. You can stop playing or reading because you know you need the right amount of sleep.

God wants you to be able to control yourself. Then he can use you to serve him better. You will also be better able to help others. Maybe someone will ask how you learned to have self-control. You can say that it is the Holy Spirit who helps you because you are a Christian. You might then be able to tell that person about Jesus. Are you allowing God to develop self-control in your life?

We are already God's children. . . . When he comes we will be like him.
1 John 3:2

YOU CAN PRAY:
Dear God, thank you for the fruit of the Spirit. Help me to have self-control in all I think, feel, and do. In Jesus' name. Amen.

HOW CAN OTHERS SEE SELF-CONTROL IN YOUR LIFE?

December

15

I CAN DO ANYTHING WITH GOD'S HELP!

One Bible writer says, "O Sovereign Lord! You have made the heavens and earth by your great power. Nothing is too hard for you!" (Jeremiah 32:17). Another one says, "I can do everything with the help of Christ who gives me the strength I need" (Philippians 4:13).

All of us need help from time to time. Sometimes God may use another person to help you. A friend may pray for you when you're sick. Your teacher may help you with a problem at school. There are other times when only God can help you do something hard, like saying you're sorry or being kind to someone who has hurt you. The Bible says that God created the world, and he can give you strength to do anything. God can help you do whatever you need to do.

How do you get God's help? God knows when you need help. But he wants you to ask him and then trust that he will do it. Is there anything that would be too hard for God to do? No! God's Word says, "Nothing is too hard for you [God]" (Jeremiah 32:17). The next time you have something hard to do, remember that you can do anything with God's help!

We are already God's children. . . . When he comes we will be like him.
1 John 3:2

YOU CAN PRAY:
Dear God, you know when I will especially need your strength today. Help me to be strong when that time comes. In Jesus' name. Amen.

WRITE ONE THING YOU NEED GOD'S HELP FOR THIS WEEK.

MY LIFE CAN BE A WITNESS TO OTHERS!

December
16

Are you different since you trusted Jesus Christ as your Savior? The Bible says, "Those who become Christians become new persons" (2 Corinthians 5:17). When Jesus lived on the earth, his life was a witness, as well as his words. In the same way, our lives are to be a witness to others.

As you get to know God better, things in your life will start changing. You won't want to do the things you used to do that made God unhappy, like lying, fighting, or complaining. Instead, you'll want to do things that please God, like being truthful, kind, and patient.

Your friends may see that you're different than you used to be. Maybe they notice that you smile instead of complain. Perhaps they see that you are patient when you have to wait and wait and wait! Your life is a witness for God. Your friends may ask why you've changed. Then you can witness with your words. You can tell them that you've received Jesus as your Savior and he is helping you do things that please him. Let your life be a witness for Jesus today!

HOW IS YOUR LIFE A WITNESS TO OTHERS?

We are already God's children. . . . When he comes we will be like him.
1 John 3:2

YOU CAN PRAY:

Dear God, thank you that my life can be a witness for you. I want to help people to know you. In Jesus' name. Amen.

December

17

I CAN PUT OTHERS FIRST!

Love your neighbor as yourself.
Matthew 22:39

YOU CAN PRAY:

Dear God, it's hard to think of other people first. Help me to do it because that's what Jesus would do. In Jesus' name. Amen.

Winning is more fun than losing. Being chosen first feels better than being chosen last. When you get to do something first, you may feel important. Many people like to think they are more important than other people in some way, but should Christians think that way too?

The Bible says, "Take delight in honoring each other" (Romans 12:10). You may win first prize in a contest. That's all right. But if the choice is yours—who goes first in line, who gets the best seat, who takes the first turn in a game—give that place to someone else. Why? That's what Jesus would do.

Many Christians want to do things the way the Lord Jesus would. They try to think of what others need or would like. Other Christians think of themselves first. Which group of Christians are you like?

Jesus said, "Love each other in the same way that I love you" (John 15:12). When you love other people, you should want to put them first. This isn't always easy to do. God knows how hard it is, but he has promised to help you. Trust God the Holy Spirit to help you to be more like Jesus as he teaches you to put others first.

WHEN COULD YOU PUT SOMEONE ELSE FIRST THIS WEEK?

GOD CAN HELP ME LOVE OTHERS!

December
18

How do you love your neighbor as yourself? Start by asking, "How do I show love for myself?" Here are some ways you do this: You eat when you're hungry. You rest when you're tired. You don't put harmful things, like bad drugs, in your body. Sometimes you give yourself a treat, like ice cream!

Then ask this question: "Who is my neighbor?" Someone in the Bible asked Jesus that question, so Jesus told a story that helped this person understand that his "neighbor" was anyone who needed his help (Luke 10:30-37).

Loving yourself means doing good things for yourself, and loving your neighbor means doing good things for other people. Do you know someone who needs food or clothes? Is there anyone who could use some help with schoolwork? Do you know a child that nobody wants to play with? How could you help these people?

The best way you can help other people is by telling them about the Lord Jesus so they can have their sins forgiven. Many people around you need your help. God can show you what you can do to help them. Ask him to help you "love your neighbor as yourself." He will!

WRITE THE NAMES OF THREE PEOPLE YOU CAN HELP THIS WEEK.

Love your neighbor as yourself.
Matthew 22:39

YOU CAN PRAY:
Dear God, thank you for sending people to help me when I need it. Use me to help someone else in need. In Jesus' name. Amen.

December
19

I CAN WALK IN FELLOWSHIP WITH GOD!

Love your neighbor as yourself.
Matthew 22:39

YOU CAN PRAY:
Dear God, I'm glad you want me to stay close to you! Help me to walk in fellowship with you. In Jesus' name. Amen.

Just think! The Creator of the world wants you to spend time with him every day! That's what "walking in fellowship" with God means. How do you do it?

How did Jesus do it? Jesus often went "to the wilderness for prayer" (Luke 5:16). Do you talk to God alone as often as you can?

The Lord Jesus learned Scripture. When Satan tried to get Jesus to sin, Jesus answered with verses he may have learned as a boy. Once, he said, "Get out of here, Satan. . . . For the Scriptures say, 'You must worship the Lord your God; serve only him' " (Matthew 4:10). Are you learning the Bible verses in this book? They'll help you stay close to God.

Jesus went to the synagogue (meeting place of worship) "as usual" (Luke 4:16). Jesus prayed and worshiped God with other people. Do you try to do that every week?

When Jesus talked about God one day, he said, "I always do those things that are pleasing to him" (John 8:29). Do you always obey God?

Jesus prayed, learned Scripture, went to the synagogue, and obeyed God. These things helped him walk in fellowship with God. These are ways you can walk in fellowship with God too!

HOW CAN YOU WALK IN FELLOWSHIP WITH GOD THIS WEEK?

I NEED TO FELLOWSHIP WITH OTHERS IN GOD'S FAMILY!

December

20

Families come in all shapes and sizes! Your "family" is the people you live with. Maybe you're related to all of them and maybe not.

When you receive Jesus Christ, you're part of another family—God's family (John 1:12). Other Christians are your brothers and sisters in Christ. You need your Christian family. You can pray for each other and share what you have, such as money or food. Together, you can worship and learn more about God. Members of God's family like to get together. They pray, sing songs that praise God, study the Bible, and help each other with their problems.

Where do Christians get together to have fellowship? Sometimes they meet in each other's homes or in churches. Ask God to help you find other Christians that you can meet with often. Maybe there is a church in your neighborhood that teaches about the Lord Jesus. You could go there to have fellowship with other Christians.

The Bible says if we walk in fellowship with God, "we have fellowship with each other" (1 John 1:7). Being in fellowship with God is the best way to be in fellowship with your brothers and sisters in God's family.

WHAT IS YOUR FAVORITE THING ABOUT BEING PART OF GOD'S FAMILY?

Love your neighbor as yourself.
Matthew 22:39

YOU CAN PRAY:

Dear God, thank you for letting me be part of your family! Help me to have fellowship with my brothers and sisters in Christ. In Jesus' name. Amen.

December
21

PEOPLE ARE LOST WITHOUT CHRIST!

Have you ever been lost? Being separated from the people you're with, even for a few minutes, is scary! There's another way a person can be "lost." People who never receive Jesus Christ as their Savior are lost in sin. Because they are sinners, they are separated from God forever.

People who are lost are not part of God's family. They don't have God's peace when things go wrong. They never feel the joy God gives to his children. They don't have the assurance that God will answer their prayers.

When lost people die, they are separated forever from God. They will never be able to be with God in the beautiful place called heaven that he has prepared for those who love him. Instead, they will go to a terrible place of suffering and punishment called hell.

People who have never trusted the Lord Jesus as their Savior may not know they are lost. That's why it's important for you, as a Christian, to tell them that Jesus Christ is the only way to heaven. Jesus said, "No one can come to the Father except through me" (John 14:6). Is there someone you can talk to about Jesus this week?

Love your neighbor as yourself.
Matthew 22:39

YOU CAN PRAY:
Dear God, help me to tell someone who is lost about you. In Jesus' name. Amen.

WHAT WOULD YOU TELL A LOST PERSON ABOUT JESUS?

....

....

....

GOD WILL GIVE ME COURAGE TO WITNESS!

December
22

Jesus told his followers, "You will . . . tell people about me everywhere" (Acts 1:8). Then he returned to heaven. A witness tells what he has seen and knows is true. Jesus' followers could witness that Jesus had come back to life.

You may think that would have been easy for them. It wasn't! They had to witness to the same people who had the Lord Jesus killed! What if these people decided to have Jesus' followers put to death too?

The followers witnessed anyway! That must have taken courage. Courage is the strength to do the right thing even when it's hard. Where did their courage come from?

Jesus had also said, "When the Holy Spirit has come upon you, you will receive power" (Acts 1:8). When the Holy Spirit came to live inside Jesus' followers, they received God's power to do wonderful things! They could love Jesus' enemies. They could boldly tell them that Jesus Christ died and rose again to take away their sins.

It still isn't easy to witness! If you're God's child, he has given you his Holy Spirit too. Ask him to give you courage to tell someone what the Lord Jesus Christ has done for you.

HOW CAN YOU HAVE COURAGE TO TELL SOMEONE ABOUT JESUS?

Love your neighbor as yourself.
Matthew 22:39

YOU CAN PRAY:
Dear God, thank you for the Holy Spirit who gives me courage to be a witness for you. In Jesus' name. Amen.

December

23

MISSIONARIES ARE GOD'S SPECIAL MESSENGERS!

Love your neighbor as yourself.
Matthew 22:39

YOU CAN PRAY:

Dear God, thank you for missionaries who tell others about you. In Jesus' name. Amen.

A long time after the Lord Jesus returned to heaven, the Christians were still meeting together to worship. One day, the Holy Spirit spoke to them. He said, "Dedicate Barnabas and Saul for the special work I have for them" (Acts 13:2).

Barnabas and Saul became the first missionaries. They went to many cities and told people about Jesus Christ. They helped start churches.

The Lord Jesus wants all of his followers to tell others about him. You can tell others about Jesus where you live, at school, or wherever you are. Sometimes God chooses people to be missionaries as their life's work.

There are many different things that missionaries do. Some missionaries are pastors, evangelists, or teachers. They help adults, young people, or children to know about Jesus. Other missionaries may be doctors, builders, pilots, secretaries, or printers. They may need special training. They may have to move to a different place. Missionaries often have to depend on other Christians to give them the money they need to live and work.

Missionaries know they are chosen to do special work for God. They are God's special messengers, taking the Good News of Jesus all around the world!

WHY DO WE NEED MISSIONARIES?

GOD MAY CALL ME TO BE A MISSIONARY!

December
24

Elizabeth heard a missionary talk about his work in another land. As she listened, God showed Elizabeth that she would do that kind of work too someday.

Lucas was praying one night. God brought the name of a certain country to his mind. Lucas knew that someday he would go there as a missionary.

Martina read in the Bible where Jesus said, "You didn't choose me. I chose you . . . to go and produce fruit" (John 15:16). She knew then that the Lord Jesus Christ wanted her to be a missionary.

Elizabeth heard a missionary talk. Lucas prayed. Martina read the Bible. Each of these children listened when God "called" them to become missionaries.

God won't "call" you on the telephone to tell you if he wants you to be a missionary! He will put the idea into your mind and then help you to know deep in your heart that this is what he wants you to do.

As you grow up, God allows situations in your life to prepare you for his work. Stay close to God and obey him in the choices you make each day. One day, he may call you to be a missionary!

Love your neighbor as yourself.
Matthew 22:39

YOU CAN PRAY:

Dear God, help me to listen and obey if you call me to be a missionary. In Jesus' name. Amen.

HOW WOULD YOU KNOW IF GOD IS CALLING YOU TO BE A MISSIONARY?

December

25

HEAVEN IS A REAL PLACE!

"Heaven isn't real—it's just something people imagine!" Have you ever heard anyone say this? The Bible tells us about heaven.

Heaven is a real place. It is God's home. God the Father, God the Son (Jesus), and God the Holy Spirit are there. God's holy angels are there. The angels surround God's throne, singing praises to him. Also, those who believed in Jesus Christ as their Savior and have died are in heaven with God.

Heaven is a perfect place. God is perfectly holy, and there can be no sin where he lives. Also, there will be no sickness or death in heaven. There will be no sorrow or crying in heaven. It is a place of perfect joy and peace.

Heaven is a beautiful place. The Bible says the walls around it are made with sparkling jewels. Each gate is made of one giant pearl. Imagine a pearl big enough to be used as the gate in the city's wall! Heaven also has a street that's made of gold. The city and street are made of pure gold like glass (Revelation 21:18-21).

It's fun to picture heaven, but—just think!—it's better than anyone can imagine! And it's a real place!

There are many rooms in my Father's home, and I am going to prepare a place for you.
John 14:2

YOU CAN PRAY:
Dear God, thank you for creating a beautiful place for me to live with you forever! In Jesus' name. Amen.

WHO ARE SOME BIBLE PEOPLE YOU'D LIKE TO MEET IN HEAVEN SOMEDAY?

JESUS IS PREPARING A PLACE FOR ME IN HEAVEN!

December
26

In Bible times, when two people became engaged, the young man added a room or two onto his father's house for his wife and himself. When he was done, he went to the bride's home to get her. He took her back to his home. The wedding took place there. After that, they lived in the rooms he had prepared in his father's house. This situation reminds us of what Jesus has promised will happen to us someday.

Before the Lord Jesus died on the cross, he told his disciples that he was going away. His disciples were confused and sad that he was leaving them. Jesus comforted them by promising that he was going to prepare a place for them in heaven, the Father's house.

If you know Jesus Christ as your Savior, he is preparing a place for you, too. We don't know exactly what this place will look like, but it will be a beautiful, perfect place. One day Jesus will come back to take those who believe in him as Savior to be with him in heaven. How wonderful that Jesus is preparing a place for you in his Father's house!

WHAT DO YOU THINK YOUR PLACE IN HEAVEN WILL LOOK LIKE?

There are many rooms in my Father's home, and I am going to prepare a place for you.
John 14:2

YOU CAN PRAY:

Dear God, thank you for preparing a beautiful home for me to live with you someday. In Jesus' name. Amen.

December

27

I AM EARNING REWARDS IN HEAVEN!

The Bible says, "The free gift of God is eternal life" (Romans 6:23). You don't have to do any work to earn it. It isn't a prize you win in a contest. Eternal life is a gift that God gives to those who trust Jesus as their Savior.

Eternal life in heaven with God forever is the most wonderful gift you'll ever receive, but there's more good news! Someday in heaven you will receive rewards for what you did for God on earth!

In Bible times, athletes who won an important game received a crown made of leaves that would last only a few days. Paul said that these people worked hard to earn a crown that would not last. He also said, "We do it for an eternal prize" (1 Corinthians 9:25).

How do you earn rewards that you will receive in heaven? One way is by doing your best to please God. Another way is by always following Christ. God also promises a reward to those who look forward to Jesus' return to earth.

These rewards are described as crowns. No one knows what these crowns will look like, but you can be sure they'll be worth all your effort!

There are many rooms in my Father's home, and I am going to prepare a place for you.
John 14:2

YOU CAN PRAY:

Dear God, thank you for the gift of eternal life. Thank you for the rewards you've promised in heaven. In Jesus' name. Amen.

HOW CAN YOU EARN REWARDS IN HEAVEN?

JESUS WILL COME AGAIN!

December
28

The Lord Jesus promised his friends that he would come back again. Forty days after Jesus died and came back to life, he went up into the clouds, back to heaven. His friends watched him go. Then an angel said to them, "Someday, just as you saw him go, he will return!" (Acts 1:11).

When will Jesus come back again? The Bible doesn't tell us. However, Jesus did tell about some things that would happen so we would know when the time was near. He called these events "signs" of his coming. One of them was that "the Good News about the Kingdom will be preached throughout the whole world" (Matthew 24:14). Since then, millions of people all over the world have heard about Jesus Christ. Many of the other signs have happened too. It's clear that Jesus is coming soon!

What will happen when Jesus comes? "For the Lord himself will come . . . with a commanding shout, with the call of the archangel, and with the trumpet call of God" (1 Thessalonians 4:16). All those who have received Jesus Christ as their Savior will rise up to meet him in the air. Will you be ready when Jesus comes?

HOW DO YOU KNOW THAT JESUS IS COMING AGAIN?

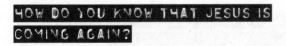

There are many rooms in my Father's home, and I am going to prepare a place for you.
John 14:2

YOU CAN PRAY:

Dear God, thank you that Jesus will soon come again. Help me to be ready for his coming. In Jesus' name. Amen.

December

29

NOT EVERYONE WILL BE READY WHEN JESUS RETURNS!

There are many rooms in my Father's home, and I am going to prepare a place for you.
John 14:2

YOU CAN PRAY:

Dear God, help me tell someone this week how they can be ready to meet Jesus. In Jesus' name. Amen.

If you were going to take an airplane trip, you'd need to have a ticket that permits you to go. You'd also have to be at the right gate at the airport on time so you wouldn't miss your flight. These important things would make you ready for your trip.

The Bible says that Jesus will return to earth to take those who believe in him back to heaven, but not everyone is ready for his return. First, you need to trust in the Lord Jesus as your Savior. That is the only way you will be permitted into heaven. Many people have heard that Jesus died to take the punishment for their sin, but they have refused to trust in Jesus as their Savior. They won't be ready for Jesus' return.

Others who have trusted the Lord Jesus Christ as their Savior will be permitted to go to heaven, but they are still not ready. They're not living in a way that pleases God. One day, they will stand before him and will be sadly disappointed to find that they have lost their rewards because they were not faithful in serving God. Have you trusted in Jesus? Will you be ready when Jesus returns?

HOW WOULD YOU TELL SOMEONE TO BE READY FOR JESUS' RETURN?

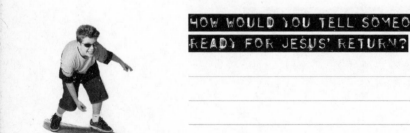

I WANT TO BE READY WHEN JESUS RETURNS!

December
30

Suppose a friend told you that he would come and take you to a favorite place. What would you do to be ready for him? Maybe you would put on clean clothes. You would probably be watching for your friend, and you'd be excited about his coming.

Jesus Christ has promised to come someday and take us to heaven. He wants us to be ready. That doesn't mean that you change your clothes and watch out the window! However, there are things you can do to prepare.

The most important way to be ready for Jesus' return is to know him as your Savior. Only those who have trusted in him will go to meet him when he comes. If you do know the Lord Jesus as your Savior, make sure you are obeying him. You need to be reading your Bible, praying, obeying his Word, and telling others about him.

The Bible says that Christians should be looking "forward to that wonderful event when the glory of our great God and Savior, Jesus Christ, will be revealed" (Titus 2:13). This is one of the greatest events that will ever happen in history. We should be ready and eagerly looking forward to Jesus' return.

There are many rooms in my Father's home, and I am going to prepare a place for you.
John 14:2

YOU CAN PRAY:

Dear God, help me to be ready when Jesus comes again by obeying your Word. In Jesus' name. Amen.

WHAT ARE SOME THINGS YOU CAN DO TO BE READY FOR JESUS' RETURN?

December

31

ETERNITY IS FOREVER!

You've made it to the last devotional in this book! You've learned a lot about God and about yourself. You've done all the activity pages! You might think that this is the end—you've learned all there is to know about God and his Word—but if so, you're wrong!

Learning about God never ends because God never ends! God is eternal—he goes on forever. If you know the Lord Jesus Christ as your Savior, God has given you eternal life. When your body dies, the real you inside (the part that thinks, feels, and decides) will live on in eternity—forever with God in heaven. What will you do for eternity? You'll be praising God for all that he is and all that he does!

There is so much more for you to learn about God! Don't stop just because you've finished this devotional book. Go back and read your favorite devotionals again. Read what you've written on the pages to see if you've done the things you wrote about. Keep memorizing the Bible verses in this book. If you have a Bible, continue having your quiet time with God every day. It will be good preparation for eternity!

There are many rooms in my Father's home, and I am going to prepare a place for you.
John 14:2

YOU CAN PRAY:
Dear God, thank you for teaching me about you. Help me to keep on learning more and more so I'll be ready for eternity with you. In Jesus' name. Amen.

WHAT FAVORITE THING HAVE YOU LEARNED ABOUT GOD FROM THIS DEVOTIONAL BOOK?

THE MEMORY ZONE

Here are some great Bible verses about what you've learned so far. Put a check mark in the box as you memorize each one!

- ❑ **Isaiah 55:8-9** " 'My thoughts are completely different from yours,' says the Lord. 'And my ways are far beyond anything you could imagine. For just as the heavens are higher than the earth, so are my ways higher than your ways and my thoughts higher than your thoughts.' "
- ❑ **Jeremiah 32:17** "O Sovereign Lord! You have made the heavens and earth by your great power. Nothing is too hard for you!"
- ❑ **I John 4:7-8** "Dear friends, let us continue to love one another, for love comes from God. Anyone who loves is born of God and knows God. But anyone who does not love does not know God—for God is love."
- ❑ **Galatians 6:10** "Whenever we have the opportunity, we should do good to everyone, especially to our Christian brothers and sisters."
- ❑ **Ephesians 2:10** "For we are God's masterpiece. He has created us anew in Christ Jesus, so that we can do the good things he planned for us long ago."
- ❑ **Romans 1:16** "I am not ashamed of this Good News about Christ. It is the power of God at work, saving everyone who believes."
- ❑ **Matthew 28:19-20** "Therefore, go and make disciples of all the nations, baptizing them in the name of the Father and the Son and the Holy Spirit. Teach these new disciples to obey all the commands I have given you. And be sure of this: I am with you always, even to the end of the age."
- ❑ **Revelation 4:8** "Holy, holy, holy is the Lord God Almighty—the one who always was, who is, and who is still to come."

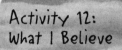

Activity 12: What I Believe

I BELIEVE

Circle the correct word to complete the sentence.

Most **All** of God's word is true.

God **always** **usually** loves me.

God **might** **won't** leave me.

I should **confess** **hide** my sins.

God **can** **can't** give me victory over sin.

I need fellowship with others **in** **outside** God's family.

People **can** **can't** be saved without Christ.

God **does** **doesn't** want me to tell others about Jesus.

I should live to please Jesus **someday** **today**.

This month God helped me make a right choice when . . .

____

THINKING IT OVER!

What I Believe

Write the answers to these questions from your devotionals in the blanks.

1. What are the parts of the Trinity?

____

2. How do you know the Bible is always right?

____

3. What should you do if you sin?

____

4. How can you show love for your neighbor?

____

5. What is Jesus preparing in heaven?

____

6. How can you be ready for Jesus' return?

____

If you need help, you can look back in this month's devotionals. The number in ( ) tells you which devotional to check for each question. 1. (1) 2. (3) 3. (11) 4. (18) 5. (26) 6. (30)

SUBJECT INDEX

Do you ever have problems? There's good news! God's Word can help you deal with the hard things that come into your life. God cares about everything that affects you. He wants to help you with your problems. The answer may be to understand God better and to trust him. Maybe you need to let God change your heart and work in your life.

The list on the next few pages can help you find answers for some of the problems and questions you have. It will tell you which devotionals to look at for help. You will see what God has to say about the things you are going through. Ask God to use the hard times in your life to help you grow closer to him.